St. Patrick's Day & Irish Collectibles

An Illustrated History

John Wesley Thomas & Sandra Lynn Thomas

4880 Lower Valley Road Atglen, Pennsylvania 19310

Other Schiffer Books by the Author:
Thanksgiving & Turkey Collectibles, 0-7643-2092-0, $29.95
Thanksgiving: An Illustrated History, 978-0-7643-3829-8, $29.99

Other Schiffer Books on Related Subjects:
The World of Wade Ireland, 978-0-7643-2618-9, $29.95

Library of Congress Control Number: 2011944351

Designed by Bruce Waters
Type set in New Baskerville

ISBN: 978-0-7643-4081-9
Printed in China

Published by Schiffer Publishing Ltd.
4880 Lower Valley Road
Atglen, PA 19310
Phone: (610) 593-1777; Fax: (610) 593-2002
E-mail: Info@schifferbooks.com

In Europe, Schiffer books are distributed by
Bushwood Books
6 Marksbury Ave.
Kew Gardens
Surrey TW9 4JF England
Phone: 44 (0) 20 8392 8585; Fax: 44 (0) 20 8392 9876
E-mail: info@bushwoodbooks.co.uk
Website: www.bushwoodbooks.co.uk

For Tommie and Joan Tuohy

Contents

Section Two: Irish and St. Patrick's Day Collectibles

Greetings from
IRELAND
GIANT'S CAUSEWAY
COLERAINE
DUNGLOE
DERRY
LARNE
LETTERKENNY
DONEGAL
ANTRIM
BANGOR
OMAGH
BUNDORAN
LISBURN
BELFAST
ARMAGH
ENNISKILLEN
MONAGHAN
SLIGO
BALLINA
ACHILL
BOYLE
CAVAN
CASTLEBAR
DUNDALK
KNOCK
LONGFORD
WESTPORT
DROGHEDA
ROSCOMMON
IRISH SEA
CLIFDEN
MULLINGAR
TUAM
ATHLONE
GALWAY
DUBLIN
BALLINASLOE
DUN LAOGHAIRE
ARAN ISLANDS
BIRR
BRAY
LISDOONVARNA
NEWBRIDGE
LAHINCH
NENAGH
ARKLOW
ENNIS
CARLOW
KILKEE
KILRUSH
LIMERICK
KILKENNY
GOREY
ADARE
CASHEL
TIPPERARY
NEW ROSS
WEXFORD
TRALEE
CLONMEL
DINGLE
WATERFORD
ROSSLARE
KILLARNEY
DUNGARVAN
CORK
YOUGHAL
SNEEM
KENMARE
BANTRY
KINSALE
SKIBBEREEN
CLONAKILTY
ATLANTIC OCEAN
©

Our Trip to Ireland

In 2005, Sandy and I embarked on a three-week trip to Ireland, not only to vacation and visit the historic sites, but to also accomplish a goal: Find my last remaining relative. Based on genealogical research, my paternal grandmother, Mary Tuohy, emigrated from Ireland in the late 1890s to the United States and, like most Irish immigrants, she resided and worked in the "Hell's Kitchen" part of Manhattan in New York City. Tommie Tuohy was a direct descendant from this family line. The mission proved fruitful and in a short period of time the Tuohys were located. They lived in an area called Knockroe, near the crossroads town of Annacarty, in County Tipperary. We were so glad to meet them and explore the surrounding areas replete with history. Regrettably, several years later, Tommie Tuohy passed away, but we have maintained an active correspondence with Tommie's widow, Joan.

When Sandy and I surprised them with a visit, the Tuohys were able to cobble together a great Irish meal, after which Tommie and I retired to "drown the shamrock" with a wee bit of Irish whiskey. Upon our departure, the Tuohys gave us a handmade gift of St. Brigid's Cross, an Irish-Christian symbol made from rushes. Our meeting definitely proved providential and well-worth the effort to seek them out. It was a great day for the Tuohy clan!

John Thomas
October 31, 2011

This collage image shows the Tuohys among past generations.

The Tuohy Family Crest.

Author John Thomas with Joan and Tommie Tuohy, 2005.

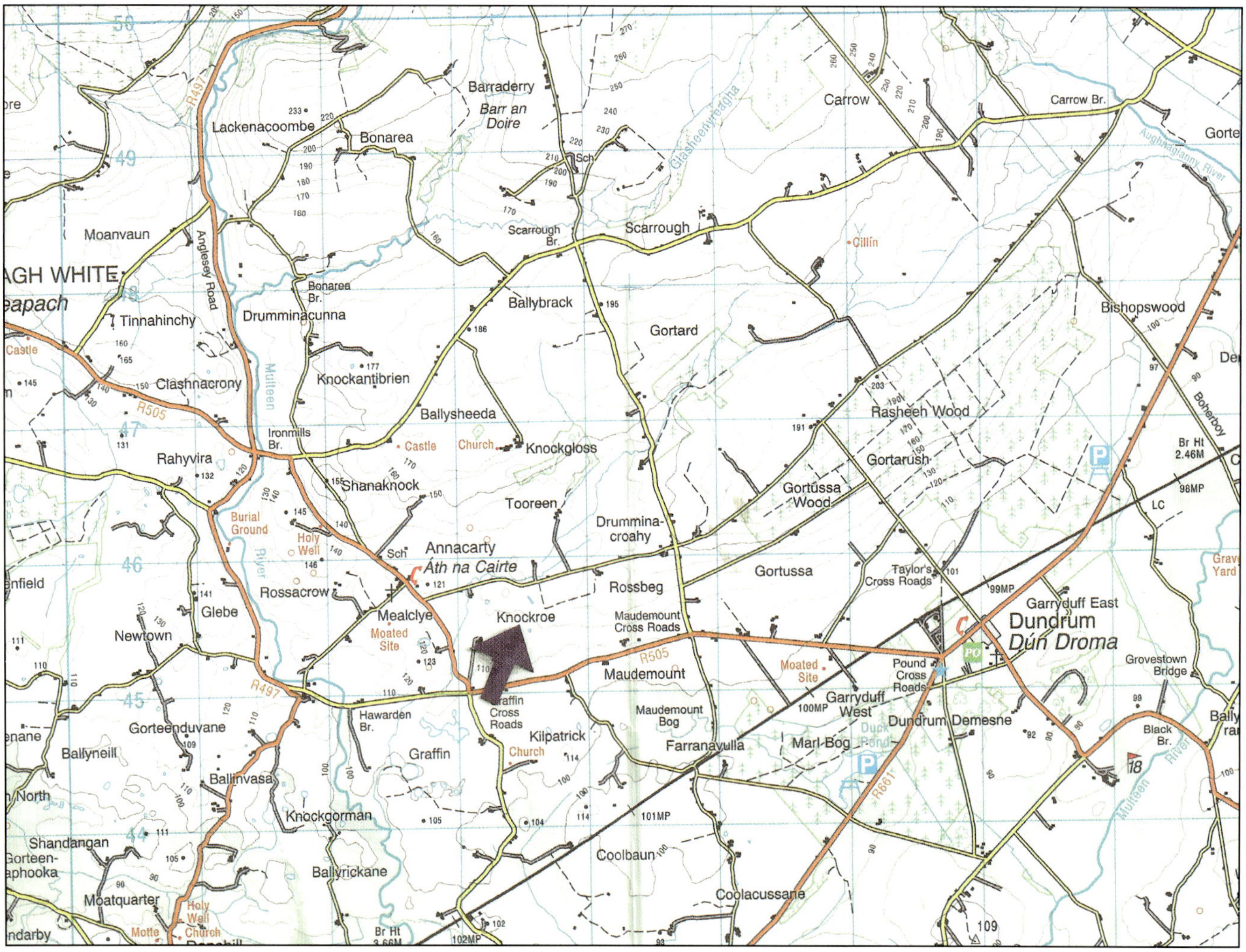

This map is of the Annacarty/Knockroe area, where the Tuohys resided.

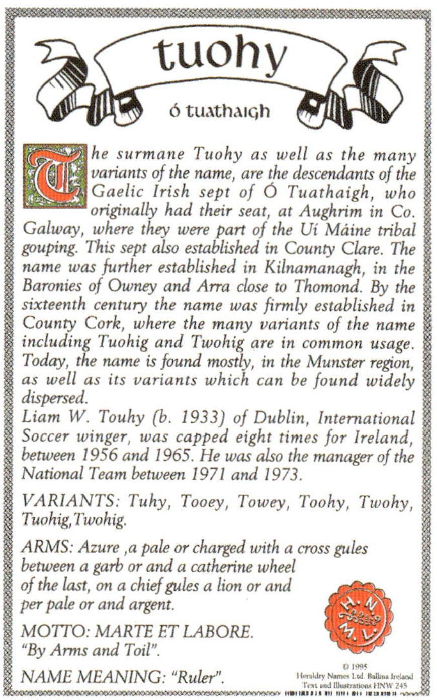

tuohy

ó tuathaigh

The surmane Tuohy as well as the many variants of the name, are the descendants of the Gaelic Irish sept of Ó Tuathaigh, who originally had their seat, at Aughrim in Co. Galway, where they were part of the Uí Máine tribal gouping. This sept also established in County Clare. The name was further established in Kilnamanagh, in the Baronies of Owney and Arra close to Thomond. By the sixteenth century the name was firmly established in County Cork, where the many variants of the name including Tuohig and Twohig are in common usage. Today, the name is found mostly, in the Munster region, as well as its variants which can be found widely dispersed.

Liam W. Touhy (b. 1933) of Dublin, International Soccer winger, was capped eight times for Ireland, between 1956 and 1965. He was also the manager of the National Team between 1971 and 1973.

VARIANTS: Tuhy, Tooey, Towey, Toohy, Twohy, Tuohig, Twohig.

ARMS: Azure ,a pale or charged with a cross gules between a garb or and a catherine wheel of the last, on a chief gules a lion or and per pale or and argent.

MOTTO: MARTE ET LABORE. "By Arms and Toil".

NAME MEANING: "Ruler".

© 1995 Heraldry Names Ltd. Ballina Ireland Text and Illustrations HNW 245

This Irish Name Card reveals the meaning of the "Tuohy" surname.

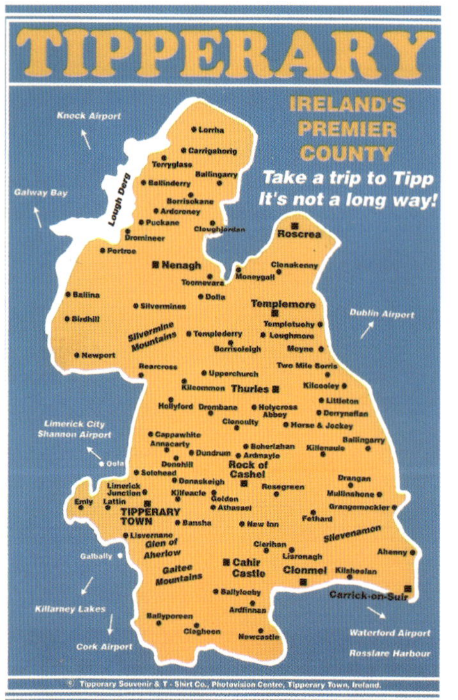

Map of County Tipperary, Ireland.

St. Brigid's Cross: Brigid Crosses are associated with Brigid of Kildare who is venerated as one of three Patron Saints of Ireland. It was traditionally believed that a Brigid Cross protects the house from evil and fire.

Introduction
"Erin Go Bragh"

During the Irish Rebellion of 1798, the well-known iconic slogan first appeared on flags: Erin go Bragh (Ireland forever). From that time forward this popular slogan has appeared on virtually all forms of written material including postcards.

Throughout the Christian world, the major religious holidays are Christmas, Easter, and St. Patrick's Day, though it is only in Ireland and two other smaller jurisdictions that St. Patrick's Day, on March 17th, is recognized as a true holiday and not just a celebration. St. Patrick's Day is enthusiastically celebrated in regions of the world where the majority of the Irish emigrated during the 1830s to the 1900s, which incorporated the peak years of the Irish Diaspora. The United States, Great Britain, Canada, Australia, and South Africa were the leading enclaves for the displaced Irish who eventually became productive citizens of those countries.

After World War II, St. Patrick's Day, once primarily a religious celebration of the Patron Saint of Ireland, became a more pronounced secular gathering of the Irish to celebrate their oneness worldwide and declare: "Proud to be Irish!" There is no better way of celebrating this than to be either a participant or a spectator in one of the many colorful parades held annually in numerous major cities. On St. Patrick's Day, the "wearing of the green" is the prescribed way for anyone to show that they are "Irish for a day!"

The authors have collected memorabilia of many important holidays, but they became interested in St. Patrick's Day over ten years ago when John was doing genealogical research on his two Irish grandmothers. This research led them to Ireland's County Tipperary, where John made contact with his last remaining living relative in 2005, and cemented their growing interest in Irish history and folklore. Soon, they began amassing a collection of memorabilia associated with St. Patrick's Day. The emphasis was on the historical and cultural aspects of St. Patrick's Day showing a progression of items from older to newer items. Today, it is the largest private collection in the world.

The authors did not want to write another "picture book" of collectibles. Instead their mission was to bring some historical perspective into the evolution and popularity of St. Patrick's Day and it is their fervent hope that the book where will inspire you to become "Irish for a day" or, perhaps, forever!

A postcard embellished with a golden border and a garland of tiny green shamrocks features the golden harp that played in Tara's Hall ringing out notes of "Erin Go Bragh" and issuing a St. Patrick's Greeting. Publisher unknown.

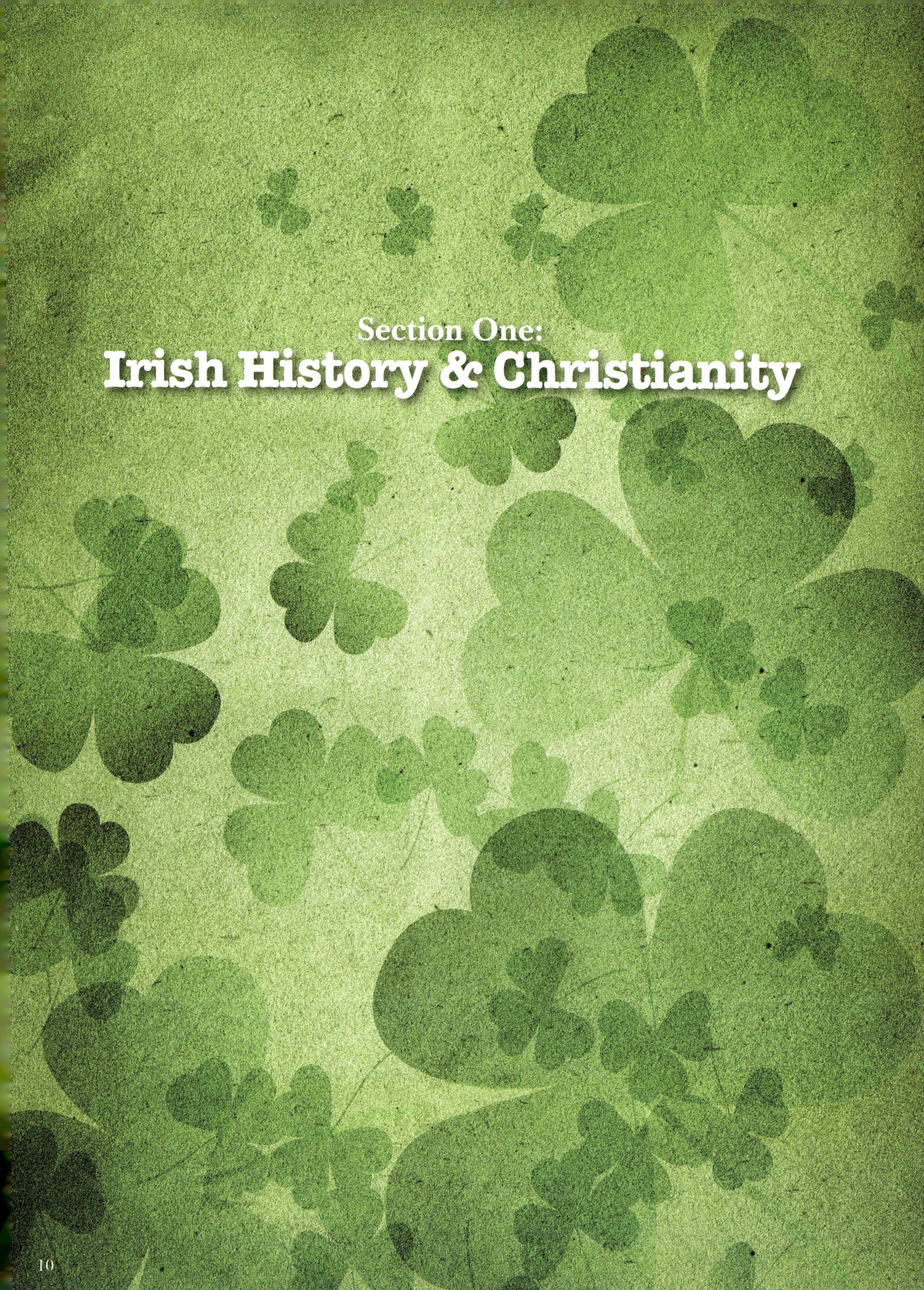

Section One:
Irish History & Christianity

Chapter 1:

The Beginning

The Ice Age

In very ancient history of our planet, before the emergence of humanoid life forms, Earth was subject to repeated "glacial ages." The commonly accepted definition of a glacial, or what is generally known as an "ice age," is an extensive reduction in the temperature of the Earth's surface and atmosphere resulting in the expansion of existing polar and continental ice sheets of very sizable dimensions.

Typically Ice ages can be divided into time frames of colder (glacial) and warmer (interglacial) periods that could last in duration from 40,000 to 100,000 years. The last glacial period within the current Ice Age lasted approximately 100,000 years, with the "last glacial maximum" (when ice sheets were at their maximum extension in North America, Northern Europe, and Asia) extending from 25,500 to 19,500 years ago. Due to massive ice sheets of over two miles in depth, the world at that time (mainly in the Northern Hemisphere) was very cold, dry, and coincided with a dramatic drop in sea levels. Ireland was no exception — virtually the whole land mass was covered with ice. Human populations that existed in Northern Europe prior to the last glacial maximum were under great pressure to migrate into warmer refuge type climate zones that included present day Southern France, fringes of Spain, Italy, and parts of Eastern Europe in order to survive. After a transitory period of deglaciation, the Earth is currently undergoing an interglacial warming period, termed the "late glacial maximum," that began approximately 13,500 to 11,500 years ago. The start of this current warming period spelled the end of the Pleistocene epoch and heralded the beginning of the Holocene epoch with the re-population of Northern European land masses.

In the early twentieth century, archeologists and cultural anthropologists devised a three-age dating system of archeology, which attempted to divide human technological and cultural prehistory into three broadly defined periods: (1) Stone Age: 2.6 million years ago to 3300 B.C.; (2) Bronze Age: 3500 B.C. to 500 B.C.; and (3) Iron Age: 1300 B.C. to A.D. 400. Among varying cultures there was much overlap, and the period of the ages could be much longer or shorter than typically agreed upon. As an isolated island, Ireland experienced the "coming of ages" much later. Most of the country's technological progress was initiated by Mesolithic colonists coming to Ireland looking for virgin land.

Ice Age Ireland. Map showing the maximum ice sheet by 20,000 B.C. Corries and eskers are geographic terms having to do with glaciated features after ice sheet withdrawal. Ireland is almost totally covered in ice.

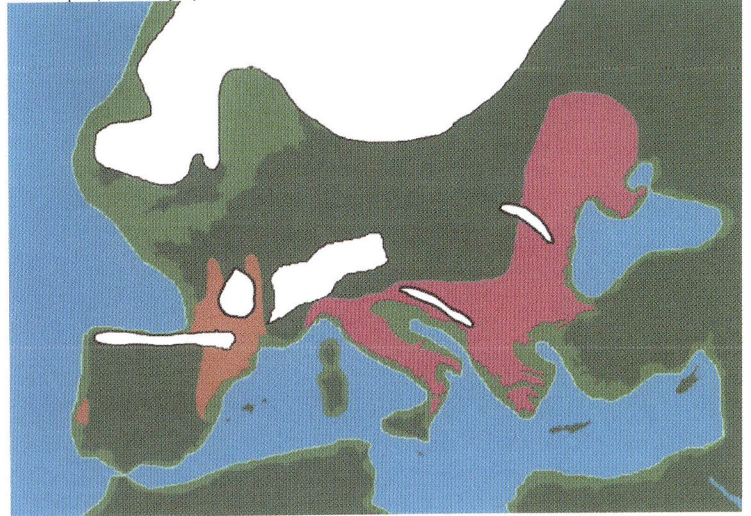

Paleolithic Era – Old Irish Stone Age (18,000-9000 B.C.)

The Paleolithic Era, dated in the same time frame as the Pleistocene epoch, was characterized by the emergence of the most primitive of hand stone tools used by hominids. These hominids, represented by genus Homo, resulted in the first true human species (Homo habilis and Homo erectus) evolved from the savannas of Africa 2.8 million years ago. Evolution continued slowly for the next 2.0 million years, resulting in the eventual migration of several ancestral species into the land mass of present day Europe and the British Isles.

Approximately 600,000 to 400,000 years ago a new species, Homo heidelbergensis, evolved with advanced tool-making skills and a primitive ability to vocalize. This became the common ancestor to Homo neanderthalensis and Homo sapiens. In Europe, H. Neanderthalensis evolved about 300,000 years ago and became extinct 25,000 years ago; H. sapiens, the first modern humans, evolved from the same H. heidelbergensis tree, but from the African branch about 200,000 to 150,000 years ago. H. sapiens began their immigration to Europe starting about 45,000 years ago, which marked the start of the Upper Paleolithic Era or the beginning of the end of the Old Stone Age.

Nothing is known about proto-human settlements in Ireland prior to the start of the most recent glaciation, which started 70,000 years ago and is referred to as the Midlandian glaciation by Irish geologists. That is because the whole land mass was effectively scoured by ice sheets measuring more than 9,850 feet (1.86 miles) in height and, in the process, eliminated all evidence of human habitation. After the Last Glacial Maximum took place between 20,000 and 16,000 B.C., an interglacial warming trend occurred from 15,500 to 10,000 B.C., which slowly transformed the permafrost of the Irish tundra into arable land, thus ending the last Ice Age in Ireland.

Imaginative depiction of the Paleolithic Era or Old Stone Age cavemen by Russian painter Viktor Vasnetsov in 1882-1885.

Mesolithic Era – Middle Irish Stone Age (9000-4000 B.C.)

After the latest Ice Age in Europe reached its zenith in 18,000 B.C. (20,000 years ago), there began a warming trend where even isolated islands like present day Ireland witnessed the emergence of indigenous flora and fauna necessary for the sustenance of human life. What land bridge existed between the British Isles and Ireland was eventually eradicated by the emergence of the Irish Sea. However, prior to that undulation, there is some archeological evidence that the Mesolithic peoples who settled in parts of habitable Ireland traveled from the British Isles over two land bridges that connected both the northern and southern parts of Ireland to the British mainland. Thus began what is called the Mesolithic Era or Middle Stone Age.

The first modern humans to reach Ireland, whether by a land bridge or wooden boats from Scotland or Britain, achieved their mission no earlier than 8000 B.C. Termed "hunters-gatherers," these primitive settlers, in order to survive, were forced to live in highly mobile, nomadic communities based on the pursuit of seasonal food sources. All hand tools and weapons were made from some sort of stone or flint whereas containers were made from hides, woven grasses, or clay pottery. Shelters were simple affairs with skin hides stretched over a bowl shaped timber frame and highly portable. The most archeologically relevant Mesolithic sites throughout Europe date from 9,000 BC while those in Britain and Ireland range from 8500 to 7000 B.C.

Due to its remoteness as a reconstituted island, Ireland was one of the last areas in Western Europe to attract migration. It is thought that the northern part of the country was settled first based on the earliest Mesolithic sites found in County Antrim and County Londonderry. Flint tools and weapons, as well as the remnants of timbered huts and charcoal from fires, were excavated and dated from 7000 to 6500 B.C. If there was any technological change in this era, it was the making of small flint and stone cutting tools that could be used for a number of situations. The nomadic lifestyle of these first Irish (few in number) did not lend themselves to permanent structures and they left few reminders of their presence.

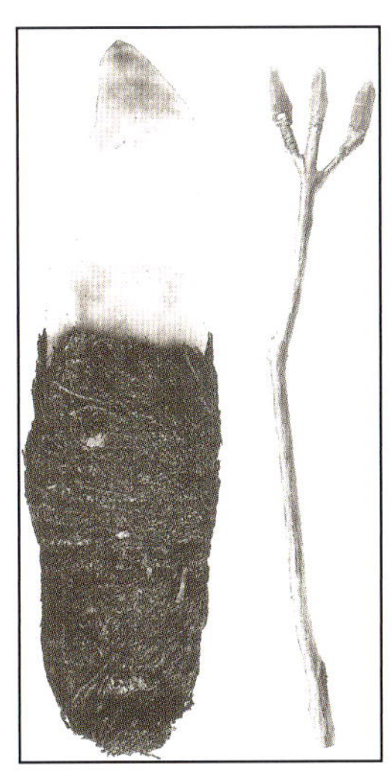

Larger single-piece weapons and tools evolved around 4500 B.C. This simple knife was made by wrapping moss around the end of a flint flake. Several flint flakes could be used in tandem to form a three-pronged spear or harpoon.

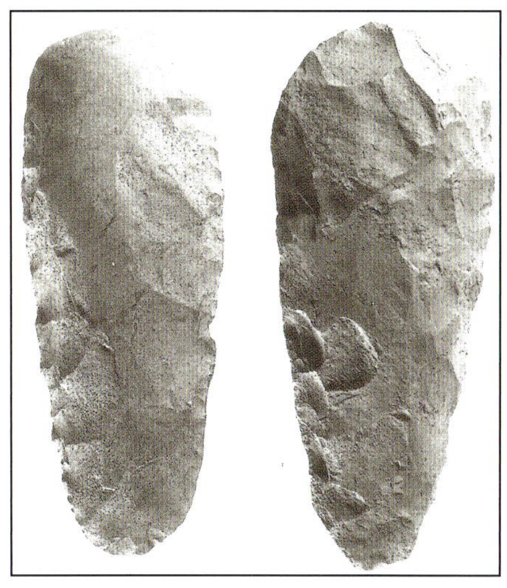

Two stone axe heads in various stages of development. *Left*: This example is in the initial stages of being ground and polished. *Right*: This example has been flaked into shape.

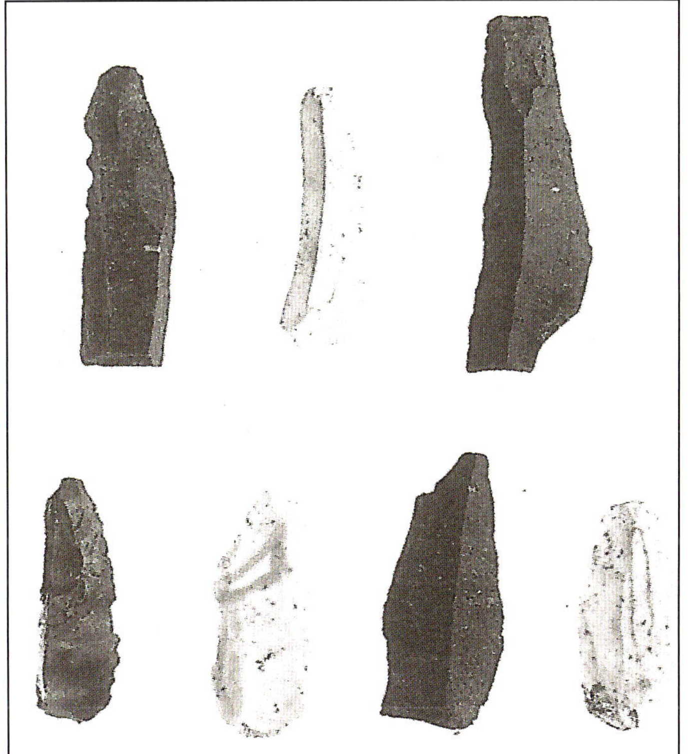

Mesolithic flint blades from Ireland. Each one is about 1" long and placed lengthwise in a wooden handle and secured to make knives and harpoons.

Neolithic Era – New Irish Stone Age (4000-2500 B.C.)

In the very late Mesolithic Era new settlers came to the north shores of Ireland through the existing Scotland-County Antrim link, which necessitated a passage across the Irish Sea. However, these new settlers were of Neolithic stock from England whose origins in the mid-Mesolithic Era emanated from the Normandy area of northwestern France. Termed the La Hoguette culture, these mixed late Mesolithic/early Neolithic peoples cultivated certain cereal grains that could be successfully grown in cooler climates. They were also well-versed in raising herds of sheep and goats.

From the origins of the first cultivation of edible plants and grain in Anatolia (present day Turkey) around 7000 B.C., the techniques of farming, harvesting, and the storage of crops slowly spread over Europe. Some 3,000 years later these techniques reached the Irish shores and, by 3900 B.C., imports of sheep, goats, cattle, and hardy cereal grains were brought in by these new settlers. The beginning of the Neolithic Era in Ireland originated with the use of domesticated animals and innovations in agrarian methods by these primitive peoples. Isolated bands of the Mesolithic "hunters-gatherers" could not adapt and were gradually replaced by Neolithic four-season farms, which also eventually supported grazing animals for fur, hides, milk, and food.

During this time, clusters of settlements sprang up among the more productive farming areas, resulting in the clearance of extensive woodland utilizing polished stone axe heads, chisels, and adzes. Another essential tool of the Neolithic farmer was quernstones, a series of two grinding stones that allowed raw grain to be crushed and ground into edible flour. These two advances in tools technology permitted the Neolithic farmer a high degree of sophistication in the cultivation of crops. An extensive Neolithic field system consisting of small farming households were marked off from one another by the construction of dry-stone walls. By the end of the Neolithic Era, Ireland was being transformed into both an agrarian and pastoral country depending upon the arable aspects of the land.

A Portal Tomb or Dolmen, County Clare, Ireland. This was a type of a megalithic single-chambered grave with a large capstone slab horizontally stacked over three or more vertically placed large stone slabs. Originally the dolmen was covered with earth although that covering has weathered away over many millennia.

With these viable means of support, the Irish lands were becoming more settled with sizable fixed populations. Attention now turned to religion, symbolism, and the afterlife. The Neolithic farmers, in order to bury and honor their dead, either built large multi-chambered tombs called Megaliths or smaller single-chambered versions called Dolmens. Today there are between 1,200 and 1,500 documented monuments, mainly located in the northern and western parts of Ireland. Megalithic tombs, which are aboveground burial chambers, consist of four basic types (dated from oldest to newest): Court tombs, Passage tombs, Portal tombs, which includes dolmens, and Wedge tombs. The Passage tombs are the most impressive and were used for complex rituals involving astronomical and ceremonial events. Dolmens were rather simple affairs consisting of three or more upright slabs of stone supporting a large flat horizontal table rock. Originally these tombs were covered with soil. While these megaliths are not unique to Ireland, their size and numbers remain a distinguishing characteristic of the Irish Neolithic lifestyle.

Passage Tomb, County Meath, Ireland. These earth-covered tombs are impressive due to their size and importance. Passage tombs are usually laid out so that they are astronomically situated to receive light into the burial chamber.

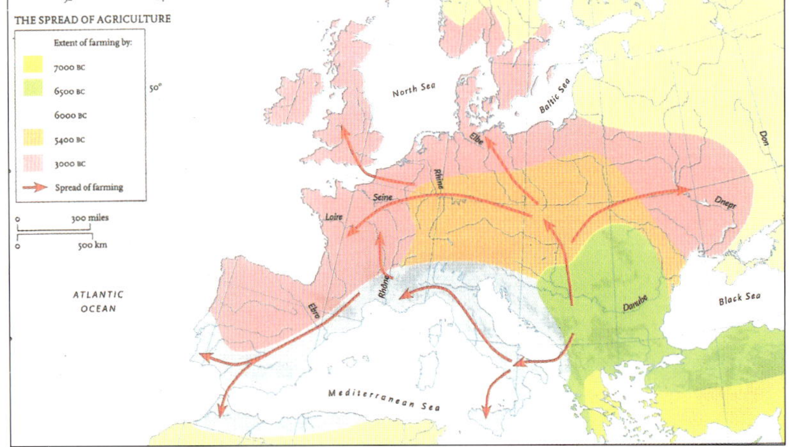

The Spread of Agriculture. Farming reached southeastern Europe c. 7000 B.C. partly due to the migration of farmers and partly due to the adoption by hunters-gatherers whose hunting grounds were being violated by Neolithic settlers. *From the Atlas of the Celtic World*.

Early to Late Bronze Age (2500-500 B.C.)

During the Stone Age era, various metals such as gold, silver, and copper were known. However, these precious metals were only used for decorative purposes since their malleable characteristics rendered them too soft to use for tools and weaponry. However, due to its availability in Ireland, copper was used fairly extensively for some tools, which resulted in a transition period from stone workings to bronze alloys termed the Copper Age, a period dated roughly from 2500 to 2000 B.C. The earliest copper tools were flat Celts or axe heads, daggers, and awls. By 4000 B.C., in the Near East, advances in metallurgy mated copper with tin to produce a hybrid metal or alloy called bronze.

The addition of tin made the resulting metal harder and easier to cast in a molten state, thereby revolutionizing metal working techniques. Archaeometallurgical studies on ancient implements have shown the ratio of copper to tin at 88% to 12%. Technological change moved slowly even in the late Neolithic Era; this knowledge of metal smelting by a crucible furnace didn't reach Ireland until at least 2000 B.C. New settlers from Normandy brought with them this ability to alloy bronze, thus initiating the start of the Irish Bronze Age, as the hardness of bronze generally replaced stone as an everyday tool and weapon. In order to ensure a dependable source of this metal alloy, mines were opened in the western parts of Ireland, where native copper was in abundance and this mineral could be extracted easily. On the other hand, since reliable sources of tin were not available in Ireland, this forced the primitive Irish people to embark in trade relationships with their British counterparts in Cornwall for its importation. Since Ireland had rich copper deposits beyond the small island's needs, it is assumed that copper and even certain bronze finished products were used in trade for tin as well as for other needs.

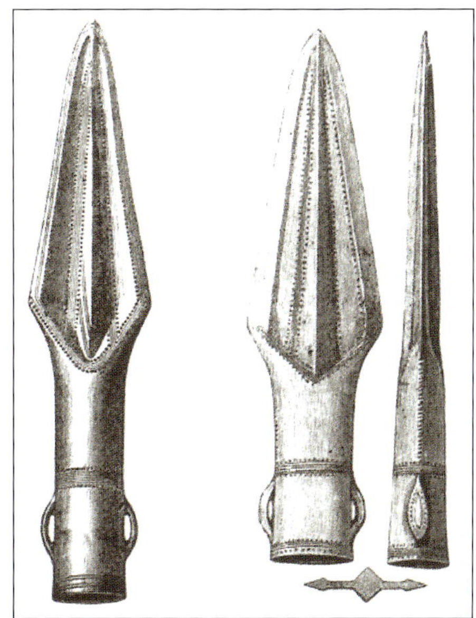

Finely wrought, fully-developed Irish Bronze Age spear-heads.

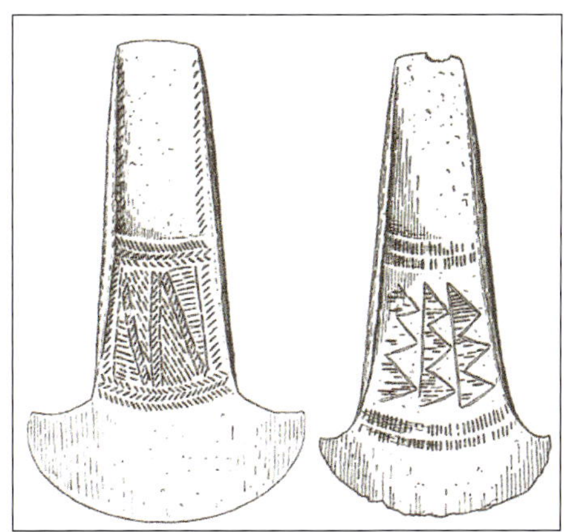

Ornamented Bronze Celts or Axe-heads. These examples still need to be attached to a wooden handle by means of a socket.

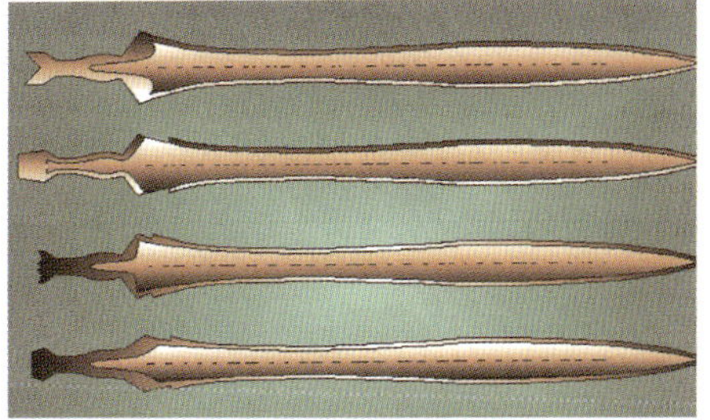

Early Irish Hallstatt period halberds or spearheads. The Hallstatt culture spanned central and western Europe from 1200 to 475 B.C., which included Late Bronze Age and Early Iron Age tools and weaponry.

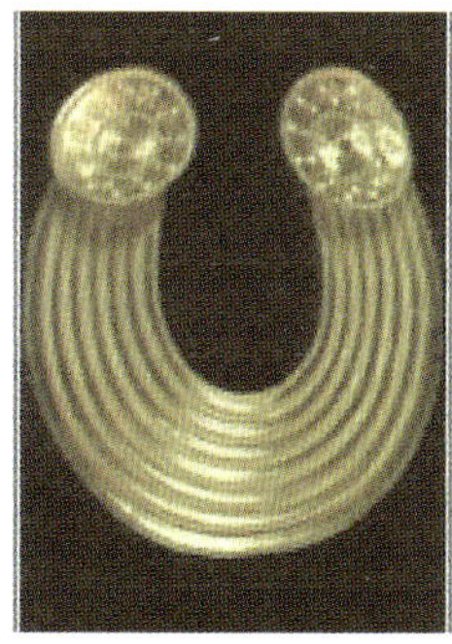

Irish Gold Gorget/Neck Collar, Middle to Late Bronze Age. The neck portion of the gorget is arranged in rows of raised ridges. The small disks at the terminus of the collar measure about three inches in diameter with concentric circles as a decorative element. This one is made from hammered gold with rope design and ribbing. They are often worn by chieftain warriors as a sign of wealth and social distinction.

Irish Gold Torc Bracelet/Small Necklace, Middle Bronze Age. Twisted gold to resemble cord tassels used on dresses.

Eminent paleoarchaeologists have documented five periods of the Irish Bronze Age, each lasting approximately 200 to 550 years, starting from the transitory Copper Age to the transitory beginnings of the Iron Age. Each of these periods showed increasing sophistication in the forging and casting of a wide range of tools and weaponry. Later in the Bronze Age casting and hammering techniques became so refined that large cooking riveted cauldrons, musical instruments such as horns and rattles, religious votive items, and a wide range of decorated prestige items were produced. Due to the availability of native gold in Ireland, many neck ornaments such as sun disks, lunulas (simple crescent shaped moon disks), torcs (twisted ribbons of gold), and gorgets (complex engraved disks) were all made from thinly hammered sheets of gold. Some of these were decorated with imported items such as jet and amber.

Irish Gold Lunula/Neck Ornament, Early to Middle Bronze Age. A hammered, gold-shaped crescent moon motif, the horns, or end, have etched geometric designs. The object of lunulae was thought to reflect light in some sort of moon rites worship.

Given the chronological range of the Irish Bronze Age lasted over 2,000 years, there appears, according to demographers, very little upward change in the population of the inhabitants numbering approximately 150,000. Even in the light of immigration from abroad, agrarian and pastoral advances in the use of arable land, improvements in cooking and housing, and a rather equalitarian society with little evidence of warfare, the population remained static. However, the one documented change was in the climate. Climatologists opine that within the Late Glacial Maximum, there was a period of a sharp downturn in climatic conditions bringing wetter and colder conditions toward the end of the Bronze Age. During the Neolithic Era, the upland forests were cleared for permanent dwellings, agriculture, and pasturage. As the forests were not very thick, stone axes were able to get the job done. However, due to the thin soil cover, deforestation, and overgrazing, the increasingly wet climate conditions contributed to the arable land becoming stagnant, acidifying, and eventually turning into blanket bogs. This type of bog (which "blankets" the land) consists of un-decomposed low lying plant life like heather that eventually transforms into peat of about ten feet thick. While this process might take up to 2,000 years to develop, it is not reversible if wet climate conditions remain the same.

Since the Neolithic upland areas were now not suitable for agriculture, the Bronze Era inhabitants were forced to clear the more heavily forested lowland areas. Bronze axes, with their stronger cutting blades, promulgated the systematic deforestation with the same bad outcome. Low lying lakes such as glacial moraine lakes became chocked by shoreline reeds. As these reeds moved out to the middle of the lake depositing peat, heather and other low lying plants grew on them, contributing more un-decomposed matter and creating a dome over the now nonexistent lake to what is called raised bogs.

By the end of the Bronze Era in Ireland, a once fairly stable and ritualistic society based on agriculture found itself "bogged" down by the capricious nature of the climate. Also the extensive deforestation contributed to the destruction of arable land, resulting in economic and cultural stagnation. However, momentous events were about to begin that would change the society of the primitive Irish inhabitants forever.

Development of Blanket Bogs in Ireland
Pine and Birch forest.
Bedrock
Soil
4000BC
Leaching
Land cleared for grazing and cultivation.
2500BC
Heather colonises the bare soil, turning it more acid.
Undecomposed peat builds up on higher ground.
Agriculture moves to lowlands.
Remaining trees choked by waterlogged peat.
500BC
Peat builds up and heather grows.
Bog
Agriculture expands in lowlands.
1000AD
Peat cut for fuel.
Conifer Plantation
Agriculture
2000AD

Blanket Bogs from Mesolithic to Present Time. In Modern times mature blanket bogs provide a form of low-quality household fuel called peat. Reclamation of blanket bog lands has been to convert them into grazing lands or to plant conifer plantations. *Courtesy: www.irelandstory.com.*

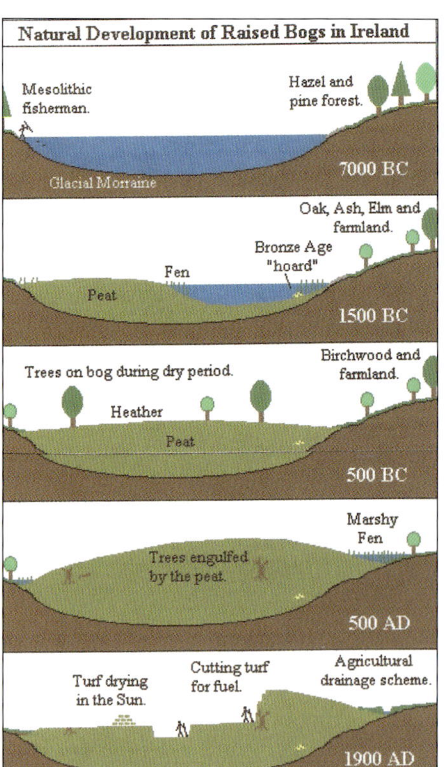

Natural Development of Raised Bogs from Mesolithic to Present Time. Raised bogs are found almost exclusively in central Ireland. After the end of the last Ice Age the glacial moraine left behind a hummocky plain with many water-filled depressions of poor drainage. Over the intervening 9,000 years these marshy hollows filled with poorly decomposed vegetable matter that turned into peat. Since the 1700s these raised bogs were exploited for cheap fuel, which is still on-going today. Within the next fifty years raised bogs will be nearly non-existent. *Courtesy: www.irelandstory.com.*

The Celts and the Roman Empire

In 700 B.C., at the start of the European Iron Age, there were five main civilizations in Europe competing for hegemony. They were the ancient Greeks, the ancient Romans, the Etruscans and Carthaginians (both soon to disappear in about 200-300 years), and the Celts. In 517 B.C., a Greek geographer first used the label "Celts" to describe an ethnic group or tribe that lived in the south of France. However, the first instance of a race called "The Celts" was the emergence of a Proto-Celt culture with its formation in and around Hallstatt, Austria. Based on archeological findings from this particular area, the first emergence of a Celtic race was labeled the European Hallstatt culture, which dated from 850 to 450 B.C. By the end of this period, out of the Hallstatt culture, there grew another more robust Celtic culture called La Tene, which existed from 450 B.C. until the Roman Republic's conquest of all Gallic tribes in the Celtic territories of Gaul in mid-first century B.C. The name La Tene comes from the archeological site at La Tene on the north side of Lake Neuchatel, Switzerland. The influence of this more advanced Iron Age culture was widespread and expanded into almost all parts of Western and Central Europe and even the far-flung islands of Britain and Ireland. More importantly, the expansive dual Celtic cultures brought with them a degree of literacy, both in the spoken and written word, to the shores of Ireland.

Of the world's language families, the Indo-European family of spoken languages is in magnitude the largest and most widespread. There are two theories that date the spread of this language family into Europe: (1) 7000 B.C. from Anatolia coincident with the spread of agriculture, and (2) 4000 B.C. from West Central Asia due to population expansion. While today the extant Celtic languages are a mere fraction of current Indo-European spoken languages, these same languages were the most widely spoken circa 300 to 200 B.C.

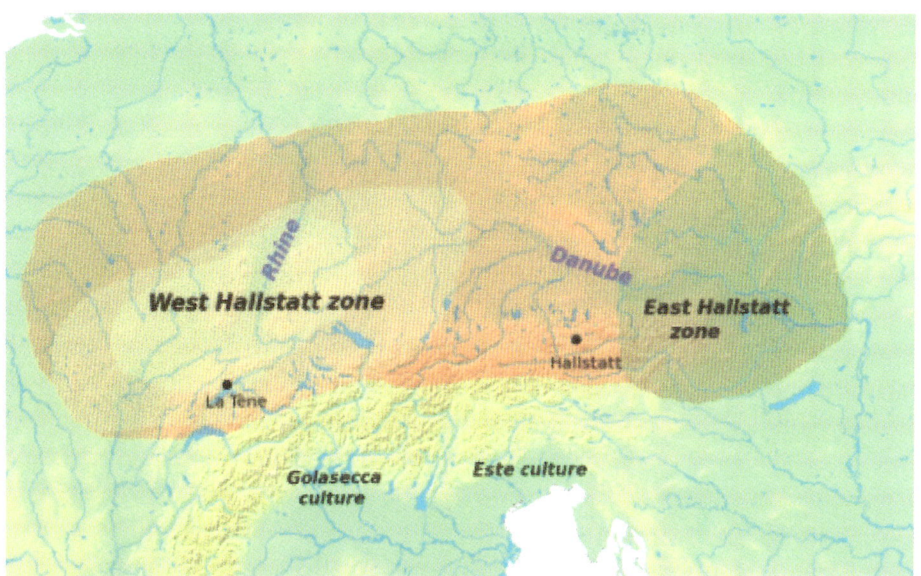

Core Area of Hallstatt Culture in Central Europe 850-450 B.C. The early Hallstatt culture was made up of small isolated chiefdoms, but with the introduction of iron as a better source of tools and weaponry, there emerged a newer, more centralized culture of wealthy chiefdoms secure in hillforts exploiting trade links to the Mediterranean basin.

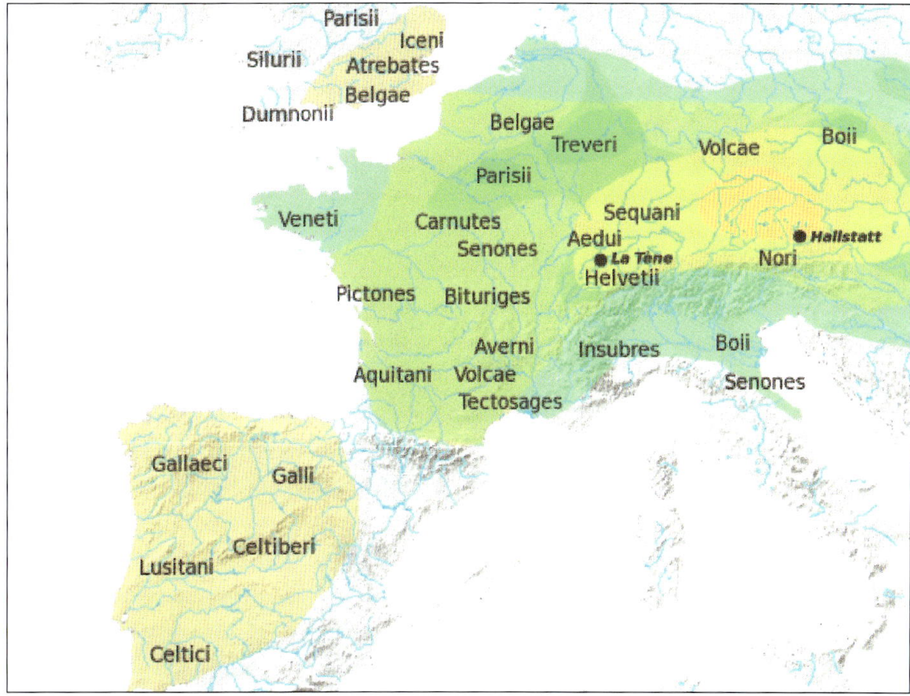

Overview of the older Hallstatt core culture (yellow) and the newer La Tene culture (green shadings). By 300 B.C., La Tene became the dominant culture across most of western and central Europe. La Tene culture and artwork tended to emphasize an aristocratic warrior society which introduced chariots as an innovation in Celtic warfare.

From the early Hallstatt period, there first emerged a Proto-Celtic language that evolved into a group of many languages called Continental Celtic. These Celtic languages, now all extinct, were spoken on the continent of Europe up to circa A.D. 200. As the Hallstatt/La Tene cultures spread westward to the Atlantic and eventually the British Isles, these are the areas where the Insular Celtic language originated. The Celtic tribes that stayed in Britain spoke a form of Insular Celtic called Brythonic whereas the Celts who colonized Ireland spoke the Goidelic variant. By the time that written records materialized in the fifth century, Archaic or Primitive Irish was the lingua franca of the Irish Celtic tribes.

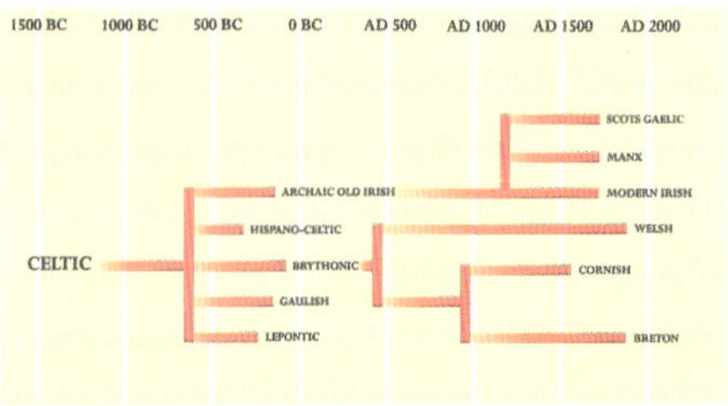

The Celtic Language Tree. While probably some form of Proto-Celtic languages (one of the successors from the cradle of Indo-European languages) were already widely spoken in Late Bronze Age Europe, it was the emergence of the very early Hallstatt Celtic culture that formed the basis of the original Celtic language tree c. 1200 B.C. *Courtesy: "The Celts"-John Davies.*

In ancient Anatolia (modern Turkey), evidence points to a successful ferrous metallurgy (iron smelting) being discovered around 1200 B.C. This was a world-changing event not only because forged iron was a superior metal to cast bronze, but also due to the high degree of technical innovation necessary to efficiently smelt oxidized iron ores in a specially designed furnace. While iron metal itself is soft and can quickly lose a cutting edge on weapons, the addition of the right percentage of carbon will turn an inferior product into a superior one that is lighter, more durable, and stronger. From out of the Hallstatt culture in 700 B.C., the expansion of the Celtic culture eastward to the Balkans and westward throughout most of central Europe, Iberia (Spain), and the Pretanic Islands (Britain and Ireland), the discovery of iron and its metallurgical attributes gave the Celts a technological edge. The time when the substituting of iron in its many forms for bronze got its start was called the Iron Age. By benefit of many innovations learned by the Celts during their conquests and assimilation of defeated European Neolithic cultures, it only took another four centuries or so to eliminate all vestiges of the primitive Irish cultures that were based on agriculture and animal husbandry.

Celtic Europe, c. 400 B.C. The Celtic culture (made up of hundreds of tribal identities) had already spread their influence into Iberia (modern Spain) by 600 B.C. and to the Pretanic Islands (modern British Isles) by 500 B.C. A few hundred years later, Ireland's Bronze Age culture was defunct and replaced by the Celtic culture.

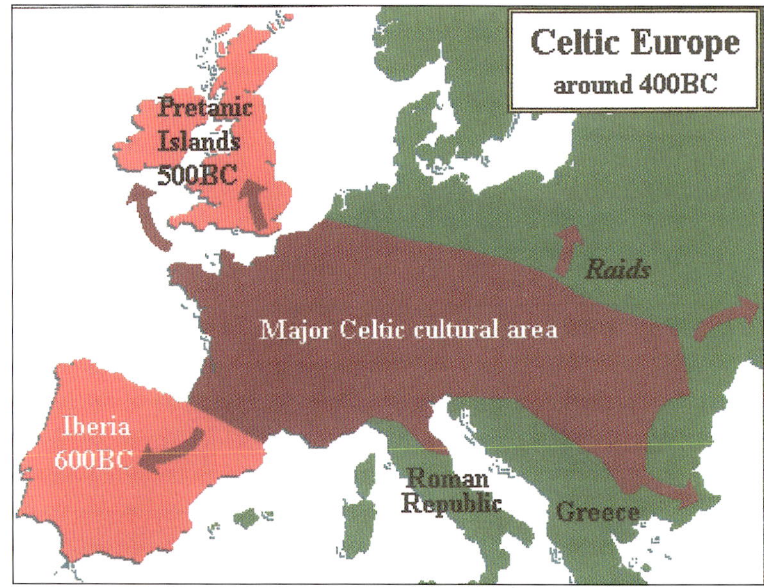

Roman Republic Conquest of Italy, 500-260 B.C. From its small base in Rome, the Republican armies in the space of 250 years conquered all of the tribes of the Italian Peninsula, including the Etruscans, the Latins, and the Samnites. By 260 B.C., Rome had a strong stable government with the whole of Italy under its control, secured by the promise of citizenship to add to the manpower ranks, free lands for the Roman army veterans, and ample resources from conquests.

At the time of the Celtic expansion in 700 B.C., there were stirrings of an even greater metamorphosis of an existing civilization — the ancient Roman Monarchy. This Roman kingdom was initiated in 750 BC with the founding of the city of Rome in what is modern day Italy. In 509 B.C., the monarchy was overthrown and the new Roman Republic expanded throughout most parts of the then-known world, lasting for 482 years until its upheaval in 27 B.C. From its early years, the Roman Republic embarked upon a series of campaigns of plunder and subjugation of the local tribes in order to secure its borders, expand its territory, and preserve its destiny. The first Roman Republican campaigns were aimed at protecting Rome from the surrounding Latin towns and Etruscan tribes. Later the Romans defeated the Samnites in a series of three wars, which, by 282 B.C., accomplished their goal of being the major power in all of Italia. By the end of the Roman Republic, the territorial expansionist policy of the Romans achieved almost full control of the Mediterranean Basin.

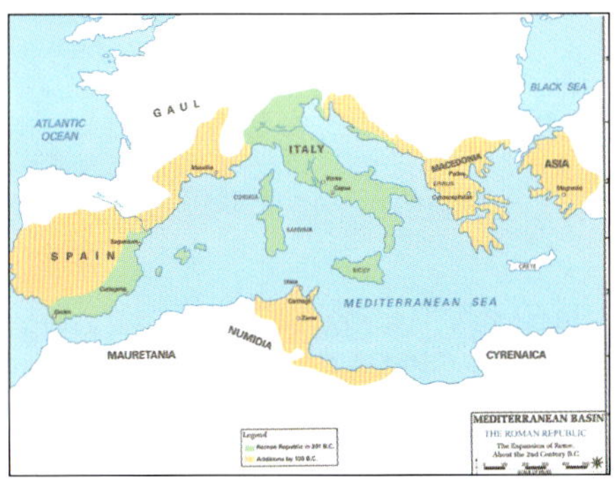

The Roman Republic, 100 B.C. The expansion of Rome throughout the Mediterranean Basin was accomplished by the time of the early Christian Era due to being victorious in the Punic Wars against Carthage, against the Celts in Spain and Gaul, and against the Mithridates in Asia Minor.

While the Emperor was the supreme leader of the Roman Republic, a Consul (two only) served as the highest elected official. In 59 B.C., Julius Caesar was elected consul. At that time Caesar was also appointed to a five-year term of Governor/Proconsul for certain Celtic parts of Gaul. In 121 B.C., the Romans first came into contact with two Celtic tribes and defeated them with seeming ease. In order to consolidate his power in Rome, Caesar felt he needed to subjugate the whole of Gaul (France), so he embarked upon a series of putative actions from 61 to 51 B.C. termed the Gallic Wars. By 50 B.C., all of European Gaul was in the Roman Republic's domain. Caesar's subjugation of Gaul was so complete that it never regained its Celtic identity and was a loyal subject until the end of the Western Roman Empire in A.D. 476.

Two waterborne expeditions undertaken by Caesar's legions over the treacherous English Channel into the southern and eastern half of Britain in 55 B.C. and 54 B.C. softened up the Island's Celts. After settling with the Briton warlords for hostages and an annual tribute, Caesar left the island with all of his men. Because of the time, expense, and efforts to successfully invade and placate Ireland, Caesar decided it was not worth the struggle for little perceived gain, so he decided to return to Gaul and eventually Rome due to increasingly adverse political situations that threatened his leadership as Consul. As we know from history, Julius Caesar, dictator for life, was assassinated in 44 B.C., which sparked a series of civil wars leading to the dissolution of the Roman Republic and the transition to the Roman Empire.

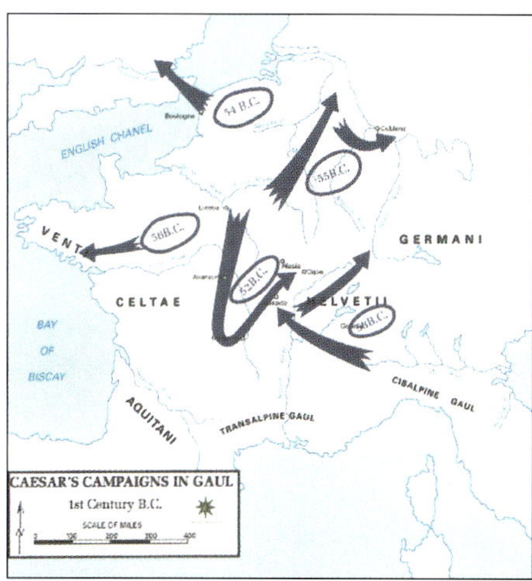

Caesar's Campaign's in Gaul, 1st Century B.C.. From 61 to 51 B.C., Julius Caesar embarked upon a series of punitive expeditions against the Gaulish tribes called the Gallic Wars, which resulted in the expansion of Rome, although at great expense both in men and materials.

Roman Republic Expansion until the Death of Julius Caesar, 44 B.C. After the assassination of Caesar, the subsequent Roman Civil Wars were fought to determine what type the next government would be and this evolved into the Roman Empire by 27 B.C.

Roman aspirations for expanding the Roman Empire (established in 27 B.C.) continued, and the Empire reached its maximum zenith in terms of land occupied under Emperor Trajan in A.D. 117. At this point in history, the Roman Empire controlled 1.93 million square miles with a total population of 88 million people of multiple ethnicity encompassing all of the Mediterranean Basin as well as the island of Britannia. It was earlier noted that Britannia controlled much material worth including tin and gold mines. Therefore Claudius, the fourth Emperor in succession of the line of the new Empire, embarked upon the invasion of southern Britain in A.D. 43 with much success, but it took the occupiers until A.D. 50 to pacify the remaining tribes. However, true peace was never realized in Britannia. For the next 367 years, there were periods of peace subverted by incursions by the British Celtic tribes and various pagan tribal invaders from Scotland and Germania. The end of the Roman Empire's rule in Britannia dissipated in A.D. 410. At that time the Western Roman Empire was in danger of collapsing, so they needed troops from Britain to quell the many pagan invasions in Europe. Wearied by the constant incursions of at least seven distinct groups of barbarians from the un-pacified areas of Northern Europe and the Asian steppes, the Western Roman Empire succumbed in A.D. 476.

The Roman Empire, A.D. 117. Under Emperor Trajan, the Roman Empire reached its maximum extent with total control of all lands comprising the Mediterranean Basin.

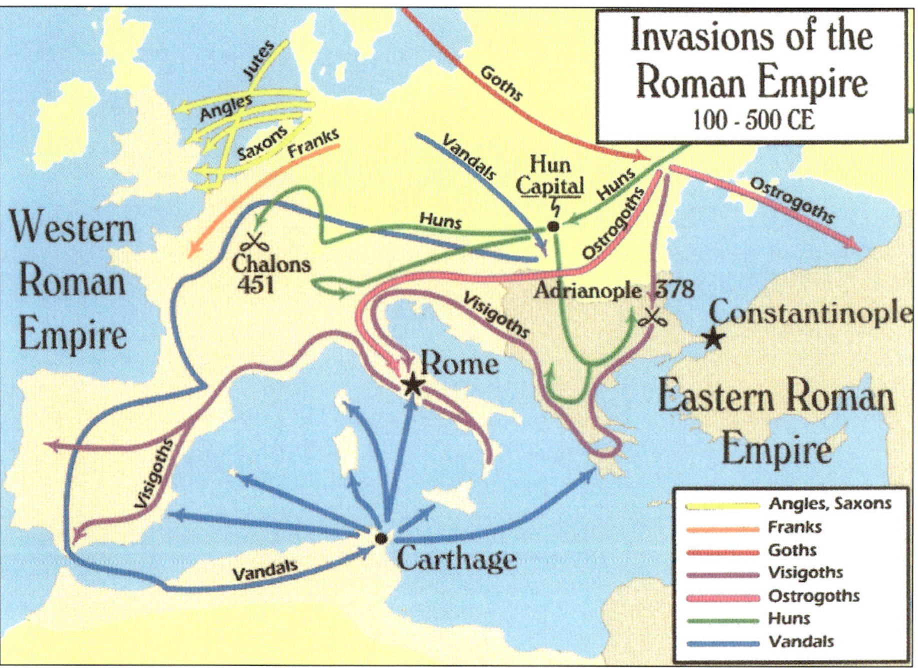

"Barbarian" Invasions of the Roman Empire. From A.D. 100 and for the next four hundred years, the Western Roman Empire was subject to seven barbarian incursions, which ultimately served to weaken and terminate the Empire by A.D. 476.

Roman Britain and the Extent of Romanization under Several Roman Emperors to c. A.D. 140.

During these times, the Irish Celts, while enjoying some trade links with Britannia, were never in danger of being invaded. Yet Ireland was relatively well-known to the Romans, who, even by 52 B.C., referred to the island as Hibernia. Based on evidence gleamed from sailors and itinerant wayfarers who had some knowledge of Ireland and its peoples, most of Ireland's tribes were known and documented. Evidence of this came from Ptolemy (A.D. 90–168), a Greek multi-faceted scientist who was born in Egypt and was a Roman citizen. One of Ptolemy's main works was his *Geographia*, a compilation of everything known about the world's geography during the Roman Empire of the first millennium A.D. Written circa A.D. 150, "Ptolemy's Map of Ireland," published as part of his *Geographia*, was considered to be a factual representation of the Celtic tribal identities known at that time. Archeological evidence also points to there being a fair amount of two-way trade between the Romans and Irish Celts, a center of trade activity being in and around modern Dublin on the Irish east coast. In fact, towards the end of the Pre-Christian period during the third to fifth centuries, when the Roman Empire's grip of its British province was in a state of decline, certain Irish tribes invaded and established enclaves on parts of the western seacoast of Britain and Scotland.

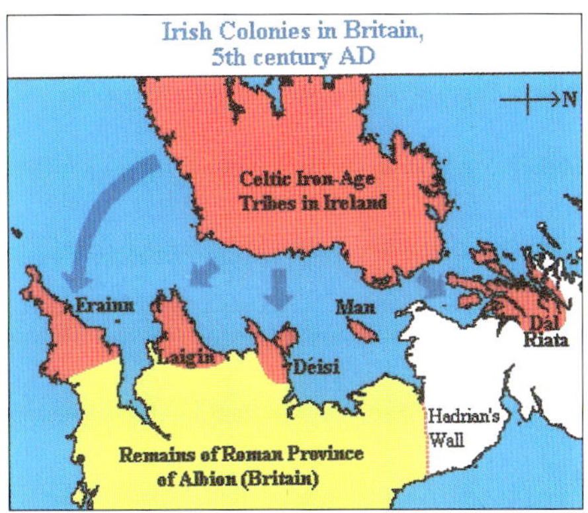

Irish Colonies in Britain, 5th Century A.D. Towards the end of the pre-Christian era, the Celtic Irish tribes began raiding and establishing enclaves on the west coast of Britain including Cornwall and Wales. To the north, the Dal Riata tribe defeated the Picts and eventually established the united kingdom of Scotland.

In the remaining centuries of Irish Iron Age culture tribal identities slowly gave way to a system of territories and kingdoms. These "territories" were defended by a series of circular hilltop earthen work forts replete with a well constructed stone wall. The larger forts, also called "royal sites," were cone-shaped buildings with a thatched roof for protection from the elements. A kingdom, or tuath, usually consisted of one or more territories that served as a residence for the local king and his extended family of warriors and servants. In those days the Irish people were not concerned as much from outside invaders as they were from each other. Therefore, Ireland, in the waning days of the Iron Age, became divided into hundreds of petty kingdoms, each intent on acquiring the property of its neighbor. It was this mentality of the Irish Celts that led to a period of economic and cultural stagnation, especially among the non-coastal tribes, which did not have much exposure to the Roman traders.

The Hill Fort of Griahan of Aileach, County Donegal. This Iron Age hill fort (c. A.D. 800-1050) was a multivallate cashel hill fort. Hill forts, a sub-category of ring forts (cashel), occupied large hilltop areas for defensive purposes and had multiple ramparts made of earth and/stone (multivallate). The circular wall was about 78 feet in diameter and, including the out-terraces, occupied an area of ten acres. This was considered to be a "royal fort" of the Kingdom of Aileach.

Ptolemy's Map of Ireland, c. A.D. 100. Written in A.D. 150, the map was based on Celtic tribal identities that were well-known due to commercial intercourse between merchants of Roman Britain and the Irish. *Courtesy: www.irelandstory.com*.

A multivallate hill fort. Viewed from the air with three concentric rings for protection.

The Coming of Christianity

Most biblical scholars place the date of Jesus Christ's birth as between 7 and 2 B.C. based on the Gregorian calendar initially adopted in A.D. 1582. Similarly the same scholars place the crucifixion and death of Jesus at Jerusalem, a major town in the Roman province of Judea, around A.D. 33. It has also been accepted that the place of Jesus' crucifixion was on Mount Calvary, where the Church of the Holy Sepulchre has been standing since the fourth century in the Christian Quarter of the Old City. This church is reputed to contain Jesus' tomb. Though Jesus' ministry only lasted for nearly three years until his death, he selected twelve disciples, or Apostles, to proselytize throughout the Mediterranean on behalf of keeping his proto-Christian community unified.

Crucifixion of Christ, painting by Michelangelo, A.D. 1540. Michelangelo was the foremost painter, sculptor, architect, and engineer of the Renaissance era. He was best known for his Sistine Chapel frescoes as well as being the architect of St. Peter's Basilica in the Vatican, Rome. His crucifixion painting was one of several he either drew or painted, as crucifixion scenes are a key element of Christian art form. He died in Rome at the age of nearly 89 in A.D. 1564.

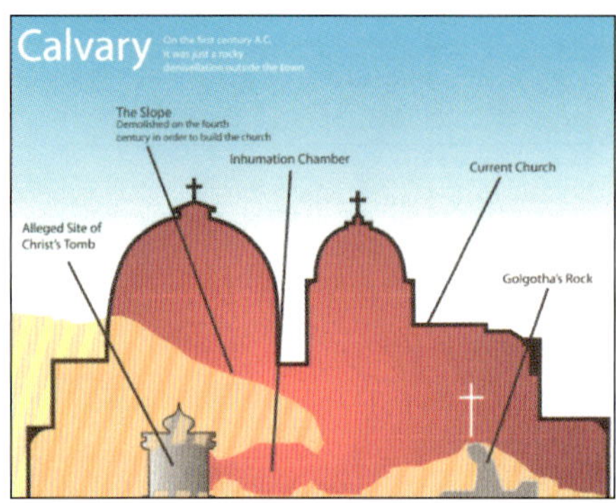

Cross section diagram of the location of the Church of the Holy Sepulchre, Jerusalem, c. 4th century in relation to the presumed original site of Calvary.

During the early Christian movement, the four Canonical Gospels written by Matthew, Mark, Luke, and John, the Acts of the Apostles, the thirteen Epistles (letters) written by Paul to the various scattered Christian groups, the eight Epistles written by others, and the Book of Revelation (Apocalypse) formed the Christian New Testament. Almost all Christian religious bodies accept the fact that the New Testament is composed of twenty-seven books of officially recognized Christian canons of Sacred Scripture. It is generally accepted that the New Testament manuscripts were written (and divinely inscribed) between A.D. 50 and 150. One of the very earliest, most prolific, and influential Christian missionaries was a Jewish Roman citizen called Paul of Tarsus.

From his conversion in circa A.D. 33 and based on his early ministry, Paul the Apostle wrote many epistles to early Gentile or Christian communities that formed part of the Roman Empire. His writings contributed a sizable portion to the makeup of the New Testament and had a major influence on early Christian thinking about not only how they should believe, but also how they should live. Pauline Christianity is today's term given by biblical scholars based on Paul's written and missionary work as forming the very first vestiges of Christianity. In fact, it was in Antioch (present day Turkey), a very influential center of early Church learning, that the early followers of Jesus were called "Christians," meaning the "followers of Christ." This new Christian label not only applied to Jewish converts, but now included non-Jewish converts called "Gentiles." While these Christian groups were thought to be, by Roman Judean authorities, as a somewhat trouble-making Jewish sect, persecutions in the form of martyrdoms were inflicted on some of the most notable Christian emissaries of mid-first century. They included St. Stephen, the first Christian martyr, in circa A.D. 35; James the Just (and brother of Jesus), the 1st Bishop of Jerusalem in A.D. 62; and Simon (St.) Peter, the first Pope, and St. Paul in A.D. 67.

"St. Paul" by El Greco, A.D. 1608-1614. El Greco (The Greek) was a nickname for Domenikos Theotokopoulos, a painter, sculptor, and architect of the Spanish Renaissance. He spent much of his mature life in Toledo, Spain, where he died in A.D. 1614 at the age of 73.

"Saint Peter" by Peter Paul Rubens, c. 1630s. Rubens was a Flemish baroque painter well-known for his monumental paintings of religious subject matter. This painting of St. Peter depicts him as Pope with the pallium (an ecclesiastical vestment) and the Keys to Heaven. Rubens was a prolific and well-regarded painter, especially among foreign patrons, for his landscapes and portraitures. He died in Antwerp in A.D. 1640.

From A.D. 66 to 70 the Jews rioted against Roman rule in Jerusalem and were almost annihilated along with the city. Caught up as a by-product of this insurrection were many "Jewish Christians" who were in the throes of an embryonic transition from Rabbinic Judaism to the primitive Christian movement. An old synagogue that survived the burning of Jerusalem in A.D. 70 became the structure that housed the first ever Christian church called Church of the Apostles. The Cenacle, or "Upper Room," of this structure is where the Apostles stayed when in Jerusalem. Many of the most important events of the New Testament were held there as well, such as The Last Supper, some resurrection appearances of Jesus, and the descent of the Holy Spirit upon the disciples on Pentecost. Next to this first church was built a larger church, the Holy Zion Church (A.D. 382-394), that, after numerous cycles of destruction from Persian invaders and reconstruction, eventually incorporated the Cenacle into part of the surviving church.

Over the next 245 years Pauline Christianity and its successor, Proto-Christianity, prospered and flourished throughout the Roman Empire in spite of intra-religious heresies, apostasies, and intermittent persecutions. The most severe persecutions by Roman Emperors were undertaken during the reigns of Valerian (A.D. 253–260) and Diocletian (A.D. 284–305), where 20,000 Christians were reputed to be killed due to their refusal to reject pantheism and offer sacrifices to the reigning Roman Emperor. These persecutions generally ended when Constantine I (A.D. 306-337) became one of four Co-Emperors in A.D. 306 under a new leadership arrangement implemented by Diocletian called Tetrarchy. In this form of governance, independent portions of the wide-ranging empire were ruled under four separate chosen leaders of equal rank. Due to the eventual internecine wars among these four leaders, the Tetrarchy was proclaimed a failure and a Diarchy was reinstated after A.D. 313, where Constantine I ruled the western part of the empire and Licinius ruled the eastern half.

"The Christian Martyrs Last Prayer" by Jean-Leon Gerome, A.D. 1883.

Present Time View of the Cenacle. At least three former churches that housed the Cenacle were destroyed in various wars. The existing Gothic-style Cenacle (divided into six vaulted bays) was probably rebuilt in the twelfth or thirteenth century, but conclusive documentation is sparse.

While the persecutions of Christians generally abated by the first decade of the fourth century, an edict (e.g. a proclamation having the full force of the existing law) was co-signed and issued by both Constantine I and Licinius in A.D. 313. *The Edict of Milan* repealed the prior Roman persecutions, initiated the return of confiscated Church property, and proclaimed an atmosphere of tolerance for all religions. In addition, it legalized Christianity as a valid religion for all of the Roman Empire.

With the rapid spread of Christianity throughout the Roman Empire as well as most of the known world, certain accommodations were made on a local or regional level that made it easier to proselytize among possible converts. These accommodations, which included merging Christian doctrine with pantheistic attitudes to achieve acceptance, occasionally permitted non-apostolic heresies to permeate official Church doctrine. However, with this situation soon becoming impossible to sustain with the many forms of "Christianities," including Gnosticism and Arianism gaining adherents, Constantine I decided to convene a council of Church bishops to provide uniform apostolic doctrine in order to resolve disagreements among the many disparate Church leaders. The First Council of Nicaea, a convocation of 1,800 invited Christian Bishops (over 300 attended), was held at Nicaea, Bithynia (present day Turkey), in A.D. 325 and was an initial effort to obtain ecumenical consensus on four issues needing Church resolve: the divinity of Christ in response to heretical theologies; a creation of a creed that would be a declaration and summary of the Christian faith; setting an annual date of Easter Sunday by independent means; and the promulgation or declaration of twenty new canons or church laws, many of which had to do with the execution of priestly duties. While the participants of the Nicean Council could not be expected to fully agree upon all matters set before them, the convocation was considered to be a success because the Bishops were able to agree on a doctrinal statement, especially in dealing with the question of the deity of Christ against prevailing heretical views. The Nicene Creed was amended to a newer version by the First Council of Constantinople in A.D. 381, which stated that anyone who did not endorse the Creed was to be excommunicated.

During the same year that the Council of Nicaea was concluded, Constantine set about unifying the Roman Empire by defeating his Co-Emperor Licinius due to the latter's resumption of the persecution of Christians. After Constantine's sponsorship of the unification of Christianity, he decided to build a new Imperial Capital away from the existing one in Rome and commenced building Constantinople in A.D. 325 on the site of an already existing city, Byzantine, located in Asia Minor on the Straits of Bosporus (where the Black Sea

Icon depicting the Emperor Constantine and the bishops of the First Council of Nicaea holding the revised Niceno-Constantinopolitan Creed of A.D. 381.

Mosaic in the Hagia Sophia (Church of the Holy Wisdom), Constantinople, A.D. 1000. A depiction of Emperor Constantine the Great holding a model of the city he had built in A.D. 325-330.

empties into the Mediterranean Sea). This expansive imperial metropolis was consecrated in A.D. 330 and, for more than 1,000 years, Constantinople was Europe's largest and wealthiest city. With his life's work accomplished, Constantine the Great, the 57th Emperor of the Roman Empire, died after a short illness in A.D. 337. Just prior to his death he was baptized a Christian and was buried in the Church of the Holy Apostles in Constantinople. Thus he became the first Christian Roman emperor.

After the death of Constantine I, civil war broke out among Constantine's three sons, each of whom claimed a portion of the Emperor title for his own. These wars had the effect of undoing most of Constantine I's work in reuniting the Empire and thus the Empire again was split, this time into three parts. In the ensuing twenty-seven years and after two more emperor changes, in A.D. 364 the Roman Empire became more formally split between the West and the East. The Western Empire, located in Rome, was under onslaught by many barbarian tribes, stretching its resources. In the Eastern Empire, the economic, as well as political, situation was much better due to well-established trade routes, on both land and water, to and from Asia and Arabia. However, both parts of the Empire were always under some form of attack from the Germanic and Hunnic tribes from A.D. 100 to 500.

"The Conversion of Theodosius by St. Ambrose" by Pierre Subleyras, A.D. 1745.

"The Baptism of Constantine" by the student of Raphael, A.D. 1520-1524. As Constantine was the first Roman Emperor to convert to Christianity, through his Edict of Milan, he proclaimed religious tolerance for all beliefs throughout the Roman Empire.

In A.D. 379, in the Eastern Empire, an important protector and facilitator of the Christian faith, Theodosius I, became emperor. Even after Constantine's efforts to unify the Christian Church through the Council of Nicaea, there existed some heretical factions of the Christian faith as well as several Roman paganism sects located in Rome. The most persistent of these heretical factions was Arianism, which espoused the theology that Jesus was a created being and inferior to God the Father; therefore, they were of similar but not the same substance. Opposed to the Nicene Creed, which espoused the absolute divinity of God the Father and God the Son, Arianism was beginning to achieve some traction.

In A.D. 374, St. Ambrose (Aurelius Ambrosius) became Bishop of the Archdiocese of Milan. As one of the original four Doctors of the Christian church, St. Ambrose was not only an extremely important counselor to Emperor Theodosius, but also an avid defender of the faith against Arianism. Since Christianity had only just become the state religion fifty years before, Theodosius decided to put to an end such schisms involving Christology. In A.D. 380, Theodosius, along with two emperors of the Western Empire, issued the *Edict of Thessalonica*, which declared "Catholic Christianity" the only legitimate Imperial Roman religion. Thus, Nicene Trinitarian Christianity became the law of the land — all Roman subjects now had to profess the Catholic (e.g. universal) faith of the bishops of Rome and Alexandria where the Nicene faith was most prevalent.

Later in this same year Emperor Theodosius I was baptized into the Christian faith by St. Ambrose. To further reduce any ambiguity concerning the new state religion, in May A.D. 381 Theodosius convened a new ecumenical conference called the First Council of Constantinople in order to repair the schism that had occurred between the Western and Eastern Empires due to the pressure of having the Nicene Orthodoxy forced upon many subjects professing other faiths. Once this state religion was firmly established, the Christian persecution of Roman paganism began in late A.D. 381. In A.D. 391, under pressure from St. Ambrose, Theodosius issued his famous "Theodosian Degrees," which effectively terminated any form of pagan ritualistic behavior, such as animal sacrifices and haruspicy. Pagan temples were destroyed, visits to important pagan sites forbidden, and pagan holidays were removed from the calendar. By the time this was accomplished in A.D. 392, Emperor Theodosius had become the sole Emperor of the Roman Empire until his death in A.D. 395.

Unfortunately, due to inherent weaknesses caused by demographic and economic instability, the Western Roman Empire finally succumbed to barbarian invasions in A.D. 476. When the political powers of the remaining emperors broke down, along with the collapse of the Roman Empire, the Church in Rome and its leaders endured as the dominant influences in post-Empire Roman politics and culture. From A.D. 325, when Constantine unified the Christian religion, to A.D. 600, the wildfire spread of Christianity was fostered by zealous clergy and laypersons that brought the "good word" to all major cities and towns out to the far margins of the Roman Empire. The Eastern, or Byzantine Empire, fared better and lasted until A.D. 1453 when Constantinople was overrun by the Ottoman Empire Turks. By then Christianity made good use of eight hundred years in which to proselytize and convert the inhabitants in the many regions of Armenia, Arabia, Asia Minor, Africa, and even India.

After the total defeat of the various Gallic tribes by Julius Caesar in 50 B.C., Gaul became a very compliant vassal province of Rome. The pacification of Gaul allowed the first Christian missionaries, probably from Asia Minor, to evangelize the area, which was populated by many pagan tribes. The first written instance of Christianity in Gaul was in A.D. 177, when it was mentioned that forty-eight Christian martyrs were killed for their faith in Lyon. It, therefore, can be assumed that Christianity gained a foothold in Gaul some years prior. For the next three hundred years until the final collapse of the Western Roman Empire, the Church in Gaul advanced rapidly with bishoprics in every metropolitan population center. However, among the rural populace, ancient Celtic religions, as well as Greco-Roman paganism, had very strong support. It was very hard for missionaries to persuade the local peasantry of the foolishness of believing in magical spells and charms, superstitions, divinations, and other aspects of rural idolatry. As a result, most of these evangelization efforts did not bear much fruit until several Gaulish heresies were beaten back at the start of the sixth century.

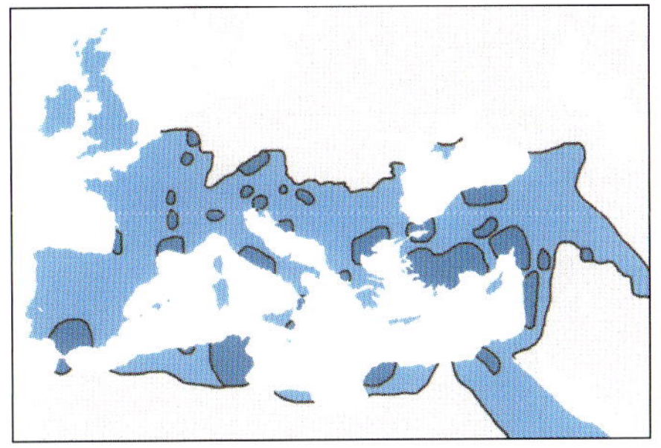

Spread of Christianity in Europe. Dark blue shows its spread to A.D. 325; light blue to A.D. 600.

Chapter 2

Early Christianity in the Pretanic Islands

Britannia (Britain)

As in Gaul, there is no written record as to when Christianity reached the shores of Britannia. It can be assumed that after Emperor Claudius finally rendered the various Briton Celtic tribes subservient to Rome by A.D. 43 that Christian missionaries, merchants, and traders eventually felt safe enough to embark upon some form of proselytism by mid-second century. However, Christian adherents came up against three separate pagan entities with which they had to do battle over the conversion of the minds and hearts of the ancient Britons: Roman pantheism and polytheism; native born Celtic deities; and a priestly form of Celtic deities called Druidism, a form of pagan religious practice that first became known during the Iron Age and of which there was word-of-mouth evidence of practice throughout Gaul, Britannia, and Hibernia. According to learned scholars, there is very little known about the Druids, as no archeological evidence or written records survive them. However, it has been assumed from literary sources that the Druids, as a priestly caste, practiced some form of human sacrifice, believed in certain forms of reincarnation, and were thought to practice prophesy, astrology, and magic.

With the Gallic Wars over, the Roman victors, starting with Julius Caesar and continuing with Claudius, firmly suppressed and banned all forms of Druid religious practices to include barbaric human sacrifices that were an anathema to the civilized Romans at that time. According to Julius Caesar, the Druids were alleged to practice animal and human sacrifice by imprisoning the unfortunates into an effigy of a large wicker human-like edifice and then setting it on fire. While the ancient Druid religion was banished, Druid written mythologies persisted into the Middle Ages, especially appearing in early Irish folklore and sages until the coming of Christianity.

Imaginative tinted illustration of "An Arch Druid in His Judicial Habit," 1815. *From The Costume of the Original Inhabitants of the British Islands.*

An eighteenth century engraving of a thirty-foot high Celtic "Wicker Man" that the Druids allegedly used for human sacrifices. *From the Commentaries of Caesar, translated by William Duncan and published in 1753.*

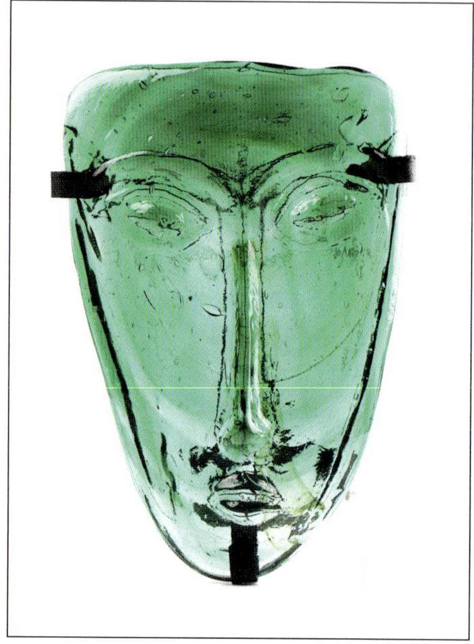

Reproduction of a Druid Mask, green glass-Irish.

Archeological evidence indicates that by the time Constantine I legalized Christianity throughout the Roman Empire in A.D. 313 there was confirmation that the early British Church was already prospering with appointed bishops in three large towns. As a result, with the mandate by the edict of Emperor Theodosius in A.D. 381 that Christianity was the only form of religion tolerated within the borders of the Roman Empire, British Christian missionaries were well disposed to begin their optimistic evangelization of Hibernia (present day Ireland). Christian worship and teachings reached the shores of pagan Ireland between A.D. 380 and 410. These dates coincide with increasing intensity of raids into Roman Britain by the Angles and Saxons (Germanic tribes), the Jutes (Danish tribes), the Picts (from Northern British areas not ruled by Rome), and the Scoti (Irish invaders).

Prior to these raids, Hadrian's Wall (named after Emperor Hadrian), a 73-mile-long fortification, was built between A.D. 122 and A.D. 128 across a narrow part of Northern Britain ostensibly to contain these invaders. Depending upon the location, the dimensions of this stone wall, as well as turf, measured 11-1/2 to 20 feet high and 10 to 20 feet wide. This wall was also protected by a wide ditch. For 285 years, Hadrian's Wall and other similar fortifications were strong enough to control incursions and smuggling, but the barbarian raids came seemingly without end from many directions. As a result, with the weakness of the Western Roman Empire at ebb and its resources spread quite thin, by A.D. 410 the Romans abandoned Britain forever forcing the Romano-Britons to fend for themselves.

The Romans Cause a Wall to be Built for the Protection of the South. By William Bell Scott, A.D. 1857; the painting shows a centurion supervising the building of Hadrian's Wall.

A stretch of Hadrian's Wall, viewed towards the East from Vercovicium, known as the Housesteads Roman Fort, which was an auxiliary fort built in A.D. 124.

Hibernia (Ireland)

When the first Christian missionaries reached the hinterlands of Ireland in the late fourth century, they found only pagan Celtic tribes and very little evidence of prior Roman activity. By the end of the Iron Age, the Celtic society that had been established in Ireland, Britain, and Gaul was based on a warrior aristocracy. With no urbanization (i.e. towns of any size) in Ireland, the established Celtic society was based almost entirely on the raising of cattle, sheep, and some indigenous swine. The many petty kingdoms that made up the five to ten original Kingdoms or Provinces were based on a cohort of pastoral communities bound together by mutual defense alliances that protected one another from cattle raids.

In Celtic Ireland, the culture of the warrior aristocracy was based on the ownership and maintenance of large cattle herds. All land — and what was herded and grown on it — was owned by families and not individuals. Individual wealth, therefore, was measured in terms of cattle and other cloven hoofed animals. Each individual, whether warrior, free men, or peasant, had a status of wealth based on their position in society. If a crime was committed against any other individual, a fine was usually paid in cattle to that individual based on that person's status. Therefore, the stealing of cattle from another kingdom's herd was not only an easy way to accumulate wealth, but also a way to add to one's warrior status.

Besides the hierarchical and class-based warrior society, Celtic culture was heavily influenced by members of the Druid priesthood. As in Britain, the Druid priests were considered to be a special class of ritualistic intellectuals who acted as intermediaries between the various Celtic polytheistic divinities and the individual. Celtic ritual life, as fostered by the Druid caste, was centered on the natural environment with special religious significances attached to pools of water, lakes, and small groves of oak trees. It was in these groves that the Druids practiced their ritual activities of casting spells, which may have included a form of animal or human sacrifice. The Druids left no written literature of their activities and, therefore, anything written about Druidian practices is conjecture.

Engraving from "The Image of Irelande" by John Derrick, A.D. 1581. The image is that of a typical hit-and-run cattle raid with the description: "An armed company of the kerne (light infantry), carrying halberds and pikes and led by a piper, attack and burn a farmhouse and drive off the horses and cattle."

Early Irish Ecclesiastical & Political History

In the very first years of the fifth century, based on hearsay reports from "unofficial Christian missionaries" returning from Ireland that the unblemished pastoral society was ripe for evangelization, the reigning Latin Pope (St.) Celestine I decided to send a high church official to "spread the good word." In A.D. 431, the Pope sent the recently ordained Bishop Palladius on an ecclesiastical mission to Ireland to minister to the "Scoti, i.e. The Irish, who believed in Christ." The wording of this passage indicates that there were already Christian inhabitants of Celtic Ireland.

Palladius arrived in Leinster, one of five kingdoms or provinces at that time, where he founded three churches. However, due to Palladius' lack of communication and bonding with the local extant Christians and various Pagan chiefs, his proselytizing efforts were not well received. Since he was also experiencing failing health, Palladius sailed to the Pictish area of Scotland, but died early in A.D. 432, although other sources have him dying some twenty years later.

From the time St. Patrick first set foot on Irish soil in A.D. 432 until the first Viking Raids in A.D. 795, he and his fellow missionaries forever dramatically changed the Celtic culture that arrived during the Iron Age. Since St. Patrick was and is such an important part of Irish culture, he is hailed as the Patron Saint of Ireland. *(See next chapter for a full development of St. Patrick).*

Unlike the failed efforts of Palladius, Patrick and the missionaries who followed in his footsteps had a profound effect on the spread of Christianity in a predominantly pagan country. Ireland, at the beginning of the fifth century, consisted of many petty tribes (clanna) and small kingdoms (tuatha) bound somewhat under the aegis of rudimentary provinces ruled by a dynastic form of kingship. As resources were seemingly always scarce and cattle rustling a coming-of-age sport among noblemen, there were constant altercations, vendettas, incursions, and hit-and-run raids amongst these tribal units. Warfare that used a combination of infantry and cavalry were usually carried out between provinces with the goals of acquisition of land, plunder, and hostage-taking being the norm.

Before the time of Patrick, there were five main Irish provinces: Ulster, Midhe or Meath, Munster, Leinster, and Connacht. While this political distinction was termed a pentarchy, the borders as such were very fluid and there were no set chieftains. However, as time progressed over the next 225 years to A.D. 650, several tribal associations, or clanna, banded together as tuatha to form powerful dynasties, which exerted influence over wide areas within these former provinces due to the almost constant warfare of which most was endemic in nature. The outcome was that some of these ancient provinces were split up, absorbed, or changed names to reflect on-going political realities. For instance, over time Meath was split up, with a part being absorbed by Leinster and a part to Ulster. In today's modern Ireland (to include Northern Ireland), there are four provinces consisting of thirty-two counties.

Stained Glass of Saint Patrick, a Romano-British Christian Missionary and the Patron Saint of Ireland.

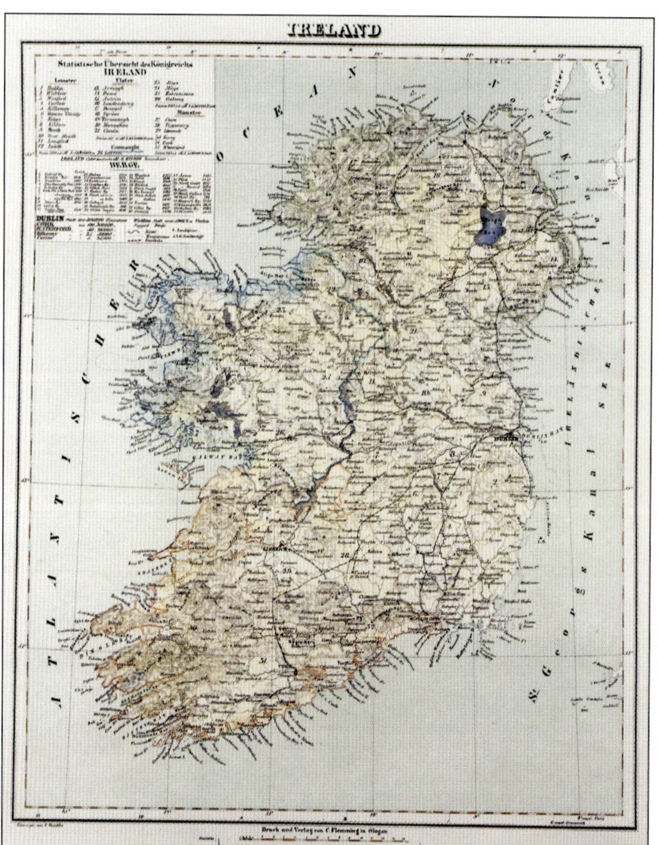

A German-made map of Ireland showing the four provinces with a total population of 8,891,000, c. 1870s.

The chronology of ancient Irish historical tradition is, in many cases, thought to be fabricated and spurious. Many of the dates of the births, successions, and deaths of major figures are either erroneous or have a mythological intent. With that in mind one major figure in early Irish history was alleged to have the most important impact on the spread of Christianity in Ireland without even realizing it. Niall Noigiallach (c. 375/380-450/455) was a traditional High King (Ard Ri) of Ireland. The epithet Noigiallach stands for "having nine hostages" in the Old Irish language. In order to keep the kingdoms under his domain peaceful, he required that an important personage from each kingdom be given as a hostage.

Originally from the Province of Connacht, Niall and his seven sons originated the Connachta Dynasty, one of the most important and strongest in early Irish history. Niall and three of his sons expanded their dynastic rule over much of western, northern, and central Ireland, which included the Provinces of Ulster and Midhe. This hegemonial expansion of territory formed a new dynasty, Ui Neill (i.e. sons of Niall), which persisted in one form or another for five hundred years. The northeastern coast of Ireland was close enough to the western shores of Scotland (north Britain) to make raids a profitable enterprise. Tradition marks the fact that Niall Noigiallach led a series of raids leading to the capture of Patrick and his sisters in the late fourth century. This serendipitous action by Niall brought Patrick to the Irish countryside as a heathen. However, after six years in captivity, Patrick escaped and sailed to the coast of Gaul as an enlightened person who became close to God due to his tribulations.

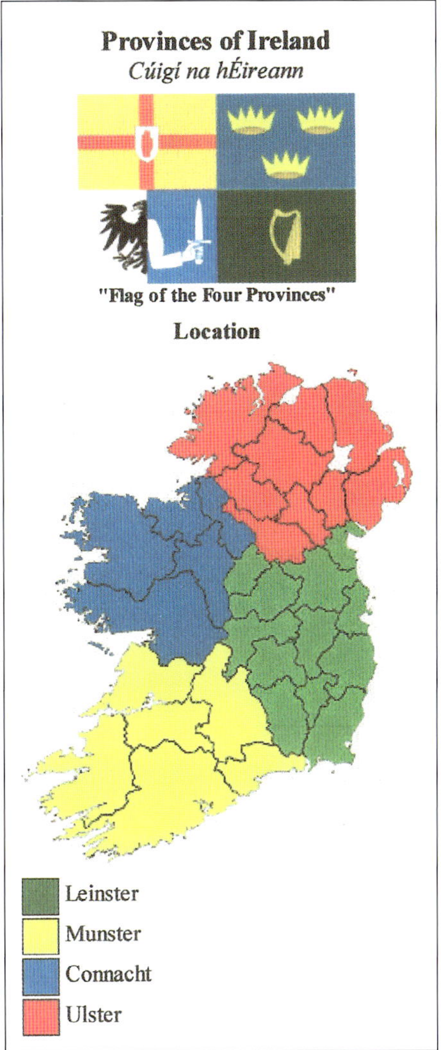

Location of the four provinces of Ireland consisting of thirty-two counties and a population of approximately 6.1 million as of 2010.

Fanciful representation of Niall Noigiallach and his men embarking on a raid on the eastern coastline of Ireland.

Chapter 3

Saint Patrick: The Man & the Myth

St. Patrick, c. A.D. 387–461 or c. A.D. 387–493: The differences in dates are just one of the many "facts" that historians have used to anoint their version of the historical record of St. Patrick. Historians are, in many cases, prone, when little documentation is available, to embellish events to reconstruct history. A good example of this is the information supporting facts surrounding the First Thanksgiving Feast in Plymouth, Massachusetts, in 1621. Two contemporaneously written books in the early 1600s by Edward Winslow and William Bradford (both Governors of the Plymouth Colony) provide the only primary sources of the "First Thanksgiving" that exist. Yet many fables have been written about this event since then that now are regarded as fact.

St. Patrick's Cross. A replica of the oldest of the great Irish High Crosses, 7th Century, Carndonagh, County Donegal, 10 feet high. Three sections of the cross: *Bottom*, three pilgrims; *Middle*, Christ with the four Evangelists; *Top*, interlacing pattern used in Celtic art to suggest the ineffable. From St. Patrick's Breastplate hymn: "Christ be with me/ Christ be before me/ Christ be behind me/ Christ be within me." Brass-painted, hand-cast resin by the Wild Goose Studio, Kinsale, County Cork, Ireland, 8.5" h.

THE DAILY GRAPHIC

AN ILLUSTRATED EVENING NEWSPAPER.

39 & 41 PARK PLACE.

VOL. 1---NO. 12. NEW YORK, MONDAY, MARCH 17, 1873. FIVE CENTS.

ST. PATRICK.

The Daily Graphic, An Illustrated Newspaper, New York City, March 17, 1873. Shown as a bishop wearing a mitre (the ceremonial head-dress of bishops being a tall folding cap rising to a peak) and holding a crozier (a stylized pastoral staff), this engraved drawing shows St. Patrick casting out the serpents from Ireland. Mitres were not worn in the Western Christian world by bishops until approximately A.D. 1000. Croziers evolved from simple wooden staffs to ornate gold or metal rods or staffs (c. 11th century) that have a curved or hooked top not unlike a shepherd's crook with the obvious symbolism that the bishop is the shepherd to his flock. Virtually all engravings and images of St. Patrick show him wearing and holding the traditional bishop's insignia of a mitre and a crozier.

Similarly, the historic record of St. Patrick is contained in only two first-person documents, written by the Saint, and one prayer. The two attributed documents are his *Confessio* (My Declaration), written when Patrick was elderly, and *Epistola Militibus Corotici* (A Letter to the Soldiers of Coroticus). Both were written in Latin as were most of the learned works of the day. The *Confessio* recounts facts about his early life and his ecclesiastical mission to Ireland. The *Epistola* pleads with Coroticus, a nominal Christian British chieftain, to free some recent Irish converts that he and his soldiers had recently captured and brutalized. Lastly, a beautiful prayer, "St. Patrick's Breastplate," or the "Lorica of St. Patrick," is a ten-stanza hymn composed by St. Patrick in anticipation of his victory over the forces of Paganism. The first and last stanzas are the same:

"I bind to myself today
The strong virtue of the an invocation of the Trinity
I believe the Trinity in the Unity
The Creator of the Universe"

For many years following Patrick's death, Irish Christians sang this hymn about the three-personed God embedded within the concept of the Trinity.

Patrick's Confessio (of Past Life)

In c. A.D. 450, Patrick, in his own words and when well into his years, wrote a 62-paragraph autobiographical "confession" that not only records his early life as a youth, but also the events leading up to his evangelism of Ireland for Christianity. Much of the known facts concerning Patrick are contained in his *Confessio*, with many other facts the subject of conjecture. The following are some key excerpts from his *Confessio*:

1. "I, Patrick, a sinner, a most simple countryman, the least of all faithful and most contemptible to many, had for father the deacon Calpurnius, son of the late Potitus, a priest of the settlement of Bannavem Taburniae; he had a small villa nearby where I was taken captive. I was at that time about sixteen years of age. I did not know the true God; and I was taken into captivity in Ireland with many thousands of people..."

4. "For there is no other God, nor ever was before, nor shall be hereafter, but God the Father...and we worship one God in the Trinity of holy name."

9. "And therefore for some time I have thought of writing, but I have hesitated until now, for truly, I feared to expose myself to the criticism of men, because I have not studied like the others" (i.e. embarassed at lack of education).

16. "But after I reached Ireland (as a captive) I used to pasture the flock each day and I used to pray many times a day. More and more did the love of God, and my fear of him and faith increase, and my spirit was moved so that in a day I said from one up to a hundred prayers, and in the night a like number..."

17. "And it was there of course that one night in my sleep I heard a voice saying to me: 'You do well to fast: soon you will depart for your home country.' And again, a very short time later, there was a voice prophesying: 'Behold, your ship is ready.' And it was not close by, but as it happened, two hundred miles away... And shortly thereafter I turned about and fled from the man with whom I had been with for six years, and I came, by the power of God...until I reached that ship."

Patrick talks the captain of the ship into taking him abroad and makes friends with the barbarian crew.

19. "And after three days we reached land, and for twenty-eight days journeyed through uninhabited country, and the food ran out and hunger overtook them; then one day the captain began saying: 'Why is it, Christian? You say your God is great and all-powerful; then why can you not pray for us?'" *Patrick did pray and at that moment a herd of swine appeared on the road, which the crew killed for food and thereafter never wanted for food again.*

21. "And a second time, after many years I was taken captive." *But a divine prophecy said to Patrick that he would be captive for two months and then set free.*

23. "And after a few years I was again in Britain with my parents and they welcomed me as a son..."

Patrick then had a vision in the night of (an angel) Victoricus coming from Ireland; Victoricus showed him letters, one of which was 'The Voice of the Irish,' from which he heard many with one voice: 'We beg you, holy youth, that you shall come and walk again among us.'

27. "They (church elders) brought up against me after thirty years an occurrence (a grave sin committed at age 15) that I had confessed before becoming a deacon." *A childhood friend broke his confidence and Patrick's youthful degradation returned to haunt him.*

In paragraphs 28-36, Patrick speaks of his sorrow about being rebuked and how God protected him, which allowed Patrick to continue his mission to Ireland so...

37. "...that I might come to the Irish people to preach the Gospel and ensure insults from unbelievers... and endure many persecutions to the extent of prison; and so that I may give up my birthright for the advantage of others..."

41. "So, how is it that in Ireland, where they never had any knowledge of God but, always, until now, cherished idols and unclean things, they are lately become a people of the Lord, and are called children of God; the sons of the Irish and the daughters of the chieftains are to be seen as monks and virgins of Christ?" *Patrick completed his triumph over Paganism.*

In paragraphs 42-61, Patrick explains how he was blessed to be doing the work of his Lord and that he would be willing to die for his faith in that he...

42-61. "...would commend his soul to God who is most faithful and for whom he would perform his mission in obscurity."

62. "But I entreat those who believe in and fear God, whoever deigns to examine or receive this document composed by the obviously unlearned sinner Patrick in Ireland, that nobody shall ever ascribe to my ignorance any trivial thing

that I have achieved or may have expounded that was pleasing to God, but accept and truly believe that it would have been the gift of God. And this is my confession before I die."

Within the context of Patrick's *Confessio*, he can be seen and viewed as a Convert, a Missionary, a Teacher, and a Pilgrim, tasks for which he was uniquely suited "in servitude to the Gospel."

St. Patrick in cameo. Published by Geschutzt and printed in Saxony.

St. Patrick in cameo holding a crozier and a shamrock. Published by Fred C. Lounsbury.

A younger St. Patrick holding a crozier with a shamrock in the background. Gold embossed image postcard published by M. B. 200.

The dates for Patrick are not uniformly accepted. From his birth date of c. A.D. 387, it is known from his *Confessio* that he was sixteen years old when captured (c. A.D. 403) and six years later at age twenty-two (c. A.D. 409) when he escaped. It has been written that Patrick, now a Bishop, returned to Ireland in c. A.D. 432 to start a drive to bring Christianity to that pagan island. Therefore, twenty-three years ensued where he returned back to Roman Britain to visit his parents, traveled to Gaul to study under Germanus, Bishop of Auxerre, to become a deacon, and then was ordained a priest/bishop. Patrick was assumed to be forty-five years old at that point. He wrote his *Confessio* in c. A.D. 450 "in his old age" after eighteen years proselytizing throughout Ireland, which would make him approximately sixty-three years old. If he died in c. A.D. 461, he would have been seventy-four years old, and if he died in c. A.D. 493, that would make him a venerable 103 years old. Regardless of the date of his death, St. Patrick is said to be buried at the Cathedral Church of the Holy and Undivided Trinity (Church of Ireland), Downpatrick, County Down, Northern Ireland.

A non-traditional image of St. Patrick in a monk's robe standing astride the world. H. B. Griggs. Published as part of L & M Series 2230.

St. Patrick wearing a bishop's mitre. Card embossed in gold. Publisher unknown, Series 7041, printed in Germany.

Reputed gravesite of the remains of St. Patrick located in the graveyard of the Down Cathedral of the Church of Ireland, built in A.D. 1183, Downpatrick, County Down, Northern Ireland.

The Book of Armagh: Patrick's Legends and Myths

Books written about St. Patrick centuries after his time not only added to his good name, but also to the legends and myths surrounding him. Early medieval hagiographers, usually plying their skilled trade out of monasteries, compiled biographies of saints that included, besides a life story, a description of the saint's deeds and/or miracles and details of the saint's martyrdom if valid. Most of these hagiographies were recorded based on little or no written documentation. Therefore the hagiographer had to rely upon stories passed from mouth-to-mouth over a span of centuries in which some exploits became exaggerated and despoiled from bias. Ireland, due to its famed seats of learning based in its many monasteries, had a rich hagiographic tradition. The most important Irish hagiographies dealt with St. Patrick, St. Brigid, and St. Columba, as all three are considered the Patron Saints of Ireland.

The written reliquary that contains two seventh century texts relating to St. Patrick is *The Book of Armagh*, known as *The Canon of Patrick*, which was written in the ninth century. The first text, "Confession – A Life of Patrick," was written by Muirchu Maccu Machteni, a seventh century Irish historian and Leinster monk. Muirchu admits that while writing the text that fills out Patrick's *Confessio* he cannot be sure of the validity of some of these facts, but deemed it important to pass on other legends and traditions that were becoming part of the persona of Patrick. One apocryphal story has Patrick winning over Loegaire, a fierce pagan king who ruled the kingdom Tara, (County Meath), which was the ritual site of the ancient high kings of Ireland. Due to divine intervention, Patrick conquered the magic of the druids and wizards of this king. Now convinced that Patrick had the true faith, King Loegaire was baptized a Christian.

The second text, by Tirechan, a seventh century Irish bishop and biographer of Patrick, is untitled, as it was written in the first-person as Patrick. This text also has a story concerning King Loegaire and his two beautiful daughters who were converted by Patrick at the well of Clebach. Tirechan compares Patrick to Moses, where Moses fasted for forty days and forty nights on Mount Sinai. In the western half of Ireland, in County Mayo, there is Croagh Patrick (2510' high), which is an important site of pilgrimage especially on Reek Sunday, the last Sunday in July, where over 15,000 pilgrims climb to the summit. Some of the more zealous pilgrims attempt the climb in bare feet. At the top there is a small church, St. Patrick's Oratory. According to Tirechan, God commanded Patrick to: "Climb, O holy man, to the top of the mountain which towers above and is higher than all the mountains to the west of the sun, in order to bless the people of Ireland." It is here that legend says that Patrick also fasted for forty days and forty nights. After his fast was over, Patrick threw a silver bell down the slope, knocking the she-demon, Corra, from the sky and causing the snakes to flee from Ireland due to the loud ringing of the bell.

Two of the many long-standing and enduring myths surrounding St. Patrick are: the concept of using the green shamrock as a simple way to explain the Trinity, and that he banished all snakes from Ireland.

CROAGH PATRICK, MAYO

SCENE OF CROAGH PATRICK, COUNTY MAYO, IRELAND. The old Irish name for Croagh Patrick is Cruachan Aigli, meaning "conical mountain." A three-mile path over white quartzite rock leads steeply to the 2,510-foot summit. Published by John Hinde, Ireland.

The Oratory - Summit of Croagh Patrick

THE ORATORY-SUMMIT OF CROAGH PATRICK. *Top*: This small chapel was built in 1905 at which time the annual pilgrimage to the summit was revived and now takes place on the last Sunday in July, known locally as "Reek Sunday." Publisher unknown. *Bottom*: Interior view of the chapel. *Photography by the authors*.

"ST. PATRICK'S DAY 1979" DECORATIVE PLATE. This monument, on the slopes of Croagh Patrick overlooking Clew Bay, County Mayo, Western Ireland, is annually besieged by many thousands of pilgrims. Crown Staffordshire Fine Bone China, 7.5" diameter.

St. Patrick in a shamrock cameo with the draped flags of Ireland and the United States. Published by Fred C. Lounsbury, Series 2059-2.

St. Patrick casting out serpents with Erin Go Bragh greetings. Publisher unknown; gold embossed image.

As a way for St. Patrick to gain some gravitas among the pagans he encountered, he had to explain the Holy Trinity, the foundation upon which Christianity rests. According to legend, Patrick used the ubiquitous green Irish shamrock, a three-leafed clover, to teach his audience about the mystery of the Holy Trinity. He demonstrated that from a single stem of the plant there were three leaves representing the one-in-three union of God the Father, God the Son (Jesus), and the Holy Spirit. Thus the green shamrock became a very important symbol of Saint Patrick and his contribution to Irish Christianity.

After the end of the last Ice Age in Europe, in which the maximum extent of the ice sheet covered 95% of Ireland, it was assumed that virtually all indigenous snakes that existed were eliminated. While there have been some attempts to reintroduce snakes to Ireland since then, they have not thrived and Ireland today is free of all of the scientific Suborder Serpentes. The single most well-known miracle attributed to St. Patrick is his banishment of all snakes, venomous or not, from Ireland. The snake-banishment miracle has been portrayed for over 1,000 years and shows a stern St. Patrick wearing a bishop's mitre and holding a crosier or pastoral staff with slithering and squirming snakes at his feet. It has been said that the ridding of Ireland of these reptiles is a metaphorical story purporting to show that the snakes symbolize the various pagan faiths that Patrick drove out of Ireland in order for Christianity to flourish.

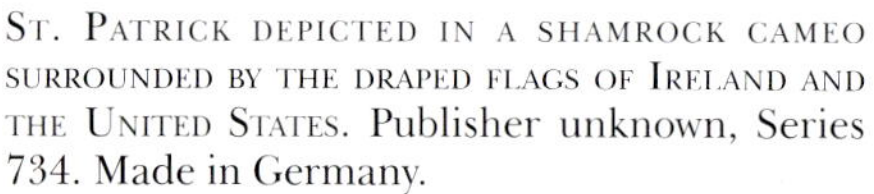
St. Patrick depicted in a shamrock cameo surrounded by the draped flags of Ireland and the United States. Publisher unknown, Series 734. Made in Germany.

St. Patrick in a stained glass motif casting out serpents. Publisher unknown.

Engraving depicting St. Patrick banishing serpents from Ireland onto a small boat — this is the most enduring myth about the saint.

Two hundred years after St. Patrick's death, the last of the pagan chieftains were converted and Ireland became a bright candle in the Christian world. The contributions made by St. Patrick (and those who followed him) were many: he established churches and monasteries all throughout the inhabited parts of Ireland and ordained over 350 bishops who would insure that his good works would survive him.

As Ireland was still a rural Christian outpost with little concentration of population, monasteries became, in many cases, the first settlements and eventually became the scholastic and religious centers of the Irish culture. The many priests and monks who served time in these monasteries brought back to Europe an abiding and enduring love for the Christian faith that begot more students enrolling in the monasteries, ensuring that the legacy of St. Patrick endured and prospered. According to *The Book of Armagh*, St. Patrick, his life's work accomplished, passed away on March 17th. Hence that date has become a day of spiritual and secular celebration in the Christian world in remembrance of a job very well done.

A non-traditional image of St. Patrick in a monk's robe holding a shillelagh while rousting out serpents from Ireland. HBG postcard published by L & E, Series. 2230.

St. Patrick giving the traditional blessing with his right hand while holding his Bishop's hooked crozier and wearing three layers of vestments. Hand-cast painted resin, 10"h.

Replica of an ancient image of St. Patrick in traditional attire holding the Bishop's crozier. As Patron of Ireland, he made medieval Ireland unique in the western world by blending its pagan past with its Christian future. Brass painted hand cast resin, 6.5"h. The Wild Goose Studio, Kinsale, County Cork, Ireland.

St. Patrick in traditional Bishop's attire casting out serpents. Hand-painted resin, 8"h. including base. Made in China.

Chapter 4

The Celebration of Saint Patrick's Day

The reasons why the Irish, Irish-Americans, people of Irish ancestry in other countries, and people who consider themselves "Irish" only on St. Patrick's Day celebrate this patron saint's feast day on March 17th are deeply rooted in the annals of medieval as well as recent history.

In 1607, some 1,150 years after the death of Patrick, March 17th was recognized as the anniversary of his death by its placement on the Irish legal calendar. The inclusion of this date meant that March 17th was officially recognized as a religious day of importance and, soon after, Patrick was elevated by the Vatican to the status of Apostle and Patron Saint of Ireland. In 1631, Pope Urban VIII added the feast of St. Patrick to the liturgical calendar of the Catholic Church. Even though there was always some form of religious expression honoring St. Patrick from the seventh to the seventeenth centuries, once he became the Patron Saint of Ireland, more and more adherents made the date of March 17th a special day of adoration and celebration.

The Illustrated London News, March 13, 1847. "An Allegorical Representation of the Celebration of St. Patrick's Day." Artist: James Mahony.

ST. PATRICK'S DAY.—1847.

[The Illustration upon the previous page is from a design by Mr. James Mahony. In the centre of the composition is a medallic representation of the Birth of St. Patrick; surrounded by a St. Patrick's Cross of Shamrock. To the left is St. Patrick, with his attendant Missionaries, banishing the "frogs and varment" into the bogs; whilst the aborigines of the country are struck with amazement at his miraculous power; and here, too, are the Irish Court, afterwards his converts to Christianity: to the left is one of his priests preaching; and in the distance is a long procession to a rude temple; and beyond it an ancient round tower, backed by lofty mountains, behind which is the setting sun, emblematic of the fall of idolatry in the country. In the lower left foreground is a picture of the Evils of Intemperance: a drunken "Paddy"—the row; the fire; the military called out; Bridewell; and in the extreme distance, the gibbet; all traceable from the flowing can, the beloved bottle, and the noggin. Thus far, the *dark side*. The opposite shows Father Mathew, "the Apostle of Temperance," administering the pledge to anxious crowds, with a long "Temperance" procession from the distant hills. Instead of the decayed hamlet and the pagan pile of stones, we have the neat village and its Christian church, backed by mountains, and the rising sun to indicate emancipation from a dark age. As a contrast to the old mode of keeping St. Patrick's Day, in the lower right foreground, is the innocent recreation of the dance; and beneath, is the happy tea-party, indicative of the regeneration of Ireland, and bringing the miseries and crimes which spring from Intoxication into powerful contrast with the peace and joy accruing from Temperance.]

Alas! though the clouds of misfortune may hover
Green Isle! o'er thy mountains and vallies so fair,
Through darkness and death thy true soul will discover
The sunbeams of Hope which shall conquer despair.
Cold, cold is the heart, in this hour of dire sorrow,
That fails to accord thee blest sympathy's ray;
And colder the harp which one stigma would borrow
To brand the brave Shamrock on Patrick's Day.

Thou type of the Trinity! through thee the glory,
Love, goodness of God was proclaimed to the land;
The King and the Kerne, the blooming and hoary,
All loved the good Saint whose apòstolic hand
Expell'd viper-vice, and uncleanness before it,
Redeem'd the fair Island from paganish sway.
And long as the teardrops of Heaven stream o'er it,
Shall Erin pay homage to Patrick's Day.

But wild was the homage. The vice of all others
Most baleful arose from the festival bowl,
And men became foes who but lately were brothers,
"The joy of the fight" baffled Friendship's control.
Raise, raise ye the statue to good Father Mathew,
His trophies o'er vice shall not soon fade away;
He taught a whole nation t'eschew death's potation,
And yet be most happy on Patrick's Day.

Oh! soon may the day dawn, sweet Isle of the Ocean!
Whose warm smile will banish the tear from thy cheek,
When scorning the breakers of factious commotion,
The true good and fame of thy sons thou wilt seek;
When the 'prentice of Derry shall love Pat of Kerry,
And both with the Saxon be prudent and gay;
When plenty and peace and the arts may increase
To honour our Empire on Patrick's Day.—L.

"St. Patrick's Day – 1847." The description of the allegories is as follows: *Center*: The birth of St. Patrick. *Left*: St. Patrick, with his attendant missionaries, banishes the frogs and varmint into the bogs. *Right*: Shows Father Mathew, the "Apostle of Temperance," administering the abstinence pledge to a long procession of people. *Lower Left*: Showing the evils of intemperance with a drunken "paddy" emblematic of the "dark side." *Lower Right*: The innocent recreation of the dance along with a happy tea party indicative of the regeneration of Ireland. Three other views are close-ups of the Left allegory with St. Patrick and the bottom allegory and description of the allegory and a four stanza poem concerning hope for the future of Ireland.

During this time the Protestant Reformation reached Ireland during the reign of England's King James I and the Anglican Church of Ireland became the "official" religion of that country. Hence, Irish Catholicism became unofficial and illegal. In 1685, James II, a self-proclaimed Catholic, succeeded his Protestant brother Charles II to the throne of England. James than began to dismantle many of the restrictions on the religious observances of Irish Catholics. However, in 1688, he was deposed by the Protestant William of Orange from the Netherlands under pressure by Irish Protestant militants and he fled to France.

Two years later, in 1690, James II returned to Ireland as the head of a newly formed Jacobite army, but the invasion was poorly handled in terms of trained men and equipment. As a result, James II suffered a disastrous defeat at the hands of William of Orange at the Battle of the Boyne (River) located in North East Ireland. For the Jacobites this largest battle ever fought in Ireland was for Irish sovereignty from England, religious toleration for Catholicism, and the return of seized lands taken after Cromwell's conquest of Ireland from 1649 to 1653. The defeat of James and his Jacobite forces guaranteed the continuation of official Protestant supremacy for another 230 years.

Throughout the eighteenth and nineteenth century, "official" state-supported celebrations of St. Patrick were held by the Church of Ireland in Dublin. Since St. Patrick, as Patron Saint of Ireland, was considered to be "owned" by both the Church of Ireland and the Catholic Church as their saint, religious celebrations on March 17th were held by each denomination. By the early 1800s, the celebration of St. Patrick's Day was a permanent annual event for all the religious and social groups in Ireland. For Catholics, St. Patrick's Day was (and is) a Holy Day of Obligation and requires attendance at Mass.

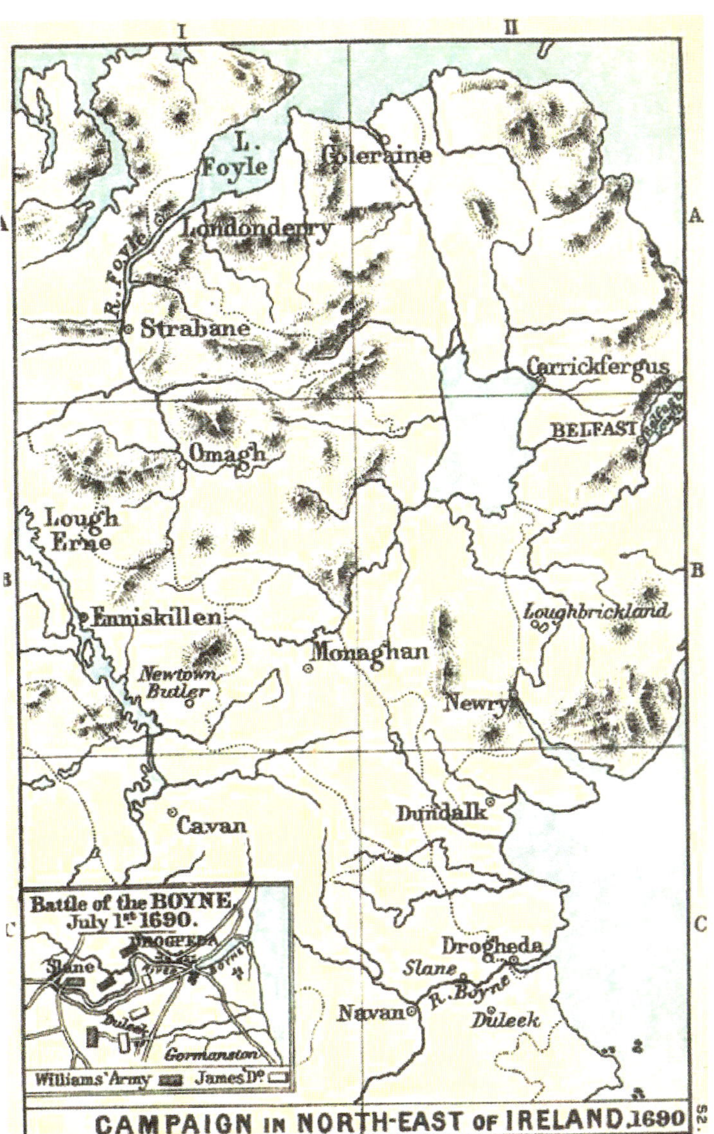

BATTLE OF THE BOYNE, JULY 11, 1690. The Williamite Army of 36,000 under William of Orange opposed the Jacobite Army of 23,500 under James II. The Williamite Army had superior numbers as well as having the latest flintlock muskets compared to the Jacobites' obsolete matchlock muskets.

Battle of the Boyne between James II and William III, 11 July 1690; painting by Jan van Huchtenburg, c. early 1700s.

Irish War of Independence

England's and the Church of Ireland's dominance in their economic and religious affairs could no longer be tolerated by the Irish citizens, resulting in many calls for Home Rule. The citizens' bitterness came to a head in Dublin during Easter Week 1916, when Irish republican leaders instigated an insurrection by proclaiming an Irish Republic independent of Britain. This Easter Rising lasted one week and resulted in 450 deaths on both sides including civilians, extensive property damage, and sixteen official executions of rebel officers by British authorities.

While this Rising was in reality the inception of the Irish War of Independence, the intervening years between 1916 and January 1919 were relatively quiet. However, due to increasing raids on loyalists' barracks and ambushes by IRA members for arms and booty, the war heated up and became one of attrition — a bitterly fought sectarian guerrilla war of ambushes, pitched battles, and summary executions involving the Irish Republican Army (IRA), a left of center paramilitary group, versus the Royal Irish Constabulary (RIC) and British troops. A truce was finally brokered in 1921, but some violence continued until December 1922 when the Irish Free State was created.

The war resulted in effectively partitioning Ireland along political and religious lines by establishing the Catholic and nationalist dominated Irish Free State of twenty-six counties against the Protestant and unionist dominated Northern Ireland, which retained six counties and became one of four countries (including Wales, Scotland, and England) that make up the United Kingdom. After fifteen years, the Irish Free State came to an end in 1937, when the citizens voted by referendum to replace the 1922 constitution. With the new constitution of December 29, 1937, the Free State part of Ireland finally became a Constitutional Republic and a sovereign state called Ireland (or Eire in the Irish language). As like before, the Republic of Ireland consists of twenty-six counties and Northern Ireland, which had chosen to remain with the United Kingdom, has six counties.

Replica of the "Irish Republic" flag that flew over the General Post Office in Dublin during the Easter Rising 1916.

POBLACHT NA H EIREANN.

THE PROVISIONAL GOVERNMENT OF THE

IRISH REPUBLIC

TO THE PEOPLE OF IRELAND.

IRISHMEN AND IRISHWOMEN In the name of God and of the dead generations from which she receives her old tradition of nationhood, Ireland, through us, summons her children to her flag and strikes for her freedom.

Having organised and trained her manhood through her secret revolutionary organisation, the Irish Republican Brotherhood, and through her open military organisations, the Irish Volunteers and the Irish Citizen Army, having patiently perfected her discipline, having resolutely waited for the right moment to reveal itself, she now seizes that moment, and, supported by her exiled children in America and by gallant allies in Europe, but relying in the first on her own strength, she strikes in full confidence of victory.

We declare the right of the people of Ireland to the ownership of Ireland, and to the unfettered control of Irish destinies, to be sovereign and indefeasible. The long usurpation of that right by a foreign people and government has not extinguished the right, nor can it ever be extinguished except by the destruction of the Irish people. In every generation the Irish people have asserted their right to national freedom and sovereignty; six times during the past three hundred years they have asserted it in arms. Standing on that fundamental right and again asserting it in arms in the face of the world, we hereby proclaim the Irish Republic as a Sovereign Independent State, and we pledge our lives and the lives of our comrades-in-arms to the cause of its freedom, of its welfare, and of its exaltation among the nations.

The Irish Republic is entitled to, and hereby claims, the allegiance of every Irishman and Irishwoman. The Republic guarantees religious and civil liberty, equal rights and equal opportunities to all its citizens, and declares its resolve to pursue the happiness and prosperity of the whole nation and of all its parts, cherishing all the children of the nation equally, and oblivious of the differences carefully fostered by an alien government, which have divided a minority from the majority in the past.

Until our arms have brought the opportune moment for the establishment of a permanent National Government, representative of the whole people of Ireland and elected by the suffrages of all her men and women, the Provisional Government, hereby constituted, will administer the civil and military affairs of the Republic in trust for the people.

We place the cause of the Irish Republic under the protection of the Most High God, Whose blessing we invoke upon our arms, and we pray that no one who serves that cause will dishonour it by cowardice, inhumanity, or rapine. In this supreme hour the Irish nation must, by its valour and discipline and by the readiness of its children to sacrifice themselves for the common good, prove itself worthy of the august destiny to which it is called.

Signed on Behalf of the Provisional Government,

THOMAS J. CLARKE.

SEAN Mac DIARMADA. THOMAS MacDONAGH.

P. H. PEARSE. EAMONN CEANNT.

JAMES CONNOLLY. JOSEPH PLUNKETT.

THE EASTER PROCLAMATION OF 1916 posted during the Easter Rising. After the seven-day insurrection was overcome, most of the signatories of this document were captured and executed. The first paragraph reads: *"IRISHMEN AND IRISHWOMEN In the name of God and of the dead generations from which she receives her old tradition of nationhood, Ireland, through us, summons her children to her flag and strikes for her freedom."*

"BIRTH OF THE IRISH REPUBLIC," WALTER PAGET, C. 1920s. The painting depicts events at Dublin's General Post Office held by the Irish Republicans during the Easter Rising, an armed insurrection, staged in Ireland during Easter Week 1916.

"Beannach na Feile Padrais." Part of the postcard's message reads: "On this St. Patrick's Day pledge yourself to help to undo the dismemberment of St. Patrick's Island." IRA postcard published by B. & N., Ltd. Dublin.

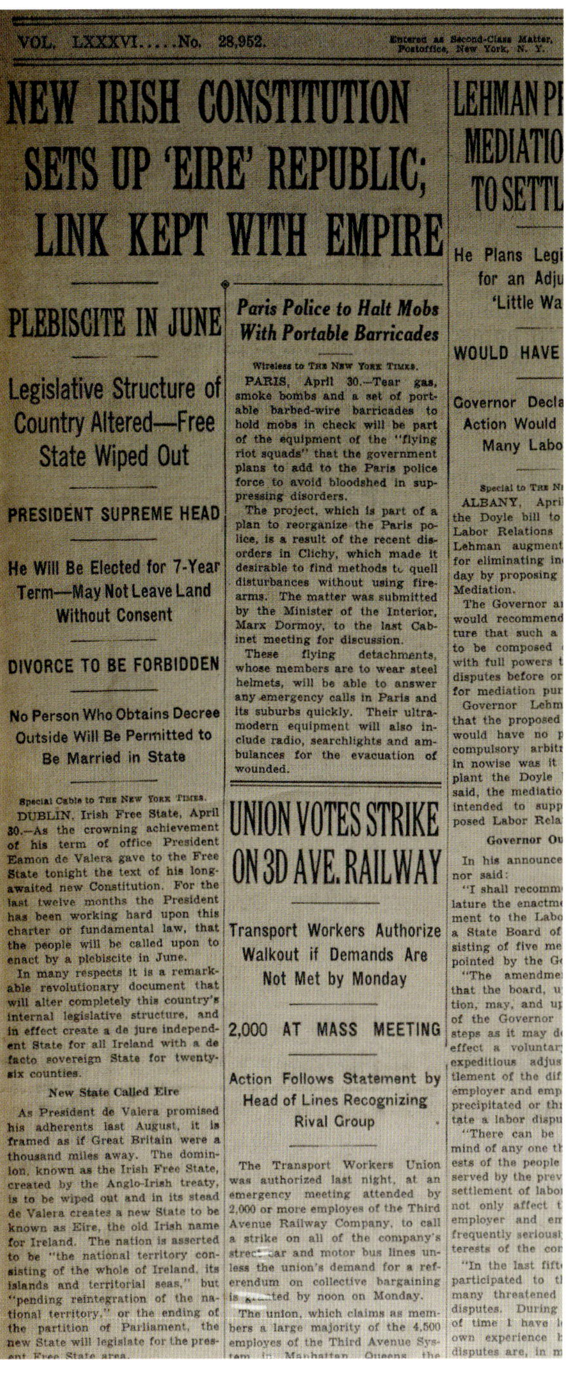

VOL. LXXXVI.....No. 28,952.

Entered as Second-Class Matter, Postoffice, New York, N. Y.

NEW IRISH CONSTITUTION SETS UP 'EIRE' REPUBLIC; LINK KEPT WITH EMPIRE

PLEBISCITE IN JUNE

Legislative Structure of Country Altered—Free State Wiped Out

PRESIDENT SUPREME HEAD

He Will Be Elected for 7-Year Term—May Not Leave Land Without Consent

DIVORCE TO BE FORBIDDEN

No Person Who Obtains Decree Outside Will Be Permitted to Be Married in State

Special Cable to THE NEW YORK TIMES.

DUBLIN, Irish Free State, April 30.—As the crowning achievement of his term of office President Eamon de Valera gave to the Free State tonight the text of his long-awaited new Constitution. For the last twelve months the President has been working hard upon this charter or fundamental law, that the people will be called upon to enact by a plebiscite in June.

In many respects it is a remarkable revolutionary document that will alter completely this country's internal legislative structure, and in effect create a de jure independent State for all Ireland with a de facto sovereign State for twenty-six counties.

New State Called Eire

As President de Valera promised his adherents last August, it is framed as if Great Britain were a thousand miles away. The dominion, known as the Irish Free State, created by the Anglo-Irish treaty, is to be wiped out and in its stead de Valera creates a new State to be known as Eire, the old Irish name for Ireland. The nation is asserted to be "the national territory consisting of the whole of Ireland, its islands and territorial seas," but "pending reintegration of the national territory," or the ending of the partition of Parliament, the new State will legislate for the present Free State area.

Paris Police to Halt Mobs With Portable Barricades

Wireless to THE NEW YORK TIMES.

PARIS, April 30.—Tear gas, smoke bombs and a set of portable barbed-wire barricades to hold mobs in check will be part of the equipment of the "flying riot squads" that the government plans to add to the Paris police force to avoid bloodshed in suppressing disorders.

The project, which is part of a plan to reorganize the Paris police, is a result of the recent disorders in Clichy, which made it desirable to find methods to quell disturbances without using firearms. The matter was submitted by the Minister of the Interior, Marx Dormoy, to the last Cabinet meeting for discussion.

These flying detachments, whose members are to wear steel helmets, will be able to answer any emergency calls in Paris and its suburbs quickly. Their ultra-modern equipment will also include radio, searchlights and ambulances for the evacuation of wounded.

UNION VOTES STRIKE ON 3D AVE. RAILWAY

Transport Workers Authorize Walkout if Demands Are Not Met by Monday

2,000 AT MASS MEETING

Action Follows Statement by Head of Lines Recognizing Rival Group

The Transport Workers Union was authorized last night, at an emergency meeting attended by 2,000 or more employes of the Third Avenue Railway Company, to call a strike on all of the company's street car and motor bus lines unless the union's demand for a referendum on collective bargaining is [illegible] by noon on Monday.

The union, which claims as members a large majority of the 4,500 employes of the Third Avenue System in Manhattan, Queens, the

The New York Times, Saturday, May 1, 1937. Article: "New Irish Constitution Sets Up 'Eire' Republic; Link Kept with Empire." "Plebiscite in June-Free State Wiped Out."

Irish Famine and Diaspora

The greatest natural tragedy ever to befall Ireland was the arrival of the potato plant disease Phytophthora infestans, commonly known as late blight or potato blight. This fungus-type disease first made its appearance in 1844 in a shipment of seed potatoes sent from Peru to Belgium farmers and then on to Ireland. The spores of this fungus, which are carried by winds, develop quickly in temperate and wet conditions for which Ireland is well known. Blight is a very aggressive plant pathogen that turns healthy potatoes into a foul smelling, watery black, inedible mush. Since the pathogen can hibernate over winter, it will affect the seed potato crop next season with the same disastrous results. Once this infestation was introduced, with no effective controls in place, the virulence was so great and widespread that by 1846 virtually the entire potato crop in Ireland was infected and wiped out.

The result of this widespread infestation led to the greatest human tragedy ever to befall Ireland — the Great Famine or the Irish Potato Famine. This national disaster occurred between the years of 1845 and 1852 due to successive potato crop failures. At the advent of this blight in 1845, Ireland's population was estimated at 8.51 million, of which two-thirds depended upon agriculture for their survival. The enormity of this crisis is in the numbers. Virtually all of Ireland's population depended upon the potato as the main source of their stable diet whereas 25% of this population depended upon the potato as their only source of food. In just six years, by 1851, Ireland's population had declined by 23%, to 6.55 million, of which 1.17 million were attributed to deaths alone. For many reasons it took the population of Ireland over one hundred years to begin the recovery initiated in the 1960s.

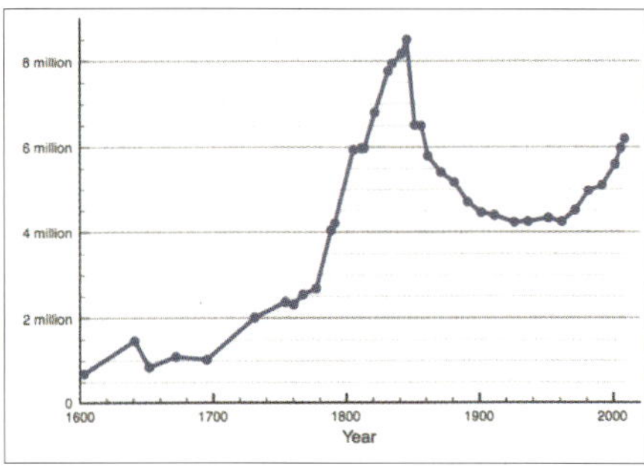

Population of Ireland since A.D. 1600. From the height of the population reached just prior to the Great Potato Famine in 1845 at 8.51 million, the low was finally reached just prior to World War II at 4.23 million, a loss of 50.3% of the island's total population. Today, as of 2012, the population has rebounded to 6.75 million.

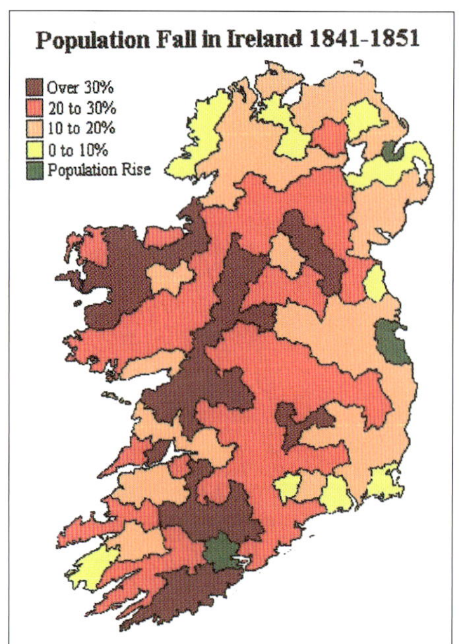

"Population Fall in Ireland 1841-1851." The Great Famine greatly affected populations in the main potato production provinces of Connaught, Munster, and the western counties of Leinster.

In mid-nineteenth century Ireland, as with most other agrarian economies, there was the "ascendancy class" made up of English absentee landlords and Anglo-Irish families that owned most of the land. The tillers of the land were the "impoverished tenants," whose entire output from the land, as well as rent, went to the owners and, eventually, the English consumer. Basically these tenant farmers had to work for the landowner in return for a small patch of non-valuable land they needed in order to grow enough potatoes and other root crops to sustain their own families. Therefore, no protein from cattle or sheep nor corn or other grains reached the tables of the "cottier" or small farmer. If this was not bad enough, the landowner could decide to put the land out for pasturage and thus evict the tenant with no recourse from the legal system. In some cases, this caused entire villages to be deserted with these poor wretches left to their own means of sustenance.

As there was no official social welfare system, many of the deaths were from starvation or infections from the effects of malnutrition. However one group of people, the Society of Friends or Quakers, realized that the situation was implacable without outside help and what the British government thought impossible the Quakers achieved by arranging for boatloads of food and transported it to the remote and most devastated areas of Ireland.

Illustrated London News, 1847. "Great Famine (Ireland)" by James Mahoney. The stretch of starving people gleaning the potato patches for some sustenance in the area of Skibbereen, West Cork.

"Another Deserted Village." This painting depicts a familiar famine scene. Artist unknown.

The Illustrated London News, December 22, 1849. Three victims of Ireland's Potato Famine.

The Great Hunger from the Quaker Tapestry depicting the volunteer work of the Quakers since 1650. This tapestry panel shows the relief work of the Friends during the Irish Famine.

With no hope for their future betterment and no ties to the land they did not own, the Irish peasantry reluctantly took the only natural step available to them: emigration. The Great Famine of the 1840s was the engine that precipitated the Irish Diaspora. A diaspora is the wholesale movement, migration, or the scattering of people away from an established or ancestral homeland or people dispersed by whatever cause to more than one location. Prior to the 1840s, migration from Ireland to the United States was rather substantial with 207,000 Irish relative to 599,000 total immigrants during the 1831 to 1840 period. From 1841 to 1850, it more than tripled: 781,000 Irish immigrated to America out of a total 1,713,000 immigrants. For the census periods of 1850, 1860, and 1870, Ireland was the number one country in terms of emigrants to this country accounting for 43%, 39%, and 33% respectively with Germany in second place. For the census periods of 1880, 1890 and 1900, Ireland was a close second behind Germany accounting for 28%, 20%, and 13% of all immigrants. In the 1900 Census throughout the United States there were 4,968,182 persons who claimed at least one Irish-born parent. From 1901 through 1908, Irish immigration averaged 32,500 per year. By 1910 immigration from Ireland slowed down to about 10% of all immigrants living in the country.

Whereas the prime mover of Irish migration was the desultory effects of the Great Famine, it was not the only reason. Earlier in the 1800s the agrarian Irish populace faced discrimination based on their religion (80% were Catholic), the removal of some basic civil rights, increased rents that caused more evictions and the further division of land holdings. Of the latter, one-third of all Irish small holdings could not support their families after paying the required rents. It is estimated that from 1830 to 1914 the Irish Diaspora alone contributed approximately 5 million people to the population of the United States, but perhaps these census statistics understate the actual Irish immigrants. From the period of 1821 to 1890, more than 3 million persons immigrated to Canada, of which approximately 50% were of Irish background. It is estimated that over 50% of all of these immigrants from Canada eventually entered the United States. In this twenty-first century, it is calculated that 80 million persons worldwide claim some Irish ancestry, of which 44 million or 55% of the total are Americans who claim Irish as their prime ethnicity.

"Emigrants Leave Ireland." Illustration by Henry Edward Doyle, A.D. 1868. *From the Preface to the first edition of An Illustrated History of Ireland from A.D. 400 to 1800.*

The Amalgamation of the Irish into American Society

While the Irish Diaspora was also responsible for sending emigrants into Canada, Britain, Australia, and South Africa, the sheer volume of emigrants into the United States overwhelmed the existing social structures, especially in the northeastern part of the country. For the first two hundred years of America's history, British emigrants, starting with the Pilgrims, settled what were the original thirteen colonies. British culture and conservative forms of Protestantism are the foundations on which America was built. Even today British-Americans are the largest ethnic group in America, with more than 100 million Americans having some British ancestry in their lineage.

The exodus of the Irish into a literate conservative framework caused massive resentment among the existing American working class. The average male Irish immigrant was 90% Catholic, over 70% illiterate (thanks in part to the Catholic Penal Laws of the eighteenth century), and a farmer with little or no industrial skills. These woe-be-gone Irish immigrants landed at Castle Garden in the Battery, which served as New York State's immigration station until 1890. After a transition period, Ellis Island opened in January 1892 with a fifteen-year-old Irish lass being the first immigrant processed. The typical immigrant was malnourished, sick, and traumatized after a three- to six-week ocean voyage in steerage class. So, with little or no money and no skills, these immigrants flooded the largest cities of the Northeast, quickly turning their living quarters into squalid hovels.

In 1855, New York City's native born Irish population accounted for 28% of total inhabitants. In 1860, New York City had the sobriquet as the largest Irish city in the world. The same statistics applied to Boston, 31% Irish, and Philadelphia, 21% Irish, of their respective populations. To the observer, little had changed for the Irish immigrant: their economic and social status remained the same, except that they were able to practice their religion as they saw fit. However, what applied to the Irish male did not necessarily apply to the Irish female immigrant (which constituted almost one-half of all Irish immigrants). Irish women had been quite industrious back in their homeland, maintaining a large family on little food and very little else, and these skills were very marketable for a lifestyle as domestics for the landed gentry of the American upper class, termed Wasps.

The Irish are bound for America in these two cards "Coming to America" and "I'm Just A Little Bit IRISH Myself." Published by Fred C. Lounsbury, 1909; Series 2098-3 and 2098-1.

Emigrants Leaving Queenstown (now Cobh), County Cork, for New York, 1874. The introduction of steamship on the Atlantic route dramatically reduced the length and hardship of the voyage.

The mass immigration to America of Irish Catholic males with little proficiency both in literacy and working skills was violently opposed. As early as the 1850s, anti-Catholic prejudices reached a peak, fronted by a Protestant "nativism" faction that formed a short-term political party known as the "Know Nothings," whose aim was to oust Catholics from positions of power and, for some of the early years, they had success.

When the typical Irish male looked for any type of work, he ran into the traditional animosity towards Irish Catholics, which resulted in institutionalized discrimination and injustice. The so-called American welcoming attitude toward "the tired, the poor, and huddled masses yearning to breathe free" no longer applied. The result was that segregation was openly practiced as "Help Wanted – No Irish Need Apply" and "No Irish Need Apply" signs and notices appeared in most businesses and boarding houses. However, because many Irish men were willing to accept any type of wage, in many cases a form of "reverse discrimination" set in where the second-generation American workingman found himself without work.

"The Republican Idea of Protection," *Puck*, October 3, 1888. Text reads: "A High Tariff on the Monopolist's Wares, Free Entrance for Pauper Labor, and a Lock Out of the American Workingman." This article attacks businessmen for welcoming large numbers of low paid immigrants, leaving the American workingmen unemployed.

The racial stereotyping of the Irish, specifically the male immigrant, was bigoted and prejudicial to the extreme. The typical view of the Irish was one of social inferiority. Characteristics attributed to the Irish male was that he was a lazy vagrant, prone to heavy drinking and violence, as well as having boorish personal habits. Nicknames like "Paddy" or "Mick" (e.g. because of the first two letters of many Irish names begin with the letters Mc) were deemed to be derogatory to males of Irish heritage. Printed caricatures of Irishmen in leading newspapers portrayed them as having simian (ape-like) features to enhance bigoted claims that the Irish were of inferior ethnicity. Many of these illustrations, some drawn by famous illustrators, usually portrayed a gang of Irish males involved in some sort of violent or drunken debauchery. In some cases the caricatures of violence and gang-like behavior were justified due to the activities of some Irish hoodlums during the New York Draft Riots in 1863 or the St. Patrick's Day Parade altercation in 1867. In the 1880s to 1910s, vaudeville acts contributed to the popular images of African-Americans and "off-the-boat" immigrants, whose specific comedic features and characteristics became widely accepted as accurate portrayals. Many "humorous" postcards that were sold in the early twentieth century used these images to foster this assertion and were actually popular among Irish-Americans.

"Reminiscence of St. Patrick's Day," *Harper's Weekly*, April 4, 1874. Artist: M. Woolf. A depiction of a simian-like Irishman, roughly dressed and with a whiskey bottle peaking out of a basket on the table, commenting on St. Patrick: "Arrah, thin, it's a great pity yer not alive this day to see how yer decindents honor yer memory!" This is a typical anti-Irish message on the public perception of the behavior of Irish-Americans on St. Patrick's Day, famous for frequently being the occasion of serious riots.

"The Usual Irish Way of Doing Things," *Harper's Weekly*, September 2, 1871. By Thomas Nash, a virulent Anti-Catholic and Anti-Irish illustrator and cartoonist; the cartoon depicts a simian-like Irishman holding a bottle of spirits with a lighted torch sitting on a barrel of Uncle Sam's gunpowder.

In spite of continual emigration from Ireland due to the on-going grinding economic deprivation, there was now enough infrastructure construction jobs in America to absorb much of the needed immigrant manual labor. In New York City alone, the Brooklyn Bridge built in 1870-1883, the steam-powered elevated railroad system built in 1870, the Interborough Rapid Transit subway built in 1904, and the laying of thousands of miles of transcontinental track all used quantities of immigrant labor whether they were Irish, German, or Chinese. While the labor was back-breaking and the pay small for Irish laborers, the Irish-American community began to coalesce and stabilize. Formidable institutions such as the Catholic Church, the Democratic Party, and any number of newly formed Irish-American societies provided the support necessary to maintain an Irish identity — and don't forget those pubs! The Irish immigrant was quickly being assimilated into the American culture and, therefore, became part of the ever-expanding "melting pot," or crucible, formed of people of many ethnic backgrounds. Therefore, to an Irishman in the mid to late nineteenth century, the one critical day to let loose and express his or her "Irishness" and cohesiveness as being part of a larger society was St. Patrick's Day and all its festivities, including a parade.

"St. Patrick's Day," *Illustrated London News*, March 19, 1853. Artist: George Thomas. A depiction of a St. Patrick's Day revelry and fighting using the form of Irish cherubs as an antithesis to the norm of drunken Irishmen.

Cover of a theatre program for the 1908 play entitled "The Melting Pot: The Great American Drama." The image of America as a "melting pot or crucible" was popularized in this play with the emphasis on cultural assimilation and acculturation.

Celebrating St. Patrick's Day

The earliest American celebration of St. Patrick's Day, of which an existing record has been found, took place on March 17, 1737. That year the Charitable Irish Society was organized in Boston, Massachusetts, by Irish Protestants with twenty-six original members. By 1742, Roman Catholics were also admitted. The Society is still in existence and the role of the Society remains the same: to cultivate a spirit of unity and harmony among and to promote the interests of the Irish people and their heritage, and to alleviate suffering and render aid to its members or other worthy recipients. Since 1996 the Society has used its influence in fostering a program to encourage Irish residents to become American citizens. In 2011, the Society hosted its 274th Annual St. Patrick's Day dinner.

According to records, St. Patrick's Day was celebrated in New York City as early as 1762. In the *New York Mercury*, dated March 15, 1762, the following notice appeared: "The Anniversary Feast of St. Patrick is to be celebrated on Wednesday the 17th Instant, at the house of Mr. John Marshall, at Mount Pleasant, near the college." On March 17, 1784, the Society of the Friendly Sons of St. Patrick was founded in New York City upon the end of the Revolutionary War.

On March 17, 1771, the Friendly Sons of St. Patrick or the Society of the Friendly Sons of St. Patrick for the Relief of Emigrants from Ireland was founded in Philadelphia, Pennsylvania, as an American social organization for Irish-Americans. The Friendly Sons, of which there are sister societies in other large American cities, just celebrated their 240th anniversary.

"Be Gorrah." A caricature assessment of a "typical" Irish immigrant. (The phrase means a mild oath for "by God.")

Many other societies formed as benevolent organizations to assist Irish immigrants. However, most of the information about these societies and their good works would never have reached the streets of metropolitan areas except for the smattering of Irish newspapers that commented on such activities as well as detailed information about St. Patrick's Day festivities. The Irish of New York, Boston, and other areas with large Irish immigrant populations realized that if they wanted to read about events important to their respective lives in their adopted country, as well as some information about Ireland, they would have to write and comment about it themselves. The first Irish weekly in New York City was *The Shamrock*, which had a short run from late 1810 to 1817 with several interruptions in the interim.

A freehold qualification to vote for a member of parliament, was lately sold in Scotland, by public sales, for L1425—6333 dollars.

IRISH MARKET PRICES.

Dublin, January 11.

Butter in casks,	L3 14 0	to L4 00 0	cwt
Green Pork,	1 10 0	1 12 6	
Bacon,	2 10 0	2 14 0	
Hams,	2 00 0	2 06 8	
Apple potatoes	0 05 0	0 05 6	
Black potatoes,	0 03 4	0 04 0	
Beef,	0 00 4½	0 00 5¼	lb
Mutton,	0 00 6¼	0 00 7½	
Pork,	0 00 4½	0 00 5	
Veal,	0 00 8	0 00 9	

Waterford, Jan. 8.

Oatmeal,	L1 02 0	to L1 04 0	cwt
Barley,	1 00 0	1 05 0	bl.
Oats,	1 00 0	1 01 6	
Potatoes,	0 00 5½	0 00 7	[per stone.

The Shamrock. A short-lived Irish immigrant weekly newspaper. Many of the articles were indicative by the use of vindictive wording as evidence of anger against the reigning English presence in Ireland. Other examples show Irish prices for foodstuffs and, from the March 29, 1817, issue, a report on The Friends of St. Patrick Society celebration of St. Patrick's Day, March 17, 1817, in Albany, New York.

The Shamrock.

108 THE SHAMROCK

The evening's entertainment was accompanied with appropriate and patriotic airs from the Albany military band, under the direction of Mr. Moore. Several national songs were sung by the company; and at the annunciation of each toast, fireworks and rockets were set off, by Mr. Buckmaster, in honor of the national jubilee.

TOASTS.

1. *The Day*—Sacred to the impulse of national feeling—to the virtuous memory of the Saint whose name it bears, and to the hospitality which he cherished in the "Emerald Isle." Music, *St. Patrick's Day.*

2. *Ireland*—" Pale, but intrepid; sad, but unsubdued." Her spirit shall yet burst forth in its native energy; the fame of her departed heroes and patriots shall be vindicated and her freedom and independence achieved by their survivors and successors in the path of glory.—*Hail Columbia.*

3. *Our adopted Country*—The constitution guarantees equal rights to all. May the genius and enterprise of her citizens, whether *native* or *adopted*, never be excluded from equal privileges.—*Hail Columbia, happy land.*

4. *The Union of the States.*—The late election of a chief magistrate has testified their consolidation, *fourteen to four*; notwithstanding the association of *blue-lights* and *Orange hushees*, sanctioned by the authority of the Hartford convention. *Arnold's March.*

5. *The constituted authorities*—May they never forget who made them.

6. *James Monroe, President of the United States*—His inaugural speech is the echo of the constitution, and the chart of wisdom, virtue and patriotism. May it never fail to be the guide of its illustrious author, in every political emergency.—*President's March.*

7. *Daniel D. Tompkins, Vice-President of the United States*—His patriotic vigilance in war, has enwreathed his brows with the renewed confidence of his country in peace. *Tompkins and Liberty.*

8. *De Witt Clinton*—The man of the people, the favourite of nature, the true politician and philosopher—May the gratitude of his fellow-citizens soon place him in a situation where his capacious genius will develope new plans of internal improvement, enlightened by a liberal policy, and thereby secure the honor and interests of the state of New-York, in defiance of the enemies of resources and the jealousies of interested demagogues.——9 cheers. *Hark! The son of Liberty advances.*

9. *The honorable John Taylor*—The independent republican and honest politician—he shrinks not in the hour of trial from the post of public responsibility. *Music.*

10. *Thomas Jefferson*—Whose mild and enlightened policy broke down the barriers erected by odious and inhospitable naturalization laws, and restored to persecuted emigrants the rights of humanity. May heaven continue to bless his philosophic retirement, with that peace and tranquility which flow from the consciousness of a well-spent life, and a well-earned fame. *Jefferson's March.*

11. *James Madison*—Though inveloped for a time in the clouds of war and adversity, his sun, has declined as it rose, in peace and prosperity—Let us then, drink cheerfully " *To the Pilot that weathered the storm.*" 3 cheers.

12. *The Army*—Its leaders, Brown and Jackson—The heroes of Erie and New-Orleans; they shewed to the hostile myriads of England, that American bayonets and bullets proved an antidote to their insolent countersign of " *Beauty and Booty,*" *Yankee doodle.*

13. *The Navy of the United States*—The infant Hercules, which has strangled the serpent of the lakes and the Leviathan of the ocean; which has taught ancient and modern Algiers to respect the laws of civilization, and given to Columbia a name, for which when she ceases to be grateful, she will cease to be free.—Music, *the lass of Columbia.*

14. *Emmet, Orr, Tone, Fitzgerald, and their fellow-patriots*—victims in the late glorious but unsuccessful struggle for Irish freedom. While as republicans we shed a tear to their memory, as christians we may recollect, that " the blood of the martyrs was the seed of the church." *Solemn music.*

15. *Washington*—If words could speak his eulogy, our hearts would venture, tho' our tongues might fail in the attempt.—*Solemn music.*

16. *Montgomery*—Shade of departed valour—sacred be the turf where sleepeth the brave—Erin gave thee birth—the halo of glory encircles thy tomb.

17. Counsellor … ney to England … when he return … may no *benefice* … disgrace the es… of reform and … *Sprig of Shil*…

18. *The Am*… additional lus… sensibility pa… *Lovely woman*…

Volunteer Toasts will be given n… week.

CHARLESTON, (S. C.) MARCH 20.

ST. PATRICK'S DAY.

On Monday last, the anniversary of … Patrick was celebrated by the Hibern… Society of this city.

After electing their officers for the en… ing year, to wit;

SIMON MAGWOOD, Esq. President.
EDMUND M. PHELON, Esq. Vice-presid…
THOMAS MALCOM, Esq. Treasurer.
THOMAS STEPHENS, Esq. Secretary.

Committee of Charity—Edmund Phelon, John Haslett, and Charles O-H… Esq's.

They sat down to an excellent din… prepared at the Carolina Coffee-House … ter which, the following toasts were dr… accompanied by the Music of a se… band.

TOASTS.

1. *Ireland*—Whose genius *should* m… tyranny blush, and whose valor *will* m… tyranny tremble. Air, St. Patrick's D…

2. *The United States of America*—… country of mankind. Hail Columbia…

3. *The immortal memory of St. Pat*… ——As a beam o'er the face of the … ters.

4. *The Exiles of Erin*—Why are … driven from the scenes of their yo… Why are they driven from the tomb… their sires?——Erin go Bragh.

5. *The President of the United Sta*… May the peace and prosperity which … den the commencement of his career … tinue till its close.——Carolan's Conc…

6. *The memory of the great Washin*… —Without a model in antiquity, wi… an equal in modern times.——The … rose of summer.

7. *The American Government*—Fel… ly in the blessings it bestows.——Le…

8. *The memory of Fitzgerald, Orr* … *Emmet*—Patriots, Heroes, Martyrs … Alleen Oroon.

9. *Religious Liberty*—Who shall deny the Almighty the homage o… creatures?——Meeting of the wate…

10. *The Governor and State of South* … *olina.*——Coulin.

… *Navy and A*… …n, and the … Paddy W… …*e gallant* … melted on … ll flourish fo… …e cold grou… *only be val*… *from Heave*…

ST. PATRICK'S SOCIETY.

Albany, March 17, 1817.

Agreeably to their custom, the members of St. Patrick's Society convened at the house of Mr. John Carroll, and elected the following gentlemen, officers for the ensuing year.

MR. JOHN CASSIDY, President.
MR. WILLIAM KEARNEY, Vice-Pres't.
MR. WILLIAM D. CARLL, Treasurer.
MR. GEORGE WHITE, Secretary.

The Society then adjourned, and met again at Benjamin's City-Hotel, at six o'clock in the evening, to participate in the celebration of the day sacred to the memory of their patron saint.

An elegant repast was prepared for the occasion, and nearly one hundred persons as well members of the society as distinguished citizens from different parts of the state, sat down to the entertainment: among whom were recognised the hon. De Witt Clinton. their honors the Mayor and Recorder of Albany, hon. Cornelius Heeney, sheriff Hempsted, Doct M'Nevin, the Rev. Dr. Gorman, Isaac Dennison, Esq. William James, Esq. John Townsend Esq. Solomon Southwick, Esq. Colonel Visscher, Mr. Jesse Buel, Mr. George Sharpe, Justice Rhodes, Justice Vernor, &c. Mr. J. Cassidy took the chair assisted by Mr. Kearney, Major Noon, and Capt. Maher, as vice-presidents.

The Ancient Order of Hibernians (AOH) today is not only the oldest Catholic lay organization in America, but it is also the largest Irish-Catholic society in the world with 80,000 members in Divisions across the United States and AOH ties in Ireland, England, Scotland, Wales, and Canada. The AOH was founded in New York City on May 4, 1836, by a group of coal miners from Pennsylvania who espoused similar interests with Irish Catholic New Yorkers to protect the clergy and churches from the violent American Nativists who attacked Irish immigrants and Church property.

In the early 1800s, due to the large number of Irish arriving in America, anti-Catholic bigotry emerged in a nativist prejudice against immigrants. In most cases, the prejudice took the form of "Paddy Making," which consisted of the parading of an effigy of St. Patrick or a simian-like figure meant to be Irish through the streets on March 17th. In New York City, an ordinance was passed imposing a fine on anyone who sought to disturb the peace by inciting their Irish neighbors. However, with the formation of nativist gangs, violence reared its ugly head, resulting in churches and a convent being torched and burned. Also these gangs intruded upon Irish neighborhoods, causing major street riots that lasted for days. With the massive influx of Irish immigrants during the great Diaspora of the 1840s and 1850s, these nativists' organizations coalesced in 1854 as the "Know Nothings." While this political party eventually withered away, in many cases it was replaced, most notably by the Ku Klux Klan in the South.

Cloth Badges: Ireland; Ancient Order of Hibernians.

"St. Patrick's Day in Atlanta, GA," *LIFE*, March 13, 1924. The Ku Klux Klan is out in force to watch representatives of two ethnic backgrounds they vilify marching.

"Two Harps That Beat As One," *LIFE*, St. Patrick's Number March 13, 1924.

By 1850, the major Irish benevolent societies were banding together on St. Patrick's Day to not only honor the Patron Saint of Ireland, but also to demonstrate their right to hold parades as full American citizens. From 1851 through 1899 there was an annual St. Patrick's Day parade in New York City, which even continued throughout the American Civil War years.

VOL. XII—NO. 3582.

ST. PATRICK'S DAY.

In the Morning, at Noon, and at Night.

Military and Civic Celebrations, Processions, Balls, Dinners and Speeches.

The Friendly Sons of St. Patrick and the Knights Thereof at a Cheerful Reunion.

Speeches of James T. Brady and John Van Buren.

The Irish all Right, and not a Copperhead in their Ranks.

The Day Here, There, and Everywhere.

No "friendly" Celt can this year complain of the way in which St. Patrick and his memory green were treated by the heavens above or the earth and all that are in Gotham. A finer day than yesterday the happiest Irishman never desired, and what with the smiling sun, the favoring breeze, the popular cheer, and the universal good nature that prevailed, it was within the power of every Green-Erinite to celebrate St. Patrick's Day, not only "in the morning," but all through the day and night, and far into to-day.

The intention, announced by the moving spirits of the proceedings in honor of the Holy Departed Saint, to celebrate the day this year with more than usual pomp and ceremony, was fulfilled to the letter. The day was finer, the procession larger, the streets fuller, the jollity more universal, the balls more numerous and the private potations deeper than at any time within reportorial recognition.

For many years it was a matter of dispute as to what day of the month was entitled to the honor of St. Patrick's nativity, but, as all well-informed in Celtic literature will remember, one Father Mulcahey settled the dispute in a manner at once original, unique and characteristic of his nation. The story is well told in the following favorite

BALLAD.

On the eighth day of March it was, some people say,
That St. Patrick, at midnight, he first saw the day;
While others declare on the ninth he was born,
And 'twas all a mistake between midnight and morn.

At last both the factions so positive grew,
That each kept a birth day, so Pat then had two:
'Till Father Mulcahey, who showed them their sins,
Said no one could have two birthdays but twins.

Says he, "Boys, don't be fighting for 8 or for 9,
Don't always be dividing, but sometimes combine;
Adding 8 with 9, and 17 is the mark,
So let that be his birth day—" Amen, said the clark."

The New-York Times.

NEW-YORK, WEDNESDAY, MARCH 18, 1863.

Bagley, acting Colonel of the 69th regiment, and Staff, mounted.
Troop L, Brigade Lancers, Capt. O'Hara
Co. C, 70th New-York State Militia, mounted.
-ninth regiment, preceded by a drum corps and band, under command of Capt. Thomas Clark.
troops of 1st New-York Cavalry, consisting of Co. A, Capt. Leary; Co. D, Capt. McManus; Co. H, Capt. McGouldrick. Lieut.-Col. D. C. Minturn in command.
-ges containing officers of Irish brigade now at the war, among them Capt. Dunlevy, of the Sixty-ninth, and Capt. Thos. W. Casey.
-ix Zouaves, preceded by a band, and bear- Irish flags.
Staff, and rank and file of the Duignan Guards.
-nnon Volunteers of 1782, bearing an American flag with the inscription, "We still live."
A detachment of the Hibernian Greens.
Connolly and John Wynn in an open barouche.
-ee companies of the Limerick Guard, with band.
Hibernia Benevolent Society, with band.
-ter's R. C. Temperance Society, Sylvester Burns, Esq., President; Patrick Nixon, Marshal; and Morris O'Hearne, Treasurer.
-s Francis Meagher Club—Edward Duffy, Marshal; Edward Mulligan and Wm. Elleff, Aids.
-ry Benevolent Society—Michael Daley, Marshal.
-idget's Benevolent Society—Patrick J. O'Connor, Marshal; George McAlvay, Aid.
-lent Society United Sons of Erin—Daniel Grinnen, -rshal; Paul McGinn and Francis Deegan, Aids.
Matthew U. B. T. A. B. Society, New-York—Edward L. Carey, Marshal.
Matthew Temperance Societies of Brooklyn—Patrick Horan and John Price, Marshals.
-nes R. C. T. A. B. Society—John Dwyer, Marshal; Edward Shannon and Wm. Smith, Aids.
-ermen's United Benevolent Society—Roger McGrath, Marshal; Daniel Sullivan, Aid.
-t Order of Hibernians, New-York—James Sand- John Tucker, and John McCann, Marshals; -ward Curry, John Traverse, Owen Hunt, Patrick Dugan, John Johnson, Aids.
-cient Order of Hibernians, of Long Island—Peter -with, Marshal; Hugh Monahan, Denis Maher and John Wall, Aids.
-ck Benevolent Society—Richard Halpin, Marshal; James McCue, Aid.

-ly all of the associations were preceded by -and the effect was really grand. The excite- the people knew no bounds, and the huzzas, on every possible occasion were shouted -were like peals of thunder. The affair was -editable to all concerned, and passed off with- -ident to mar, or unpleasant incident to alloy -lute success. All along the line of route from

plause.] Let me, my friends, add, that nothing noble in America fails to derive benefit from having Irish seeds deposited in its soil. [Applause.] I accept these as the emblems of young men of Irish extraction within the sound of my voice. [Applause.] But there is a poetry about it which I could not do less than recognize; for, within the sacred precincts of St. Patrick's Cathedral, in the City of New-York, where the roll of the omnibuses disturbs the ashes of those who died as long ago as my parents—within the sound of that, if death has ears, my parents are listening to American sounds, for they are in American graves. I deem it specially fit that they should be there. Without intending by the remark to have uttered a sentiment to the prejudice of any man present, I accept this as an illustration of the grave which I would love to occupy, reposing in native earth with the shamrock of Ireland growing over me. [Applause.] I will detain you no longer, but will introduce you to a little eloquent speech and the first regular toast:

St. Patrick's Day and all who honor it.—(Cheers and music.)

The next regular toast, which was received with great enthusiasm, was,

The United States—"Whom God hath joined together, let no man put asunder."

Recorder HOFFMAN, in responding to the toast, said that within the past few moments he had received the first intimation of the desire of the President that he should speak to the sentiment. He thought some reflection was necessary to do justice to such a great patriotic toast; but when he heard that if he did not respond to it, it would be passed in silence, he felt bound, though unprepared to perform that pleasing duty. The moment they decided to shatter or divide the North from the South, their happiness, their prestige and their future were gone. [Applause.] The speaker then alluded to the marriage service of the church, uniting the couple at the hymenial altar, and compared it with the Union of the States. He likened the North to a consort who was bound irrevocably, for good or ill, to the South, and declared the right of the former to demand that, after he had given all that love or duty should exact from him, the partner united with him should still be in his household. [Applause.] There were times when even those united in marriage, who proposed to separate, their children rose and demanded that for their sake there should be no separation. [Applause.] The speaker then alluded to the services of the Irish in the army, in connection with Gen. MEAGHER and

in Ireland, and not in America. [Applause.] That whatever might be their feelings as Irishmen, if the great United States of America required them to forego and forget, such should be their duty. [Applause.] He reminded them of the readiness which Gen. JACKSON evinced to forego and forget—to stop fighting when the time came, as well as fight with a will, to divide his opponents, to unite his friends, and bring the contest to a short, sharp and quick conclusion. When ordered to New-Orleans to defend the city, JACKSON did not stop to consider the color of anybody who was to defend it. [Applause.] He brought to his aid black troops, who defended New-Orleans with as much vigor as white ones. He even pardoned LAFITTE the pirate, and made good use of him. He cautioned them to do one thing at a time, and above all devote their whole attention to that, and when that was disposed of, they would have time to attend to some other business. [Applause.] He paid a high compliment to the unswerving loyalty of the Irish citizens—in the war with Great Britain, in the Mexican war, and during the rebellion. [Applause.] He prophecied the ultimate success of the Union arms, the speedy fall of Vicksburgh and Port Hudson, and the opening of the Mississippi, and said that when a loyal stream runs through the heart and the body of rebeldom, it won't take long to purify the arteries and veins. [Great applause.] In view of this contest, parties fall into insignificance. The great work was to subdue the rebellion, and it did not look much like a wish of a man to see that done when that man kept saying, "Oh, you can't subdue the South." It reminded him of the story of the woman who said, when defending her life, "I never will submit, unless you are stronger than I am, and I know you are. In conclusion, Mr. VAN BUREN again complimented the loyalty of the Irish race in this crisis, mentioning, as illustrations, the worthy efforts of the Chairman, the gallant CORCORAN, the Sixty-ninth, the Irish Brigade and Gen. MEAGHER. [Applause.]

Mayor OPDYKE responded briefly to a toast to "The City of New-York," and other toasts, speeches and songs, kept the company until a late hour, or rather, an early hour this morning of SHILOH'S DAY.

Dinner of the Knights of St. Patrick.

The second annual dinner of the "Knights of St Patrick"—an association formed a little over a year ago—was given at the Chinese Assembly Rooms,

FROM THE ISTHMUS OF PANAMA.

Arrival of the Champion with $249,514 in Treasure.

Important News from Central America.

Battle Between the Guatemalan and Salvadorian Troops.

TOTAL DEFEAT OF THE GUATEMALANS.

A General Central American War Expected.

Affairs in the United States of Colombia.

The Provisional Presidency Resigned by Mosquera.

The steamship *Champion*, Capt. WILSON, from

Opposite Page: The New York Times, March 18, 1863. An optimistic report by the usually negative *Times* on the St. Patrick's Day festivities, as the first column reads: "No 'friendly' Celt can this year complain of the way in which St. Patrick's Day and his memory green were treated by the heavens above or the earth…to celebrate St. Patrick's Day in the morning, at noon, and at night."

For the most part, except for the usual bad weather that occurred in the early Spring, the parades prompted little controversy — until the 1867 parade. A large-scale riot broke out between the metropolitan police and some of the AOH marchers over a horse-drawn truck that would not move out of the marcher's way. This and other smaller incidents, in some cases having to do with the over-consumption of drink, gave the Irish marchers of having reputations of bullies, fighters, and drunks. Many of the political drawings of those years persisted in illustrating the Irish as low-life's having simian-type appearances.

"St. Patrick in New York," *Harper's Weekly*, April 2, 1870. This anti-Irish cartoon shows a wife preparing her husband for the St. Patrick's Day parade.

PUCK.

ST. PATRICK'S DAY, 1885.

St. Patrick was a gentleman,
And came of decent people—
He built a church in Dublin town,
And on it put a steeple.

II.

Thus all the records are agreed
About the late lamented
Great saint who flourished ages ere
Was dynamite invented.

III.

We don't, however, hear that he
For patriotic uses
Bestrewed the sister island's ways
With murder-starting fuses.

IV.

And never of that gentleman
Has anybody stated
That where he went his path was strewn
With dwellings devastated.

V.

He did not feed his neighbor's cows
With hay crammed full of needles,
Nor kill poor casual passers-by
To blow up English beadles.

VI.

St. Patrick was a gentleman,
But oh, his pleasant manners,
Would seem much out of place beneath
Parnell's ensanguined banners.

VII.

Remember, Patrick's sons, to-day,
His memory's the brighter
Because he was a gentleman,
And not a dynamiter.

B. M.

"St. Patrick's Day 1885," *PUCK*. This 9-verse poem, consisting of four lines each, was printed with a decorative border drawn by the famous cartoonist "Zim" (Eugene Zimmerman) of a St. Patrick's Day parade of Irishmen. The poem begins by saying that St. Patrick was a gentleman who came from decent people, and contrasts his stature with the Irish of that current day, who are portrayed as murderous dynamiters.

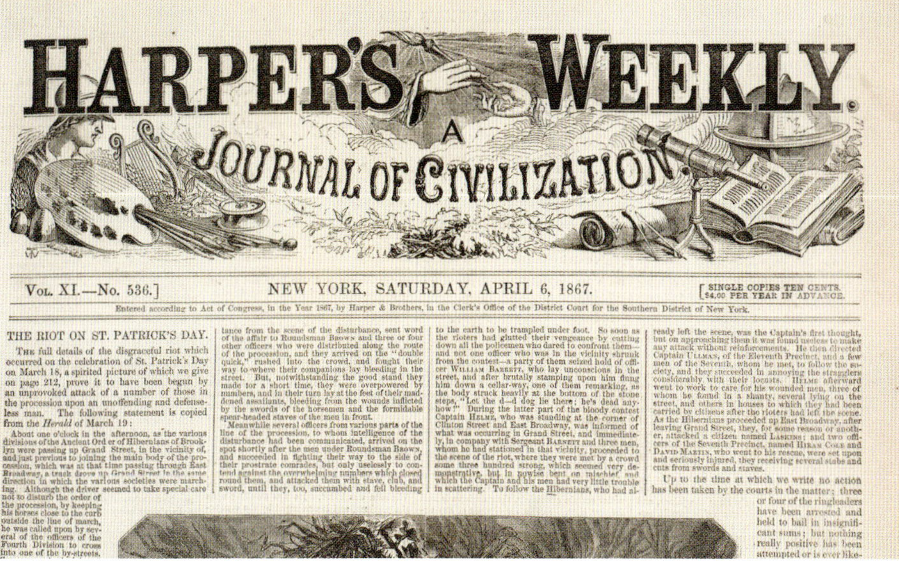

HARPER'S WEEKLY.
A JOURNAL OF CIVILIZATION.

VOL. XI.—No. 536.] NEW YORK, SATURDAY, APRIL 6, 1867. [SINGLE COPIES TEN CENTS. $4.00 PER YEAR IN ADVANCE.

Entered according to Act of Congress, in the Year 1867, by Harper & Brothers, in the Clerk's Office of the District Court for the Southern District of New York.

THE RIOT ON ST. PATRICK'S DAY.

THE full details of the disgraceful riot which occurred on the celebration of St. Patrick's Day on March 18, a spirited picture of which we give on page 212, prove it to have been begun by an unprovoked attack of a number of those in the procession upon an unoffending and defenseless man. The following statement is copied from the *Herald* of March 19:

About one o'clock in the afternoon, as the various divisions of the Ancient Order of Hibernians of Brooklyn were passing up Grand Street, in the vicinity of, and just previous to joining the main body of the procession, which was at that time passing through East Broadway, a truck drove up Grand Street in the same direction in which the various societies were marching. Although the driver seemed to take special care not to disturb the order of the procession, by keeping his horses close to the curb outside the line of march, he was called upon by several of the officers of the Fourth Division to cross into one of the by-streets, tance from the scene of the disturbance, sent word of the affair to Roundsman BROWN and three or four other officers who were distributed along the route of the procession, and they arrived on the "double quick," rushed into the crowd, and fought their way to where their companions lay bleeding in the street. But, notwithstanding the good stand they made for a short time, they were overpowered by numbers, and in their turn lay at the feet of their maddened assailants, bleeding from the wounds inflicted by the swords of the horsemen and the formidable spear-headed staves of the men in front.

Meanwhile several officers from various parts of the line of the procession, to whom intelligence of the disturbance had been communicated, arrived on the spot shortly after the men under Roundsman BROWN, and succeeded in fighting their way to the side of their prostrate comrades, but only uselessly to contend against the overwhelming numbers which closed round them, and attacked them with stave, club, and sword, until they, too, succumbed and fell bleeding to the earth to be trampled under foot. So soon as the rioters had glutted their vengeance by cutting down all the policemen who dared to confront them—and not one officer who was in the vicinity shrunk from the contest—a party of them seized hold of officer WILLIAM BARRETT, who lay unconscious in the street, and after brutally stamping upon him flung him down a cellar-way, one of them remarking, as the body struck heavily at the bottom of the stone steps, "Let the d—d dog lie there; he's dead anyhow!" During the latter part of the bloody contest Captain HELME, who was standing at the corner of Clinton Street and East Broadway, was informed of what was occurring in Grand Street, and immediately, in company with Sergeant BARNETT and three men, whom he had stationed in that vicinity, proceeded to the scene of the riot, where they were met by a crowd some three hundred strong, which seemed very demonstrative, but in nowise bent on mischief, and which the Captain and his men had very little trouble in scattering. To follow the Hibernians, who had already left the scene, was the Captain's first thought, but on approaching them it was found useless to make any attack without reinforcements. He then directed Captain ULLMAN, of the Eleventh Precinct, and a few men of the Seventh, whom he met, to follow the society, and they succeeded in annoying the stragglers considerably with their locusts. HELME afterward went to work to care for his wounded men, three of whom he found in a shanty, several lying on the street, and others in houses to which they had been carried by citizens after the rioters had left the scene. As the Hibernians proceeded up East Broadway, after leaving Grand Street, they, for some reason or another, attacked a citizen named LASKINS; and two officers of the Seventh Precinct, named HIRAM COLE and DAVID MARTIN, who went to his rescue, were set upon and seriously injured, they receiving several stabs and cuts from swords and staves.

Up to the time at which we write no action has been taken by the courts in the matter; three or four of the ringleaders have been arrested and held to bail in insignificant sums; but nothing really positive has been attempted or is ever like-

"The Riot on St. Patrick's Day," *Harper's Weekly*, April 6, 1867. The article reads: "The full details of this disgraceful riot which occurred on the celebration of St. Patrick's Day on March 18th, a spirited picture of which we give…" There were two sides to this story: one from the Ancient Order of Hibernians, the other from *Harper's Weekly*.

Similar political drawings from the pages of the *Puck* and *Judge* magazines used rowdy parade symbolism to further one sectarian cause or another. In these years, while the parades of marching units and bands got bigger almost every year, many non-Irish Americans resented the press coverage and the interference to their daily lives that these celebrations caused. However, public sympathy to the blight of the Irish was changing for the better, especially due to the many Irish-staffed Union Army units that fought under the Irish Brigade. Comprised of the 63rd, 69th, and 88th New York Infantry Regiments, and eventually the 116th Pennsylvania and the 28th Massachusetts, the famed Irish Brigade fought in every major battle of the eastern theater of the American Civil War. Many times elements of the Irish Brigade had to fight against their Irish counterparts fighting for the Confederacy. Once the Civil War was over, these soldiers returned to their homes content in the knowledge that they fought well and now were in a favorable position to take advantage of the unlimited opportunities available to them that Ireland could never offer — and the charges of "popery" against these Irish-Catholic veterans were silently diminished.

"The Political St. Patrick's Day Parades," *Judge*, July 1896. "The gold bug and the free silverites of the Democratic party meet. Now look for a great fight." Artist: Hamilton. While this extraordinarily well-drawn and colorfully painted lithographic centerfold gives a realistic depiction of many of the political players of the day, many of the background faces were drawn with simian-like features. The crux of this engraving was that the silverites advocated free coinage of silver, which would have allowed more money to be minted causing inflation (reducing the future cost of debt), whereas the backers of the gold standard felt that protection against inflation was of tremendous importance because inflation devalues the value of savings.

From 1900 to 1922 the parades took on a more militaristic appearance due to events surrounding World War I as well as the emergence of Irish nationalism. The Ancient Order of Hibernians provided a large part of the parade's participants with many of their marching "knots."

"St. Patrick's Day, March 17th – A Fair Type of Irish Beauty." The Days' Doings, *An Illustrated Journal of Romantic Events, Reports, Sporting & Theatrical News at Home & Abroad*, March 18, 1871. At the end of the front-page illustration is a brief bit of verse: "Wit, tho' bright,/ Hath no such light/ As warms your eyes, my Nora Creina." This is the conclusion of the poem "Lesbia Hath a Beaming Eye" by legendary Irish poet Thomas Moore.

"Patriots on Parade," *PUCK*, March 22, 1899. Artist: C. J. Taylor. Colorful drawing depicting the marching Ancient Order of Hibernians; the "Patriots on Parade" poem in Irish dialect is by H. A. Crowell. "Mairch / Mairch / Sivinteenth of Mairch! Throw your shoulders back and show the public how to mairch!"

"St. Patrick, 1914." A sepia toned "real" postcard of participants in an early American St. Patrick's Day parade. Note that "St. Patrick" is holding his staff in the wrong hand. Real Photo Postcard (RPPC), divided back, KRUXO paper. Very rare card.

GOVERNOR AND STAFF REVIEW PARADE
Governor Smith of New York with members of his staff in the reviewing stand at Sixty-fourth Street and Fifth Avenue. The Governor expressed himself as greatly pleased with the showing made by the long line of marchers. At the moment this photograph was taken he was gazing at the 165th Infantry, which, as in other years, headed the procession. Many of the noted medal winners of the regiment were recognized and received an ovation all along the line.
(Wide World Photos.)

MARCHERS PASSING UP FIFTH AVENUE
Hundreds of thousands of spectators lined the streets in a crowd which was said to be the largest that has witnessed a parade in the metropolis since the return of the Twenty-seventh and Seventy-seventh Divisions from France. Some no doubt were attracted by the rumors that an attempt would be made to break up the procession by those who were not in sympathy with the new Irish Free State. Nothing of the kind happened, however, to mar the occasion.
(P. & A. Photos.)

In 1918, the first distinct all-women's unit, the Women's League, marched. Also in 1918 the first Irish Republic (though not yet formed) tricolor flags were used instead of the all-green flag of the Irish nationalists. In 1920, the first Irish head-of-state (President of the Dail Eireann), Eamonn de Valera, reviewed the parade. From 1923 to 1935 parade participation was down due to the boycott by the Irish Republicans over the Irish Free State and partition of Ireland. The American Great Depression also had a part in lower numbers.

MID-WEEK PICTORIAL, MARCH 29, 1923

St. Patrick's Day Parade on Fifth Avenue, New York City

The New York Times, Mid-Week Pictorial, March 29, 1923. "St. Patrick's Parade on Fifth Avenue, New York City" Governor and Staff Review Parade.

VANGUARD OF 69TH REGIMENT

Famous old Sixty-ninth Infantry—the 165th of World War fame — passing up Fifth Avenue during the annual St. Patrick's Day parade. The regiment received a vociferous greeting from the spectators who packed the streets from buildings to curb all along the route. The men marched with the swing and precision of veterans, their spirits heightened perhaps and their step quickened by the glorious weather that prevailed. The procession was not as large as in some former years, owing to the differences that existed between those who favored and those who opposed the present Free State Government of Ireland.
(International.)

The New York Times, Mid-Week Pictorial, March 29, 1923. Vanguard of 69th Regiment; they are traditionally the first in line in the Order of the March for the Parade.

However, with the popularity of the St. Patrick's Day parade now immersing most New Yorkers, commercialism in the form of selling parade badges, emblems, shamrocks and all sorts of green trinkets, pin back badges with Irish sayings, and ribbons first made its appearance in the 1926 parade (still continues today). Bad weather also took its toll as several of the parades were cancelled until days later when the weather cleared.

"The Grand Marshal Gets A Green Horse," *LIFE*, March 15, 1928. Artist: J. Norman Lynd. Image depicts the leader of the St. Patrick's Day parade trying to stay aboard a startled horse that has begun to buck due to a barking dog as the crowd lining the street react.

"Flag Series," c. 1916-1920. Artist Childe Hassam (1859-1935) was a prolific American impressionist painter and well-known for his flag-theme series of paintings capturing various weather and light conditions. Painting Reproduction.

Full-series of Postcards, copyright 1905 by Arthur Livingston, 1897-1907. Livingston was a stationer that began producing cards depicting warships, regional views, and comics. This series highlighted all aspects of the New York City parade: The Grand Marshal, The Color-Bearers, The Band, The Committee, The Irish Brigade, The Crowd, The Mayor, and, finally, The Morning After. All the characters in the series have simian facial features and all cards are bordered by the shamrock, harp, and a bottle of rye.

St. Patrick's Day Pin-Back Badges and Ribbons.

An array of Humorous Pin-Back Badges dated from the 1960s to the 1990s.

Since 1936, the parades have taken on the modern characteristics of life today in terms of marching units and bands. Even in 1938 over one million people watched the parade of over 50,000 participants taking four hours to pass the reviewing stand. Floats, except for the rarest of occasions, weren't allowed. As one may realize, collectible manufacturers were quick to catch on to the popularity of parades and its salable accouterments and have produced attractive items for home display.

In 1948, for the first time, the parade had as a guest — the President of the United States, Harry S. Truman. Not to be outdone the Irish got their glory in 1956 when the first Prime Minister of Ireland, John A. Costello, made his appearance. In 1951, the practice of painting a green line down the parade route was instigated. Some pranksters over the years have tried to repaint parts of the line with orange paint. From about 1969 to 1981 parade participants and spectators were subject to the sight of disorderly and sometimes drunken teenagers, a new element who were rowdy and rude with little or no identification with St. Patrick or Ireland. Finally, a massive police crackdown on having possession of or drinking spirits has generally led to a more sober parade over the ensuing years. The St. Patrick's Day Parade held in 2011 celebrated its 250th anniversary. An estimated two million spectators lined the 1.5-mile route to watch 150,000 marchers led traditionally by the United States 69th Infantry Regiment, originally part of the old Irish Brigade.

The St. Patrick's Day Parade in New York, 1988. Written by John T. Ridge, this book gives an extensive review of all St. Patrick's Day celebrations and parades in New York City from 1762 through 1987.

"St. Patrick's Day Parade, Tuesday, March 17, 1970, at 11 o'clock." This admissions ticket was for the Grand Stand at 61st to 62nd Streets, New York City.

Irish Mementos. *Top*: "St. Patrick's Day Parade," 4" l x 3"h. *Middle*: "Erin Go Bragh," 3" x 2.5"h. *Bottom*: "Lucky's Irish Souvenirs," 6" h x 4"d. Battery Operated-AC/DC Adapter. "Lighted by lucky shamrocks, this is your one-stop shop for mugs, shirts, and noisemakers-everything green. And that's no blarney." Department 56, Eden Prairie, Minnesota.

Masthead of the March14, 1971, issue of *The New York Times Magazine* and reproduction of a song sheet: "Patrick's Day Parade: An Original Sketch and Song" by E. Harrigan. Internal article: "The Last of the American Irish Fade Away." Written by Andrew M. Greeley, it states: "The Irish have finally proved to the WASP's that they could become respectable. But they paid a price...they are no longer Irish! The Irish have become just like everyone else. The parades on St. Patrick's Day are monuments to lost possibilities of which few people in the parade are even aware!"

Besides the parades held in New York City, Boston, and Philadelphia, there are also well-attended crowds in Chicago (where the Chicago River is dyed green), Savannah, Georgia (where the fountains are dyed green), New Orleans (where green Mardi Gras beads are handed out), and San Francisco and San Diego in California. In every year since 1991, March has been proclaimed as Irish-American Heritage Month by either the U. S. President or Congress due to the date of St. Patrick's Day. For Irish-Americans St. Patrick's Day is both a religious and secular celebration involving, besides church services and parades, the consumption of much food and drink, followed by Irish music, songs, and dances.

In 1903, St. Patrick's Day became an official public holiday in Ireland. The first St. Patrick's Day parade held in Ireland (Free State) took place in Dublin in 1931. For both the Roman Catholic Church and the Church of Ireland, the holiday remains a religious observation.

Today, throughout all of Ireland, St. Patrick's Day is celebrated first as a day of piety and then the country hosts up to 120 individual parades. Out of a total population of 6.17 million, 74% or 4.57 million Irish consider themselves Catholic. Therefore, there is plenty of manpower to go around for participating in or viewing the many parades. In Dublin, St. Patrick's Day is celebrated over a five-day festival that includes the world's second largest parade with over 600,000 spectators.

Program from Chicago's St. Patrick's Day Parade, Tuesday, March 17, 1964. This parade was dedicated to the memory of John Fitzgerald Kennedy (1917-1963), 35th President of the United States of America, who was assassinated in November 1963.

Program from Chicago's 20th Annual St. Patrick's Day Parade, Monday, March 17, 1975. The following years parade would be the last parade that Richard J. Daley, Mayor of Chicago since 1955 and Honorary Parade Chairman, would officiate. Mayor Daley passed away in 1976.

Program from Chicago's St. Patrick's Day Parade, Saturday, March 17, 1973. A message from the long-time President of the Republic of Ireland, Eamonn de Valera: "May St. Patrick's Breastplate be their (the Irish) protection always."

Program from Chicago's 29th Annual St. Patrick's Day Parade, Saturday, March 17, 1984. The theme of the parade was "The Heritage of the Irish." The program read in part: "Thanks to St. Patrick, the Irishmen and women who came to America were looking for a future, not a faith. They brought their faith with them. This parade is dedicated to the Irish – their activities and achievements.

Program from Chicago's St. Patrick's Day Parade, Saturday, March 18, 1961. From the program: "The St. Patrick's Day Parade in Chicago is now a city-wide tribute to the patron Saint of the Irish. In recent years two parades heralded the St. Patrick's season. In this year of the 15th Centenary of St. Patrick, it is fitting that both the South and the West Side parade organizations have joined to present a dignified salute to St. Patrick." Since the start of the parade was in 1952, this would be the 10th Annual Parade in Chicago. However, since the larger South Side parade was controlled by then Mayor Daley and brought downtown, this would count as the 6th Annual Parade.

"Irish for a Day!" Even in San Francisco, California, with its large Irish-American community, there was room for anyone to be "Irish for a Day!" During the St. Patrick's Day Parade of March 17, 1940, children from the St. Mary's Chinese School marched with large cardboard shamrocks inscribed with oriental characters that meant "Feast of St. Patrick – Celebrate Together."

Parade, San Francisco, March 15, 1948. An entry of the United States Marine Corps was a representation of a large, sinuous snake, which, according to tradition, St. Patrick drove the snakes out of Ireland.

"The Irish City." A Kodacolor photographic postcard from Shamrock, Texas, with an early 1950s scene of a St. Patrick's Day Parade. Published by Baxter Lane Co., Amarillo, Texas.

An array of necklaces, string beads, and pins given away at St. Patrick's Day parades and parties.

For the St. Patrick's Day celebration, unlike Thanksgiving, Halloween, or Christmas, there is a scarcity of magazine covers highlighting the event. Hardly one cover in the author's collection depicts a visage of St. Patrick. In fact, except for one *LIFE* magazine (the old humor magazine) cover, none of them illustrates a St. Patrick's Day parade. However, *The New Yorker* magazine, in its history of producing covers that have a St. Patrick's Day theme, has produced only parade-oriented covers except, perhaps, for one. Since the author's collection is deep and trends back to 1934 (the magazine was founded in 1925), we assume that there is a relationship between the art direction of the covers and the fact that the world's largest St. Patrick's Day parade is held in New York City. As is the case for much of *The New Yorker* covers, they are not only iconic in many ways, but also the cover theme usually bears little resemblance to the magazine's content. Therefore we have arrayed the covers by artists depicting differences or similarities of their style over time rather than chronologically.

March 17, 1934; Artist: Bea Irvin.

March 18, 1950; Artist: Leonard Dove.

March 16, 1935; Artist: Constantin Alajalov.

March 15, 1952; Artist: Charles E. Martin.

March 19, 1935; Artist: Constantin Alajalov.

March 14, 1953; Artist: Arthur Getz.

March 19, 1955; Artist: Leonard Dove.

March 18, 1961 Artist: Arthur Getz.

March 20, 1971; Artist: Abe Birnbaum.

March 17, 1956; Artist: Ilonka Karasz.

March 14, 1964; Artist: Charles E. Martin.

March 18, 1972; Artist: Charles E. Martin.

March 15, 1958; Artist: Abe Birnbaum.

March 15, 1969; Artist: Anatol Kovarsky.

March 16, 1992; Artist: Danny Shanahan.

Chapter 5

Traditional Irish and St. Patrick's Day Symbols

A symbol is defined as being a sign or emblem that is representative of some deeper abstract meaning or thought. After the advent of agriculture 10,000 years ago, tribes of Neolithic humans came together to form societies that had a set permanence relative to water, arable land, domestication of animals, and natural resources. Unlike the predecessor Paleolithic hunter-gathers who used cave paintings as representative of their lifestyle, the first humans who were able to form the earliest stable settlements now had time to reflect on their respective belief systems. Many of these tribes had supernatural beliefs, most of which would be considered myths or superstitions.

With the invention of writing around 3000 B.C., the oral tradition of communicating religious beliefs became much easier with the use of symbols inscribed in clay. Sumerian cuneiform and Egyptian hieroglyphics were the earliest form of writing using symbols. These first ideograms were used in accounting, but eventually these symbols were able to form abstract expressions that allowed people to understand and communicate religious imagery. Once the desired symbols were "written in stone," the clergy could use many together to form the basis of sacred texts in a coherent form. Today symbolism in its many guises (e.g. religious, political, and social) has universal appeal; after all, as the saying goes, "A picture (symbol) is worth a thousand words."

All major holidays and celebrations have identifiable symbols, but St. Patrick's Day is the clear leader in term of quantity. The origin of much of St. Patrick's Day symbols comes to us in the form of ancient Irish Celtic ideograms or pictograms. They are the Triskele or Triple Spiral; the Triquetra or Trinity Knot; the Celtic Knot; and the Celtic Cross. Each of these symbols had older, pre-Christian meanings, but the Celtic Christians adopted these symbols in an effort to explain by imagery the conventions of the new Christian religion.

"Symbols of Ireland." They come in many forms and are universally known. Published by Bell'acards, Whitegate, County Clare, Ireland.

TRISKELE

Also called the triple spiral, this ancient pictogram is found at many Irish Megalithic and Neolithic burial passage tombs especially at Newgrange (c. 3200 B.C.). While the meaning is unclear, triple deities and triads are very common throughout world mythology. At some point the Celtic Christians embraced the symbol to represent the Christian Trinity.

The Triskele, or Triple Spiral, showing the pre-Celtic and Celtic pagan version as well as a modern form of the spiral.

TRIQUETRA

Also called the trinity knot, this symbol originally had a pagan religious meaning, as it had been found carved on Northern European rune stones. Later the Celtic Christians adopted the Triquetra as a symbol of the Trinity because this knot incorporated three shapes that could be identifiable as Christian symbols.

The original Latin meaning of Triquetra simply means a triangle or three cornered shapes. The Trinity knot is a triquetra interlaced with a circle.

CELTIC KNOTS

A variety of plait work (a woven, unbroken cord design) emblematic of Celtic decorative art; most of these intricate knot designs found their way into early manuscripts such as *The Book of Kells* as decorative elements.

A classic and complex Celtic knot pattern.

CELTIC CROSS

This symbol combines a decorative cross with a circular ring that circumnavigates the intersection at the reverse. While it has older pre-Christian origins, these cross forms are a major part of Christian Celtic art. The circular ring is meant to represent eternity or to represent the fusion of the old ways and the new.

In the Celtic Christian world a cross was combined with a circle around the intersection.

High Crosses

The Christian Irish High Crosses are products of the Irish monasteries that flourished during and, most importantly, after the time of St. Patrick, between the ninth and twelfth centuries. One of the functions of the monks who lived in these monasteries was the studying and interpretation of the sacred scriptures. Therefore the monks' studies of the biblical scenes of the Old and New Testaments provided enough source material to be incorporated into the architecture of these High Crosses. Typically many of the individual scenes were chosen to illustrate a particular aspect of church doctrine — the High Crosses were erected as a reminder of the Passion, Death, and Resurrection of Christ.

An important Christian High Cross is located at Monasterboice, County Louth. It is called Muiredach's Cross after a so-named monk who had the cross carved and erected. It is one of the most significant and best preserved sandstone High Crosses in Ireland.

Many of the High Crosses have complex dioramas and symbolism that is hard to interpret based on a ninth to twelfth century imagination. However, the iconographical portrayal of various biblical scenes gracing the grand Cross at Monasterboice was rather easy to interpret. One of the most beautifully rendered scenes is contained at the intersection of the cross's arms and shaft. The Last Judgment is one of the best representations to survive extant anywhere in Europe. Just below The Last Judgment is St. Michael Weighing a Soul and just above is Christ in Majesty.

In Ireland, for the tourist trade, there are many representations of Christian High Crosses fabricated in ceramic, glass, and other mediums, as well as viewed through postcards. Some of the best work has been done by famous ceramic makers, such as Belleek, or glass producers, such as the now closed Waterford Crystal Company. It is in this regard that Ireland can be justly proud of its contributions to early Christian art through the placement of High Crosses. Today there are approximately 125 High Crosses throughout Ireland, of which 50% have some figural sculptural representations.

Christian High Cross at Monasterboice, County Louth, Ireland. Two views (East face) of one of the most impressive crosses located in one of the most important centers in Ireland for High Crosses.

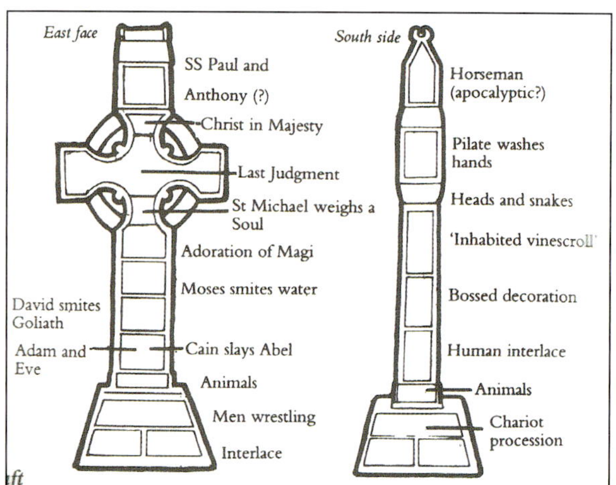

Monasterboice – Muiredach's Cross. East and South side diagrammatic views with descriptions of the figural representations carved on the Base, Shaft and Head.

Ceramic representation of a Christian High Cross, 7.5" h. Belleek, Ireland (green stamp).

"Cead Mille Failte-One Hundred Thousand Welcomes." A young Irish girl is superimposed on a Celtic Cross. Published by Gottschahaulk Dreyfuss and Davis (GDD), Series 2275.

Crystal glass representation of a Christian High Cross, 8" h. Waterford Crystal Company, Ireland.

Wearing of the Green

One of the moist famous Irish symbols that emanated from the Rebellion of 1798 was the color green *(see "Irish War of Independence," Chapter 4)*. The emblem of the United Irishmen was a green banner with the harp on it. During those times anyone found to be wearing any sort of green, whether it was a sprig, shamrock, or ribbon, were either imprisoned or sentenced to death by a method called "slow hanging."

In that same year an anonymously written street ballad, called "The Wearing of the Green," was made popular because the song enumerated the repressions being brought against Irish citizens. Therefore wearing green was a popular form of visible protest against the British government and became a symbol of the Irish rebellion. Since the Irish Diaspora, the "wearing O' the green" has become a symbol of Irish unity and cultural identity. On St. Patrick's Day, whether Irish or not, everyone tends to get into the act by being Irish for one day by wearing some sort of green-colored object or clothing.

"United Irish Patriots, 1798." Tinted engraving, artist unknown. The United Irishmen was a non-sectarian republican revolutionary group formed to press for democratic reforms and Catholic emancipation. Most of the group originally hailed from the ranks of the Presbyterians, but were joined by other disenfranchised Protestant groups as well as the Defenders, an exclusively Catholic agrarian resistance group.

"A St. Patrick's Day Vision: When Erin Conquers the 'Saxon'," *Puck*, March 17, 1881. Artist: J. A. McWoles. *Above*: A fanciful rendition of what would happen if the Irish were granted Home Rule. Ten humorous panels around the central theme contain the slogans: "Whiskey Will Run Free," "Pat Will Be His Own Landlord," "And The Puck Will Dance an Irish Jig." *Below*: Close-up of Main Panel: "The Irish Will Take Possession of the Houses of Parliament." Some of the humorous vignettes include the Head Parliamentarian wearing a bishop's mitre, Queen Victoria watching from the balcony, along with the usual rowdiness among the Irish members.

Symbol and Badge of the Society of United Irishmen. Their motto was "Equality – It is now strung and shall be heard." It displayed a Harp without the Crown and the Cap of Liberty.

"THE WEARING OF THE GREEN." This embossed, artist signed Ellen Clapsaddle card shows a beautiful young woman in all her finery. Published by International Art, Series 931.

"THE WEARING OF THE GREEN." In these artist signed Ellen Clapsaddle cards, both the lady and the gentleman, dressed in their green outfits, proudly offer shamrocks. Published by International Art.

"THE WEARING OF THE GREEN." All in green – hat, bird, flag – adorn this marching lass. St. Patrick Series No. 1. Publisher unknown.

A card decorated by the musical notes with the lyrics, "Fare-well! For I must leave thee." Publisher unknown.

A group of five, all with green hats, ribbons, and shamrocks, look as if on parade. Series 5306. Publisher unknown.

A young man sings "The Wearing of the Green" while dressed in his top hat and green and white striped pants. Published by L & E (Leubrie & Elkins Co., New York).

"The Wearing of the Green," Wolf Publishing series 253. This is possibly an unsigned Ellen Clapsaddle card, as cards produced by Wolf Publishing were usually not signed by Clapsaddle.

A circle of shamrocks surround a young couple wearing the green on March 17th. Published by S. Bergman, New York, 1913; Series 2400.

Two sweet young girls, one dancing a jig on a chair and the other carrying a basket overflowing with shamrocks celebrate the "green." One card is unsigned, but is probably by Ellen Clapsaddle. Published by International Art.

A young boy with bright red hair and wearing an orange shirt asks for forgiveness for not "wearing the green" and promises to do so from now on. Published by Barton Spooner; Series 335.

This very unusual postcard shows a gentleman leaning on his umbrella and standing on a very old hand-woven Indian rug. A real photograph, hand-tinted, publisher unknown.

Shamrock

One of the most recognizable and enduring national symbols of Ireland is the Irish Shamrock, a three-leafed clover of the *Trifolium repens* species of white clover. The Genus Trifolium means three leaflets and the Species T. repens means creeping. Therefore the shamrock is an herbaceous, perennial creeping white clover plant with three smooth egg-shaped leaves. The Gaelic word "seamrog" is defined as white clover and is the origin of the word shamrock.

In the pre-Christian era, the priestly class of Druids prized the shamrock for its mystical and healing properties. The shamrock is connected with the pagan belief that the number three is a magical and sacred number. Due to the shamrock's lush green color and trefoil charm, it enjoyed sacred status among the Druids and became symbolic of the Spring, or Vernal, Equinox that occurs between March 20th and March 21st of any year.

According to Christian tradition, St. Patrick used the shamrock in his efforts to bring Christianity to Ireland. Because Ireland in the fifth century was comprised of many small kingdoms, each with one or more Druid priests, St. Patrick first had to proceed slowly as to not antagonize this very influential group of teachers, diviners, and magicians. Eventually St. Patrick made such good use of the Irish shamrock that he converted a large number of tribal chieftains, Druid priests, and other pagans to Christianity. By the time St. Patrick passed on, most of the island of Ireland was Christian. He used the three-leafed shamrock as a way of explaining the Holy Trinity, which is the bedrock of most Christian religions. As the number three to pagans was sacred, they understood the implications of each leaf being representative of the "Father, Son and Holy Spirit."

Since St. Patrick is irrevocably entwined with the shamrock, there is one sentimental Irish song that gives credit where credit is due:

> There's a dear little plant that grows in our isle,
> "Twas St. Patrick himself sure that set it,
> And the sun on his labours with pleasure did smile,
> And the dews from his eye oft did wet it.
> It thrives through the bog, through the brake, through the mire land,
> And he called it the dear little shamrock of Ireland"

In a modern context, the three leaves of the shamrock are emblematic of the three main elements of Irish life: religious, political, and cultural. The story of Ireland is a long and contentious mix of rich heritage. Thomas Moore (1879-1852), who was considered to be the National Bard of Ireland for his lyrics and poetical abilities, penned some chosen words on behalf of the shamrock in 1812:

> Oh the shamrock, the green immortal shamrock!
> Chosen leaf,
> Of Bard and Chief,
> Old Erin's native shamrock.

Two young lasses surround the shamrock, showing their "True Irish Hearts." St. Patrick Series #3. Publisher unknown.

"The Emerald Isle," Series No. 157, published by Raphael Tuck & Sons. "The dear little, Sweet little shamrock of Ireland" circles the young woman also holding shamrocks.

In this very fine example of a projection card, the shamrock folds out showing a water scene. Publisher Winsch produced a series of these fold-out cards.

"The dear little shamrock speaks ever of home. Our hearts turn to Erin wherever we roam." A typical message on many St. Patrick Day cards, this one surrounded both by a circular wreathe of shamrocks and a border.

A maiden is enveloped in a large shamrock and surrounded by clusters of the symbol. Published by Nash, Series #11.

An attractive couple sails away, its sail resting on a shamrock. Published by Wildt & Kray, London, Series 2718.

This is a rare postcard because of the small packet of real shamrock seeds attached, probably a dear reminder of the homeland. Published by National Series.

A young woman proudly holds a green flag decorated by the harp ensign, published by International Art (likely a Clapsaddle card); dressed in green, the maiden leans on the golden harp and holds her flag with the harp emblem, published by Julius Bien & Co., Series 7404; "Are you wid us?" A pipe-smoking young lad holds his waving flag. Published by M. W. Taggart.

Irish Shamrock. Crystal glass representation 4" square, Waterford Crystal Company, Ireland.

Harp

While the shamrock is regarded as the most obvious cultural symbol of Ireland, the Harp is the national symbol of Ireland. Since the Free State of Ireland already had a tricolor flag first introduced in 1848 (green for the Irish people, orange for the English supporters of William III, and white in the middle to represent peace between the Irish people) and officially adopted in 1922, it was suggested that there should be a Presidential Flag that would retain the emblem of the former national flag without interfering with the current national flag. In 1945 the basic elements of the Presidential Standard were adopted. "The design is that of the national emblem, the harp, in gold, on a ground of St. Patrick's Blue. The harp is a replica of that on the Presidential Seal, and is represented with fifteen strings. It appears as mirror images on the two sides of the Standard…"

The harp, a multi-stringed instrument, was known to exist in the Middle East 6,000 years ago. These ancient bow-harps were probably independently invented in many cultures. Through evolution the harp acquired certain structural elements such as a triangular frame, more strings, and, in some cases, pedals. By the tenth century, the Gaelic triangular, wire-strung harp was well-known and played by all the Celtic clans from Scotland and Ireland. In fact, it was Brian Boru, the alleged High King of the whole of Ireland in the eleventh century, who popularized the instrument by playing it himself.

Throughout the rich context of Irish history, starting with the Anglo-Norman invasions in 1169 AD to the present day Republic, the harp has been used in many guises as a political symbol of both England and Ireland and has appeared on most Royal Standards. It was in 1642 during one of the English campaigns against an Irish insurrection in Ulster that the harp was first used on a field of green, making it the first recorded use of the harp emblem by the Irish vassals. From that point on, some form of the harp, usually on a field of green, was used by Irish revolutionaries throughout the following three hundred years.

This unsigned Samuel Schmucker card features an easily recognizable, beautiful, and bewitching Colleen swinging on a harp. Published by Winsch.

Both cards exhibit vibrant colors, such a change from just the green, though harps are still the dominant image. Published by The Robbin Brothers Co. (1907-1912), Boston, a publisher of New England view cards and holiday cards.

Published by Nash, Series #6.

This card featuring a gold harp has a special effect – it folds out. Published by Winsch.

A young lass holding her harp looks far away offering an Irish greeting, "ronar buan." Unknown publisher.

Shillelagh

A shillelagh is a Gaelic word for two types of heavy wooden sticks: a short, stout club or cudgel with a strap and a longer walking stick. Each of the shillelaghs was made from a heavy knotty stick with a large knob at the top. Original shillelaghs were made from oak, but as these forests in Ireland were clear cut, present day shillelaghs are made from the branches of the blackthorn hedge. The shillelaghs seen today are made either for the tourist trade or for use in celebrations such as St. Patrick's Day parades.

To the Irishman, a shillelagh was an absolute personal necessity to be carried at all times. If there was fighting about, the Irishman would use two shillelaghs held in the middle of the stick: one for defense and one for offense. In the American illustrated newspapers of the nineteenth and early twentieth centuries, caricatures of simian-looking Irish toughs fighting always showed them using shillelaghs on one another or against authority. In effect, the printed media portrayed the shillelagh as a symbol of male "Irishness" with a touch of bad behavior thrown in for good measure.

SHILLELAGH (BLACK THORNWOOD) WITH GREEN TASSEL/BOW, 15" LONG. "Genuine Irish Homeware" black stamp and varnished with Shamrock decal "Shillelagh."

A young girl and boy balance a harp much bigger than either of them. Published by Winsch, Series 1027.

This simple card conveys the importance of the shillelagh to the Irish. Published by S. Bergman, Series M512.

Pretty Colleen holds her shillelagh honoring "Ould Ireland so Green" while a young man shouts an Irish greeting. Published by B. B. London, Series E266.

A be-speckled Irishman carrying his shillelagh wishes "The top o' the morning to you and may your shadow never grow less." Published by F. A. Owen Co. (1915-1927), Dansville, New York. This book and magazine publisher also produced holiday and greeting postcards.

This Irishman, dressed in his shamrock-designed pants, looks as simian as possible waving his shillelagh. Published by the Robbins Brothers Company.

A galloping horse carries a finely dressed boy waving a shillelagh. Published by Raphael Tuck & Sons, Series #189.

Ceramic figurine of an old gent waving a shillelagh, 4"h. Light green matte. Lefton (gold/red foil sticker). Black stamp "6203 on base.

Clay Pipe

In the late sixteenth century, the smoking of tobacco in the British Isles and Europe was becoming rather widespread despite, even then, the condemnation from certain authoritative and religious bodies. When pipe tobacco became widely available among the lower classes, inexpensive clay pipes were produced in England and the County Roscommon in Ireland. By the nineteenth century, Ireland and Scotland were the primary exporters of clay pipes made in England to America to sustain pipe-smoking among the new immigrants.

Unlike the classic long-stemmed pipes with large bowls, the working classes generally preferred a short, three-inch clay and, much like the razor/razor blade business where the razor was free, clay pipes were a very simply made commodity item that was literally given away to support the tobacco market. The short-stemmed clay pipe was called a "dhudeen" and was, in many cases, associated with crude depictions of Irish drunks in several illustrated newspapers and postcards. It was thought that a smaller sized pipe smoked "hotter," therefore producing a mellower smoke. Some of the better clay pipes with larger bowls were able to employ decorative motifs such as Erin Go Bragh, the Harp, or the Flag of Ireland.

Pipe with white stem, medium green paint and white felt paper rim decoration, 5.5"l x 2.75"h. "Japan" appears in a black stamp on back of the stem.

Lapel pins made with small white pipes set with delicate filigree shamrocks.

Two rival factions, one being Ancient Order of Hibernians, smugly smoke the peace of peace while hiding either a brick or shillelagh. Unknown publisher, Series #1.

Three Irish girls are enveloped in the smoke of a pipe with the fields of Killarney below. Published by Winsch.

In this unsigned card by artist Schmucker, an Irish Colleen is surrounded by two pipes and shamrocks. Published by Winsch.

"The Piper." An older Irishman is featured in a bucolic scene with two crossed pipes in the foreground. Unknown publisher.

Two Irishmen are smoking "The 'Patrick Pipe' of Peace!" This artist signed HBG (H. B. Griggs) card is recognizable by the stylized writing. Published by L & E, Series 2269.

Top Hat

In the working classes, the typical Irishman's daily head covering was a flat cap. Only in the upper classes did the male wear a top hat with any regularity for reasons of class distinction and the expense of felted beaver fur. By the 1830s top hats became popular with all classes due to less expensive material being used such as rabbit fur. A top hat, which goes by many names such as silk hat, cylinder hat, or stove pipe hat, is a tall, flat-crown, broad-brimmed hat.

Due to the urbanization of the 1850s, the top hat was not considered useful for city life, so more serviceable styles such as bowler hats and fedoras were becoming more commonplace. The standard top hat was a hard, black silk hat, but in illustrated newspapers, magazines, and postcards, both males and females were shown wearing this hat or sometimes a bowler. Also many of the hats depicted were in green with a large buckle placed above the brim. Usually an Irish lass, leprechaun, or an Irish fairy was shown wearing this hat. The coloring and decoration did not apply to the jaunty style top hat worn by the Irish even at St. Patrick's Day celebrations.

Pipe in hand, an aging Irishman looks out from the blue sea. Artist signed Ellen Clapsaddle card. Published by International Art, Series 1450.

The top hat is the centerpiece draped in gold ribbon, a gold shillelagh, and green shamrocks. Published by Julius Bien & Co., Series 740.

The red-haired Colleen is the center of beauty in this colorful card. Unknown publisher, Series 338.

This colorful card features a Green top hat with a cornucopia of pink and red roses. Published by Santway, Series 111.

A simian looking Irishman bows with his top hat offering his greetings in this colorful card. Published by the Robbins Brothers.

A young boy with a clownish-looking face tips his hat to the audience. Artist signed Ellen H. Clapsaddle card. Published by International Art.

The Irish Pig

'Twas an evening in November,
as I very well remember,
I was walking down the street
in a drunken manner,
But my knees went all a-flutter,
so I landed in the gutter,
And a pig came 'round and laid
down by my side.

Yes I laid there in the gutter
thinking thoughts that I could
not utter
When a colleen passing by
did say:
"You can tell a man that boozes
by the company he chooses"
And with that the pig got up
and trotted away!

"Good luck ye divil!" The date 'March 17,' written in shamrocks, is eyed by two pigs. Published by Gottschahaulk Dreyfuss and Davis (GDD).

A wide-eyed boy sits in the middle of a green hat decorated with gold stars and ribbon. The card is enhanced by a matching gold border. Published by Barton Spooner.

Pig

Wild boars used the same land bridge as the Mesolithic hunter-gathers did in 8,000 BC to reach the shores of Ireland. Once there they became an indigenous food source. Wild boars and wild pigs are from the same Genus, Sus, of which the wild boar is of the species, *Sus scrofa*. In Celtic and Irish mythology, the wild boar was sacred and featured in several heroic hunting stories. The ancestor of the wild boar is the domesticated Pig, which have quite a history in the lifestyle of the common Irish farmer. Except for a small potato patch in which the tenant farmer used to feed his family, all of the output from the acreage and/or pasturage was exported to the English markets. So if the tenant farmer could afford it, he maintained one or more domesticated pigs for use in enhancing his family's diet and/or using monies from the sale of the pig for the bare necessities of life. Pigs had a good reputation among farmers who thought of them, somewhat, as a household pet with little or no upkeep as they are omnivores. Therefore pictorial drawings and illustrations of the era show pigs happy and contented. There is even a famous poem written anonymously about a pig.

This comical card features a circus act as one pig jumps through the hoop. Another pig acts as the audience waving a green flag. Publisher BW, Series 375.

Pretty Colleen fondly holds a pig draped with a green bow. Unsigned artist Samuel Schmucker card. Published by Winsch.

A young boy "walking" his pig turns his attention to a pretty Irish lass. Unknown publisher.

Two pigs having a wonderful time dancing an Irish jig. Unknown publisher.

A farm girl pushes a very large pig in a wheelbarrow. A dark green background surrounds the scene. Published by B. B. London, Series 1601.

Five pigs, dancing what seems like the "bunny hop," are all carrying shamrocks. Published by C. W. Faulkner & Co., Series 265.

A young girl trains her pig to jump over the shamrock. Published by Raphael Tuck & Sons.

Potato

The potato, a starchy edible tuber, was domesticated over 8,000 years ago from a single origin point in Southern Peru. Eventually the potato reached Europe and especially Ireland in the late sixteenth century, where it was the first country to grow the tuber on a large scale. It has been said that the poor tenant farmer with a family of six could feed themselves for a year on one and one-half acres of planted potatoes. For many Irish people, especially in the very poor sections of western Ireland, potatoes were virtually their sole diet, so when the late blight attacked the potato crops in 1845 it took a devastating toll. There was no respite from this fungal scourge for seven or more years, leading to the Great Irish Famine. Nonetheless, the potato, as a symbol of the Irish, is held in high regard because it was, in many cases, the sole source of sustenance that kept the Irish alive until late nineteenth century when other dietary items became available. The potato, as part of most Irish diets, runs the gamut from a classic dish called Colcannon to a "moonshine" whiskey called Poteen, illegally distilled from potatoes to avoid taxes.

A comical card of laughing potatoes in a pot — when the pot is lifted, fold-outs are scenes of the "places they grew." Unknown publisher.

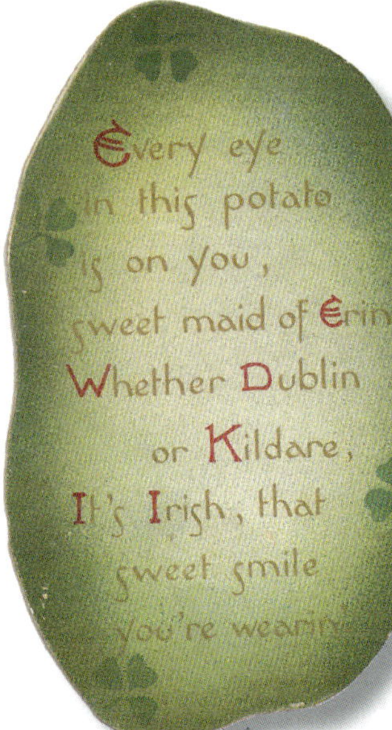

A postcard in the shape of a potato opens to the image of a beautiful woman. To honor a sweet maid of Erin, "Every eye in this potato is on you." Published by Raphael Tuck & Sons, Series 520.

Irish Fairies & Leprechauns

Irish literature has a long robust heritage spanning a trefoil of expression: serious prose and poetry; mythology; and folklore. An important part of its folklore consists of the hundreds of stories concerning Irish Fairies, which are known in Ireland as the people of the *sidhe*. According to tradition, there are two distinct classes of fairies that inhabit Ireland: the trooping fairies and the solitary fairies.

The congenial trooping fairies live and travel together in groups. Based on ancient Celtic folklore, it is thought that these sidhe people still inhabit the thousands of raths (a circular enclosure surrounded by an earthen wall used as a dwelling and stronghold) that are part of the landscape throughout Ireland. Due to superstition, many of these fairy raths are left alone in the pastures and fields for fear of disturbing these beautiful creatures.

Opposite to the trooping fairies are the solitary fairies that have the reputation of being anti-social. The most famous of the solitary fairies are the Leprechauns. Known as a "wee folk," a leprechaun is depicted as a wizened, bearded solitary old man being no taller than a small child. He is typically clad in some sort of a red coat or jacket, red breeches, black stockings, and a cocked pointed hat. The modern day version of the leprechaun has him dressed in green with a broad brimmed hat, a red beard, and buckles on his shoes — and having a much more pleasant demeanor. The industrious leprechaun spends all of his time busily making and mending the shoes for the other fairies whose chief delights are dancing and, therefore, are in constant need of shoes. The eighteenth century Irish poet, William Allingham, wrote in his poem "The Leprechaun" or "Fairy Shoemaker":

> "Do you not catch the tiny
> clamour,
> Busy click of an Elfin
> hammer,
> Voice of the Leprechaun
> singing shrill,
> As he merrily plies his
> trade?"

Leprechauns are known to be mischievous and enjoy practical jokes. Legend has it that the leprechaun has buried his pot of gold at the end of the rainbow and, if caught, has to tell his captor where the gold is buried, but beware of his trickery!

In any serious book on the history of Ireland, there is no mention of the word "leprechaun" or "fairies," but the now green-clad friendly faced leprechaun, while still mischievous, occupies a major role in the makeup of St. Patrick's Day parades and other festivities that may involve a wee bit of drinking.

A couple sits on a bench, the Irishman apparently waiting for his lass to finish peeling the potatoes. "With his witty conversation, he then forms closer relations." Published by M. W. Taggart.

This simple card illustrates the importance of the potato to the Irish people. Published by F. A. Owen & Co.

THE LEPRECHAUN. *L-R*: Leprechaun seated on a mushroom, ceramic-light green matte, 4"h, no marks. Elf sitting cross-legged, ceramic-light green gloss, 2.88"h, marked in orange is "Made in Occupied Japan." Leprechaun standing with hands folded, "Leprechaun" on base 2.50"h. Leprechaun with Pipe Sitting on Stump, "Leprechaun" on base 3.25"h. Jittey Artefacts, Kildare, Ireland.

This modern day postcard describes leprechauns as "Irish 'little people', for their help to busy housewives, mending shoes, grinding corn, and being generally useful. Elusive, they are occasionally seen under ancient trees or amongst thick vegetation." Published by Bella cards.

Section Two:
Irish and St. Patrick's Day Collectibles

The next nine chapters will attempt to illustrate the breadth and depth of the popular collectibles that not only honor and recognize the efforts of St. Patrick, but also of the Irish worldwide. For the first quarter of the twentieth century, there were few St. Patrick's Day collectibles to be found outside of the use of colorful postcards. It was not until parades became large one-day events in the mid-1920s that St. Patrick's Day collectibles started to gain traction as valued items. Starting with parades and the associated celebrations, most people subscribed to the fact that it was fun to be Irish and wear green for a day and, hence, it was the genesis of a new collectibles market.

As food, drink, music, and parades became a mainstay of St. Patrick's Day celebrations, people also began to embellish their homes with a wide assortment of colorful party decorations and extensively used the mail to pass on postcards with "Erin Go Bragh" (Ireland Forever) or "Cead Mile Failte" (One Hundred Thousand Welcomes) messages. The most valued and sought after memorabilia that exact a good premium are German and some Japanese candy containers, nodders, and small celluloid items made in the 1920s and 1930s.

In the modern era, after World War II, a plethora of collectibles came to the marketplace such as planters, music boxes, ceramic smalls, tableware, pins, ornaments, and various music and dance items. Drinking collectibles such as whiskey decanters and beer steins have always had strong collector appeal. Some of the most prized collectibles in the future may be handmade, one-of-a-kind dolls representing leprechauns and other iconic Irish images. Please enjoy the efforts of our twelve years of collecting St. Patrick's Day memorabilia, which represents the largest in private hands.

Chapter 6

Whiskey & Beer Containers

When the Irish immigrated to the United States in the nineteenth and early twentieth centuries, they did not have much to sustain them, except for their religion, their family, their willingness to accept any job, and their taste for spirits. The fact was that in Ireland in the 1830s and 1840s, due to multiple potato crop failures, Irish tenant farmers and other lower classes were spiraling into poverty, which, compounded by increasing alcoholism, was unraveling the fabric of the Irish society. While the Anglo-Irish State made some attempts to combat poverty by the establishment of some workhouses, the Catholic Church responded by initiating a campaign of total abstinence from alcohol.

In 1838, Father Theobald Mathew, a charismatic Capuchin Friar from County Cork, embarked upon a remarkably successful crusade against "the demon drink." By 1843 five million Irish citizens out of a population of just over eight million had taken "the pledge," vowing abstinence from the evils of alcohol. *(See Chapter 4 for an allegorical engraving showing Father Mathew and his temperance followers).* Without taking anything away from Father Mathew's efforts, it is suspected that due to the Irish mother and Irish wife as the center of the household, the male family members were probably prodded to take this pledge to avoid spousal recrimination. While the abstinence did adversely affect many distilleries and breweries, the strong survived on providing exports to England and elsewhere. Since then both whiskey distilling and beer brewing in Ireland have enjoyed long histories of success in providing the best of flavor and quality in Irish whiskeys as well as lagers and stout.

"ST. JAMES GATE: THE HOME OF GUINNESS." The zookeeper and his menagerie are shown before the front gate of the Guinness Brewery in Dublin.

The message on this card was written by a gentleman on an extended trip writing from Arizona, to New Mexico, and back to California; however, Louisiana had the "best scenery we have seen." I wonder if on his trip he enjoyed the food and, like the leprechaun, had "Too Much of a Good Thing." Published by J. I. Austen Co.

"LOVELY DAY FOR A GUINNESS." One of artist John Gilroy's most popular Guinness characters, the Toucan made its first appearance in 1935.

Whiskey labels past and present from Irish Distillers.

In the United States, "temperance" movements also began in the 1830s. In that year, it was estimated that the average American of drinking age consumed 1.7 bottles of hard liquor per week, three times the amount consumed today. While the prohibition or "dry" movement lost its vigor during the American Civil War, it picked up steam through the Prohibition Party in 1896 and the Women's Christian Temperance Union (WCTU) founded in 1873. The combined efforts of these groups, aided by the vigilante and axe-wielding Carrie Nation and the Anti-Saloon League, all coalesced into enough political support to force an amendment to the Constitution.

The efforts of the "prohibitionists" were definitely helped by the prejudices of native-born Americans, whose propaganda attributed crime and alcoholism to the morally corrupt behavior of the inner-city inhabitants who were part of the mass immigration during the nineteenth century. The Irish-American communities as a whole suffered from this backlash, especially since they were pro-wets. Many postcard publishers during the early twentieth century utilized the theme of tipsy Irishmen, whose images graced the more comedic postcards commemorating St. Patrick's Day. However, other postcards showed conviviality when illustrating drinking themes.

A debonair couple enjoy a drink with a shamrock backdrop. Published by United Art Publishing Co., New York, Series 1290. Printed in Germany.

An Irishman hosting a mug to his sweetheart. Published by Raphael Tuck & Sons, Series 117.

"Ay, may ye always feel as gay as do on St. Patrick's Day!" Unsigned artist HBG (HB Griggs) card. Published by Leubrie & Elkins Publishing Co., New York, Series 2230. Printed in Germany.

In January 1920, the 18th Amendment to the Constitution became law — it implemented a national ban on the sale, manufacture, and transportation of alcohol. Due to the failure of Federal enforcement of the Volstead Act (18th Amendment), the violent gang criminality associated with "bootlegging," the black market for alcoholic beverages, and the fact that large portions of the alcoholic beverage industry workforce was without employment, the amendment was repealed in December 1933, thereby bringing to an end the "Noble Experiment."

With the amendment's repeal, the St. Patrick's Day parades and associated parties became much more festive due to the imbibing of spirits. However, it was not until the mid-1950s that the collector craze for whiskey decanters and beer steins began to initiate a whole new collecting segment. In 1955, Jim Beam was the first American distilled spirits company to introduce porcelain or ceramic decanters. In the mid-to-late 1960s, other liquor manufacturers began offering limited issue decanters. Soon there were twenty or more companies each with their own creative thematic output that were collected by thousands of enthusiasts.

Whiskey Decanters

The following is a collection of figural whiskey decanters and associated items made by several distillery manufacturers starting in 1968.

"Drowning the Shamrock on St. Patrick's Night." *Harper's Weekly*, 1885. Artist: E. Fitzpatrick.

"The wee bit of shamrock we all love so well." Published by Raphael Tuck & Sons, Series 157.

Due to the reputation of St. Patrick's Day as a day devoted to food, drink, and parties in the United States, many domestic whiskey and beer producers began issuing limited edition decanters and stein specifically for this holiday celebration. In Ireland, as well as in the United States, there is a custom known as Pota Phadraig or Patrick's Pot. The custom is known as "drowning the shamrock" because it is customary to float a leaf of the shamrock in the whiskey before downing the shot.

"The Wearin' O' The Green." Decanter with Stopper, 9.25"h. Stitzel Weller Distillery (Old Fitzgerald), Porcelain, 1968. No. 1 in the series.

"Erin Go Bragh." Decanter with new Stopper, 8.25"h. Stitzel Weller Distillery (Old Fitzgerald), Porcelain, 1971.

"Songs of Ireland." Decanter with Stopper, 10"h. Old Fitzgerald Distillery, Porcelain, 1974.

"Irish Luck." Decanter with new stopper, 10"h. Stitzel Weller Distillery (Old Fitzgerald), Porcelain, 1972.

"An Irish Wish." Decanter with Stopper, 9"h. Old Fitzgerald Distillery, Porcelain, 1975.

"An Irish Wish." Decanter with Stopper, 9"h. Old Fitzgerald Distillery, Porcelain, 1975.

"American Sons of St. Patrick: 1776-1976 Bicentennial." Decanter with Stopper, 9.25"h. Old Fitzgerald Distillery, Porcelain, 1976.

"The Four-Leaved Shamrock An Irish Charm." Decanter with Stopper, 9.5"h. Old Fitzgerald Distillery, Porcelain, 1977.

"The Coins of Ireland." Decanter with Stopper, 11.5"h. Old Commonwealth (J. P. Van Winkle & Son), Porcelain, 1979. The Old Fitzgerald distillery was sold to Schenley in 1972, but the figural decanter line continued under Winkle's Old Commonwealth label.

"March 17 St. Patrick's Day." Decanter with Stopper, 10.5"h. Old Commonwealth (J. P. Van Winkle & Son), Porcelain, 1984.

"Symbols of Ireland." Decanter with Stopper, 11.75"h. Old Commonwealth (J. P. Van Winkle & Son), Porcelain, 1985.

More Irish Symbols: Back and side views of the "Symbols of Ireland" decanter seen on the previous page.

"A Happy Green St. Patrick's Day." Decanter with Stopper. Old Commonwealth (J. P. Van Winkle & Son), Porcelain, 1986. No. 19 in the series.

"Mr. Lucky." Decanter/Music Box with Stopper, 12.5"h. Hoffman Distilling Co., Lawrenceburg, Kentucky, Matte ceramic, 1973. A pipe-smoking Leprechaun holding a pot of gold and a drink.

"Mrs. Lucky." Decanter/Music Box with Stopper, 12"h. Hoffman Distilling Co., Matte porcelain, 1974. A dancing Irish girl.

"Harpist." Decanter/Music Box with Stopper, 11.5"h. Hoffman Distilling Co., Matte porcelain, 1974. A young Irishman sitting on a log playing a harp.

"Irishman Dancer." Decanter-Miniature with Stopper, 6"h. Hoffman Distilling Co., Matte porcelain, 1975. Mint flavored syrup.

"Mr. Lucky." Whiskey Pitcher, 5.5"h. Hoffman Distilling Co., gloss white porcelain, 1978.

"When Irish Eyes Are Smiling." Decanter/Music Box, 12"h. Lefton, Japan, Gloss porcelain, 1970s. Full red-bearded leprechaun holding a whiskey jug.

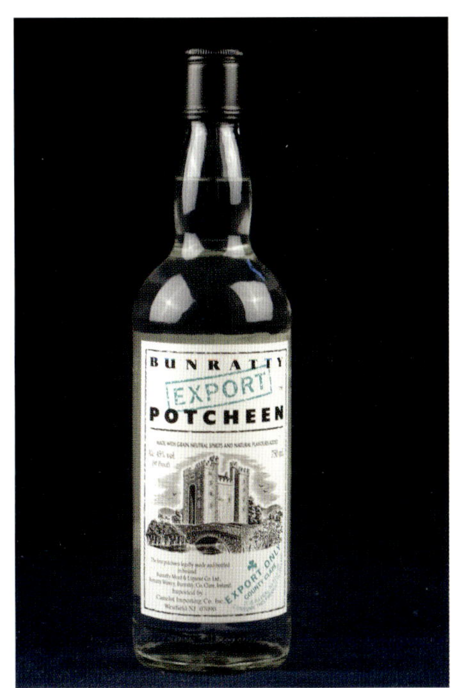

Potcheen. Full bottle of white neutral spirits distilled from grain. The original Irish word for potcheen is Poitin, meaning "little pot." These spirits are legally made for export only. In Ireland, when poitin is made illegally, it is the equivalent to America's "moonshine." Banned for domestic use since 1661. Bunratty Winery, Bunratty, County Clare, Ireland. Single distilled at 40% alcohol by volume.

"The Shamrock Whiskey." Reproduction sign, 7.75" x 12".

Full-page advertisement for Jameson Irish Whiskey: "The best selling Irish whiskey in the world." Early 1970s.

Beer Steins

Anheuser-Busch Company

In the United States, Anheuser-Busch is the largest producer of beers with a 51% share of the market. Its largest brand is Budweiser (pale lager beer), Bud Light, and Bud Ice. To take advantage of the popularity of this brand, Anheuser-Busch began issuing collectible beer steins in the 1980s. In 1991, Anheuser-Busch began issuing the first in a long series of St. Patrick's Day themed steins, of which there have been twenty-one through 2011. Presented are steins and their graphically enhanced boxes issued over the first ten years. Each of the crafted stoneware steins were made by Ceramarte of Brazil and were individually designed by an artist.

"Erin Go Bud." Leprechaun holding a mug and a shillelagh, 5.5"h. Did not come with a box. Artist: Tom Patrick. #1-1991.

"Pot of Gold-Erin Go Bud." Two leprechauns with a pot of Budweiser's, 5.5"h. Did not come with a box. Artist: March Wilson. #2-1992.

"Bottled treasure: Erin Go Bud." Trio of Leprechauns in a field of clover, 5.5"h. With box. Artist unknown. #3-1993.

"Luck O' the Irish." Pot of gold topped with nuggets and a cluster of Budweiser cans, 5.75"h. With box. Artist unknown. #4-1994.

"Tip O' Hat." Festive top hat decorated with shamrocks, 5.5"h. With box. Artist unknown. #5-1995.

"Horseshoe Stein." Clydesdale 8-horse hitch high-stepping through a stylized horseshoe, 5.5"h. With box. Artist unknown. #6-1996.

"Luck O' The Longneck." Three leprechauns have discovered in their hollow tree home an ice-cold longneck bottle of Budweiser, 6"h. With box. Artist: Ron Hubbard. #7-1997.

"Erin Go Budweiser." Six tiny leprechauns "parading" with a full bottle of Budweiser, 5.5"h. With box. Artist: Jack Whitney. #8-1998.

"The Bud That Got Away." A peaceful fishing scene with three prankish leprechauns sneaking away with the Budweiser from the fisherman's cooler, 5.5"h. With box. Artist: Thom Buttner. #9-1999.

"Leapin' Leprechauns." Seven leprechauns leaping from one Budweiser bottle cap to another, all floating in a blue pond, 5.5"h. With box. Artist: Thom Buttner. #10-2000.

"Erin Go Hamm's-O'Hamm's Salutes the Irish." This very limited and rare edition features Sascha the Beer Bear, 6"h. Dark green on a white base. Did not come with a box. 1973.

"St. Patrick's Day-O'Hamm's Salutes the Irish." Sascha the Beer Bear leads a parade, 6"h. Dark green on a white base with gold embossing. No box. 1974. Made by Ceramarte, Brazil, serial no. 005940.

Hamm's Brewery

Started in 1865, Hamm's Brewery was first sold in 1969 to a liquor company. After being resold several times, it now brews Hamm's brand of beer under its current owner, MillerCoors. Like many beer producers, Hamm's have produced ceramic beer steins for collectors. Its long-term mascot was the Hamm's Beer Bear named Sascha, which was featured on radio and television in the early 1950s. In the 1970s Hamm's issued two St. Patrick's Day thematic beer steins.

Beer Cans. *L-R*: "Irish Pride-Genuine Green Beer, 1979," August Schell Brewing Co., New Ulm, MN; "Erin go Braugh-Happy St. Patrick's Day 1979," Bilow Garden State Light Beer, Walter Brewing Company, Eau Claire, WI; "O'Keenan's Erinbrew, March 17, 1979," August Schell Brewing Co., New Ulm, MN; "Happy St. Patrick's Day 1980," Bilow Garden State Premium Beer, Walter Brewing Co, Eau Claire, WI. All cans 4.75"h.

Other Beer Memorabilia

Throughout parts of middle America, several brewing companies issued commemorative souvenir beer cans in celebration of St. Patrick's Day. Associated with the special issue beer cans were plastic drinking containers in various St. Patrick's Day motifs.

Beer Cans. *L-R*: "St. Patrick's Day 1982, 1983, 1984, 1985," Walter Brewing Company, Eau Claire, Wisconsin. All cans 4.75"h.

Beer Cans. *L-R*: "St. Patrick's Day 1986," Walter Brewing Company, Eau Claire, WI; "Walter's City Brewery-St. Patrick's Beer 1987," Hibernia Brewing Ltd., Eau Claire, Wisconsin; "McMahon's Genuine Irish Potato Ale 1992," Minnesota Brewing Company, St. Paul, MN. All cans 4.75"h.

Series of six plastic drinking containers all with Irish slogans dating from the 1980s and 1990s.

The Hard Rock Café

The Hard Rock Café is a chain of musically themed restaurants founded in 1971. In 1979, the existing restaurants began to add Rock & Roll memorabilia to its walls, which have been the norm for every newly opened restaurant since that year. To furnish the various restaurants, the Hard Rock Café archives contain over 70,000 memorabilia and artifacts of rock history including autographed guitars, traveling outfits from world tours, gold and platinum records, celebrity pictures with autographs, and others icons from the Rock & Roll era. From its first opening of a restaurant in London, England, in 1971, Hard Rock Café (now owned by the Seminole Tribe of Florida) operates over 150 theme restaurants in fifty-three countries.

Leprechaun Figural Ceramic Mug, 4.5"h. Papel Freelance, Cranbury, New Jersey. With box.

Smiling Paddy Head Figural Ceramic Mug, 4.25"h. Frankoma Pottery, Sapulpa, Oklahoma, 1980. No box.

Leprechaun Figural Ceramic Mug, 5.25"h. Hand-painted. Fitz & Floyd, 1988. No box.

Leprechaun Head with Bulging Eyes Figural Ceramic Mugs, 4.5"h. Department 56, Eden Prairie, Minnesota, 2003. No box.

Shamrock Decorated Mugs with Leprechaun Figural Handle, 5.5"h. Lefton, Japan.

Shamrock Pipe Figural Ceramic Mug, 3.25"h. Relpo #6184, Japan. No box.

Advertisement: "Real Gusto in a great light beer... Ah! The Irish sure know how to make beer. After the parade, get together with a friendly glass of Schlitz!" *The Saturday Evening Post*, 1964.

Pins

One of the features of a restaurant opening was the issuance of a "special" pin to mark the event. In the years following, an annual "city" pin for that club was issued. Pins can only be purchased at a Hard Rock restaurant or traded with other collectors. To mark different holidays, like St. Patrick's Day, special pins are made for these occasions. As a help to Hard Rock Café pin collectors, the company has issued a checklist with photos and descriptions for every pin for every club, whether in existence or not. In 1996, the first edition of the *Official Hard Rock Café Pin Collectors Guide* was issued (to commemorate the firm's 25th Anniversary). It was 207 pages in length. The following is a series of special St. Patrick's Day pins issued from various cities throughout the world from 1998 through 2009. Additionally a few sporting and miscellaneous pins are also offered.

An array of St. Patrick's Day pins dating from 1998 through 2009 issued by Hard Rock Café from different locations.

An array of St. Patrick's Day pins dating from 1998 through 2009 issued by Hard Rock Café from different locations.

An array of St. Patrick's Day pins dating from 1998 through 2009 issued by Hard Rock Café from different locations.

An array of St. Patrick's Day pins dating from 1998 through 2009 issued by Hard Rock Café from different locations.

St. Patrick's Collector's Pins. *L-R*: An undated Hard Rock Café Tijuana, Mexico, pin; Buena Vista Café, San Francisco, California, pin; Hooters 2004 pin.

Boston Celtics and Boston Red Sox St. Patrick's Day pins.

Chapter 7
St. Patrick's Day Feast

From the time of St. Patrick in the fifth century, the staple diet of Celtic farmers was cereal grains and dairy produce. The diets were supplemented to some degree by the addition of wild edible greens such as nettles, watercress, wild garlic, and wood sorrel. Protein was taken in the form of salted bacon and whatever the abundant freshwater streams could produce such as eels. This very bland but reasonably nutritious diet of oats, barley, and dairy produce for the Irish peasantry withstood the test of time and showed little change until the introduction of the potato in the late eighteenth century.

Though there were some additions to the diet due to the Viking and Norman invasions that only benefitted the upper classes in the form of fowl, rabbit, grapes, figs, nutmeats, and a large assortment of spices and cordials, since one-third of Ireland's inhabitants were subsistence farmers, the introduction of the potato was a welcome addition to their diet. In a short period of time, the potato, which could be grown very easily, established itself as the staple foodstuff. The potato, which supplanted watery porridges, was an enhancement to the nutritional value of a meal and one in which it became the sole food for over one million Irishmen.

When the potato crop experienced successive crop failures during the mid-nineteenth century, waves of Irish immigrants came to America, each bearing some favorite Irish recipe from their respective counties. Due to the abundance of available foodstuffs and spices in America, Irish recipes took on a new life, and they became the driving force behind the hearty fare for which Irish cooking is well-known. Many excellent Irish cookbooks have been introduced in the last decade or so as they explore the whole range of Irish cooking and recipes, many from a historic aspect.

Two excellent guides to Irish food and cooking: *Irish Food & Folklore* and *Irish Traditional Cooking*.

The Whiskeys of Ireland, a guide to every Irish whiskey produced, and *A Taste of Ireland in Food and Pictures*, combines old black & white photographs from the late nineteenth and early twentieth century with the old recipes of that era.

Colcannon

Similar to Champ, but flavoured, coloured and textured by the addition of cooked and shredded kale – a member of the cabbage family. Traditionally served at Hallowe'en.

500 g/1 lb kale or green leaf cabbage, stalk removed and finely shredded
500 g/1 lb potatoes, unpeeled
6 spring onions or chives, finely chopped
150 ml/¼ pint milk or cream
125 g/4 oz butter
salt and pepper

Heat a pan of salted water and boil the kale or cabbage in boiling water until very tender. This will take 10–20 minutes. At the same time heat another pan of salted water and boil the potatoes until tender. Place the spring onions and the milk or cream in a pan and simmer over a low heat for about 5 minutes.

Drain the kale or cabbage and mash. Drain the potatoes, peel and mash well. Add the hot milk and spring onions, beating well to give a soft fluffy texture. Beat in the kale or cabbage, season with salt and pepper and add half the butter. The colcannon should be a speckled, green colour. Heat through thoroughly before serving in individual dishes or bowls. Make a well in the centre of each serving and put a knob of the remaining butter in each. Serve immediately.

Colcannon, like champ, can be served as a main dish with a glass of buttermilk or as an accompanying vegetable.

COOK'S NOTES

Sometimes I blend the kale in a food processor along with the hot milk and spring onions before adding to the potatoes. This produces an even texture and overall green colour and makes an interesting alternative.

Serves 4–6
Preparation time: 15 minutes
Cooking time: 20 minutes

Did you ever eat Colcannon,
When 'twas made with yellow cream?

(Traditional Rhyme)

102 VEGETABLE DISHES

Recipe for "Colcannon," a traditional Irish dish.
From Irish Food and Folklore.

Recipe for "Irish Coffee," Buena Vista Café, San Francisco, California.

Classic Irish Fare

The celebration of St. Patrick's Day is the one time of the year where traditional Irish food is expected to be served to the Irish and non-Irish alike. Classic dishes such as Irish Lamb Stew, Corn Beef and Cabbage, Soda Bread, Colcannon, Dublin Coddle, Shandy, Cockles and Mussels Soup, Ulster Fry, and Boxty Pancakes will grace the menus of most eating establishments throughout St. Patrick's Day. Menus usually used editorial license to name various dishes after Irish names. Your choice of beverage could include Irish whiskey, Guinness beer, Irish coffee, or strong teas. Articles in magazines also provided tips for the successful hosting of a St. Patrick's Day meal with suggested menus for luncheon and dinner.

There is a traditional rhyme about Boxty that is heard often: *"Boxty on the griddle/ Boxty in the pan/ If you don't eat your boxty/ You'll never get a man."*

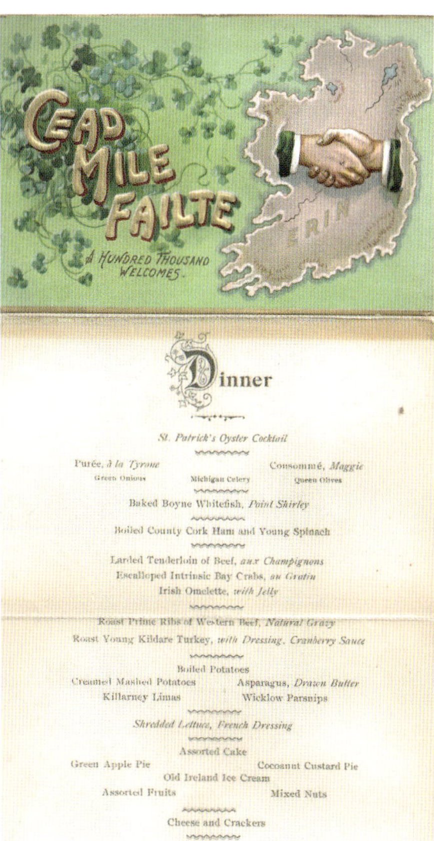

Dinner

St. Patrick's Oyster Cocktail

Purée, *à la Tyrone* — Consommé, *Maggie*

Green Onions — Michigan Celery — Queen Olives

Baked Boyne Whitefish, *Point Shirley*

Boiled County Cork Ham and Young Spinach

Larded Tenderloin of Beef, *aux Champignons*

Escalloped Intrinsic Bay Crabs, *au Gratin*

Irish Omelette, *with Jelly*

Roast Prime Ribs of Western Beef, *Natural Gravy*

Roast Young Kildare Turkey, *with Dressing, Cranberry Sauce*

Boiled Potatoes

Creamed Mashed Potatoes — Asparagus, *Drawn Butter*

Killarney Limas — Wicklow Parsnips

Shredded Lettuce, French Dressing

Assorted Cake

Green Apple Pie — Cocoanut Custard Pie

Old Ireland Ice Cream

Assorted Fruits — Mixed Nuts

Cheese and Crackers

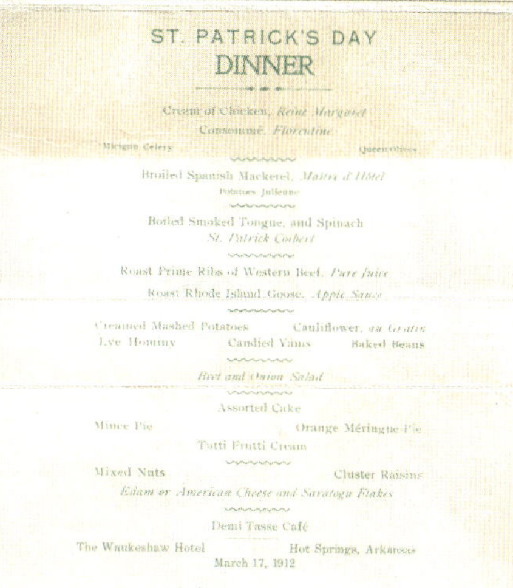

ST. PATRICK'S DAY
DINNER

Cream of Chicken, *Reine Margaret*

Consommé, *Florentine*

Michigan Celery — Queen Olives

Broiled Spanish Mackerel, *Maitre d'Hôtel*

Potatoes Julienne

Boiled Smoked Tongue, and Spinach

St. Patrick Colbert

Roast Prime Ribs of Western Beef, *Pure Juice*

Roast Rhode Island Goose, *Apple Sauce*

Creamed Mashed Potatoes — Cauliflower, *au Gratin*

Lye Hominy — Candied Yams — Baked Beans

Beet and Onion Salad

Assorted Cake

Mince Pie — Orange Méringue Pie

Tutti Frutti Cream

Mixed Nuts — Cluster Raisins

Edam or American Cheese and Saratoga Flakes

Demi Tasse Café

The Waukeshaw Hotel — Hot Springs, Arkansas

March 17, 1912

MENU FROM WAUKESHA HOTEL, HOT SPRINGS, ARKANSAS, MARCH 17, 1912. Menu is in the form of a postcard.

MENU FROM HOTEL MILWAUKEE, HOT SPRINGS, ARKANSAS, MARCH 17, 1911. The menu is in the form of a postcard titled "Cead Mile Failte."

ONWARD TO BERLIN

To Tune of "Wearing of the Green"

When the war is over, Heinie.
Just take a tip from me:
There'll be no German submarines
A diving through the sea.
For in Fatherland is Kaiser Bill,
The guy we're going to lick:
We'll have a brand new Kaiser
And same will be "Mick."

We'll change the song 'Die Wacht Am Rhine'
Into an Irish reel,
And make the Dutchman dance,
If so inclined we feel.
The police force in Berlin
Will be "Micks" from County Clare:
When we put an Irish Kaiser
In the palace over there.

Sure, in every German parkway
You'll find a sweet coleen:
And in the fields of Sauerkraut
We'll plant the Shamrock green.
No liverwurst or sausage
When the Dutchman drinks his suds:
But he'll get corned beef and cabbage
And good old Irish "spuds."

The heathens' guns and gas bombs,
We'll throw them all away:
There'll be no iron crosses,
To make the Dutchman gay.
There'll be no more goose-stepping,
Sure, the Shamrocks they will wear,
When we put an Irish Kaiser
In the palace over there.

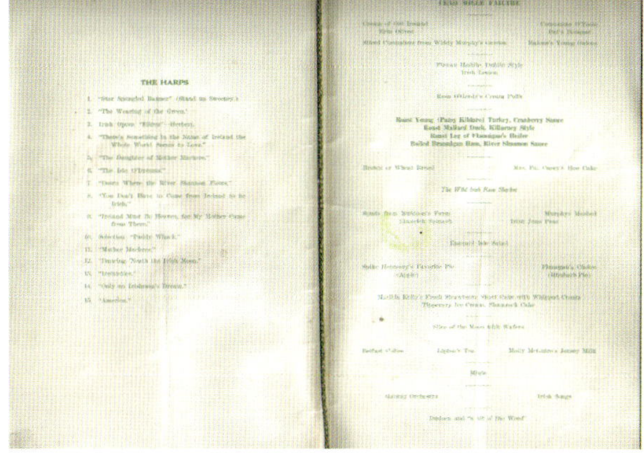

MENU FROM THE HUNTINGTON, HUNTINGTON, WEST VIRGINIA, MARCH 1918. Menu contents include a patriotic song and a list of songs played by an orchestra.

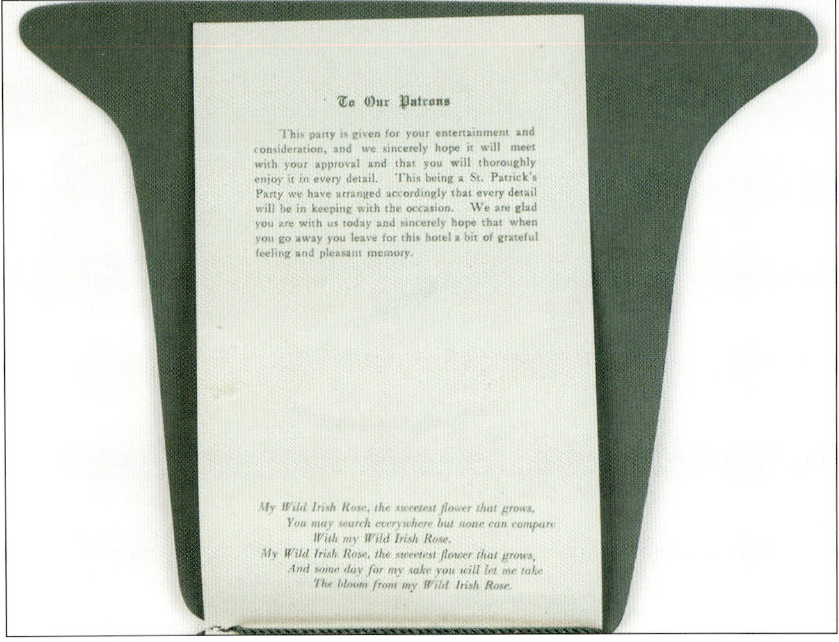

To Our Patrons

This party is given for your entertainment and consideration, and we sincerely hope it will meet with your approval and that you will thoroughly enjoy it in every detail. This being a St. Patrick's Party we have arranged accordingly that every detail will be in keeping with the occasion. We are glad you are with us today and sincerely hope that when you go away you leave for this hotel a bit of grateful feeling and pleasant memory.

My Wild Irish Rose, the sweetest flower that grows,
You may search everywhere but none can compare
With my Wild Irish Rose.
My Wild Irish Rose, the sweetest flower that grows,
And some day for my sake you will let me take
The bloom from my Wild Irish Rose.

Menu

St. Patrick's Punch
Potage Erin Go Bragh — Consomme Shannon
Pat's Bouquet — Kilkenny Shots — O'Neil's Relish

Prime Roast from Mulligan's Heifer
Baked McGettigan's Ham with Muldoon's Hoe Cake and Gallaway Sauce
Jiggs' Special Corned Beef and Cabbage
Just a Bit of Heaven

Murphys With Their Jackets On — O'Brien Potatoes

Emeralds en Creme — Banshees on a Raft

Tipperary Salad--Flannagan's Dressing
Toasted Shillalahs

Mollie McGuire's Green Apple Pie
Bridget Shallu's Churned Cow

Erin Ice Cream — Shamrock Petit Fours
Sweets of Old Erin

Maggie O'Leary's Shortcake with Whipped Cream from Dinty Moore's Cow

Blarney Stones

Blackthorn Coffee — Goat's Milk — Red Eye Tay

And When They Had It Finished They Called It Ireland

Menu from Hotel Witter, Wisconsin Rapids, Wisconsin, March 18, 1928.

O'er every land float the Irish tunes
Like a gallant flag to the breeze unfurled,
For to sweep the strings of the Irish harp
Sweeps the heart-strings of the world.

E'en the ancient Irish pipe
Wears a glory all its own,
For the lips can blow a halo
That have kissed the blarney stone.

St. Patrick's Day Party, Luncheon, or Tea, for Those Who Are Irish or Otherwise

By ELAINE, *Entertainment Editor*

IMPORTANT INSTRUCTIONS

ON RECEIPT OF 10 CENTS IN STAMPS, ADDRESSED TO ELAINE, ENTERTAINMENT EDITOR, GOOD HOUSEKEEPING, 119 WEST 40 ST., N. Y. CITY, SUGGESTIONS WILL BE SENT FOR A ST. PATRICK'S DAY PARTY, LUNCHEON, OR TEA, INCLUDING INSTRUCTIONS FOR MAKING:

1. Invitations to Smoke the Irish Peace Pipe
2. Emerald Isle Decorations
3. Irish Harp and Blarney Stone Centerpiece for the St. Patrick's Day Table
4. Notes From the Irish Harp Place Cards
5. Irish Potato Table Centerpiece
6. Irish Menu for St. Patrick's Day
7. Choosing Partners in Irish Fashion for Charades Illustrating Irish History
8. Irish Games Honoring the Famous Clan of Murphy Known and Beloved of All, Be They Irish or Be They Otherwise

The fat Irish pig
Is dancing a jig,
Is dancing a jig or two,
For he's brought home the bacon
The English had taken,
To make him an Irish stew.

On receipt of 10 cents in stamps, instructions will be sent for a Children's Party and a Bride's Shower suitable to be given at a luncheon, tea, or evening affair. Elaine, Entertainment Editor

"St. Patrick's Day Party, Luncheon, or Tea, for Those Who Are Irish or Otherwise." Article includes instructions on how to make table centerpieces, decorations, and menus. *Good Housekeeping*, March 1922.

March, 1929 LADIES' HOME JOURNAL

Menus for St. Patrick's Day Entertaining

Noonday Luncheon

FRUIT COCKTAIL
Alligator Pear Cubes Marinated in Lime Juice Dressing, Garnished With Shredded Sweet Pickle

CHICKEN LIVERS EN BROCHETTE
SCALLOPED POTATOES BROCCOLI WITH HOLLANDAISE

WHITE RADISH AND LETTUCE SALAD—FRENCH DRESSING

[illegible]
NUTS DIPPED IN GREEN FONDANT

Bridge Luncheon

FRIED CREAM PUFFS FILLED WITH SEA FOOD À LA NEWBURG
SHAMROCK ROLLS OLIVES WITH ONION STUFFING

BEAN-SPROUT SALAD WITH GRATED CARROT GARNISH

GINGERBREAD SHORTCAKE
BANANA FILLING MARSHMALLOW SAUCE
MARZIPAN POTATOES

COFFEE

Afternoon Refreshments

EMERALD SALAD
Canned Pears Molded in Green Gelatin
With
OPEN-FACED SHAMROCK SANDWICHES
Sweet Pickled Cucumber Shamrocks on White Bread Surrounded With a Fluting of Cream Cheese
ST. PATRICK COCONUT KISSES
Ordinary Kisses Dipped in Green Coconut
TEA

Evening Refreshments

PATTY SHELLS FILLED WITH CHICKEN IN PINEAPPLE SAUCE
LETTUCE SANDWICHES STUFFED CELERY

SCOTCH TOOTS FILLED WITH PISTACHIO ICE CREAM
MINT GUM DROPS

COCOA
or
COFFEE

Dinner

ST. PATRICK'S HORS D'OEUVRES
Dill Pickle Slices Topped With a Sardine
Slices of Salami Sausage With Onion Rings Filled With Chopped Cheese
Squares of Sweet Pickled Watermelon Rind
Garnished With a Shamrock of Green Pepper

STUFFED LAMB CHOPS
or
ROAST DUCKLING
Accompanied by Prunes Stuffed With Mint Jelly
or
Slices of Orange Under a Mint Jelly Cube

NEW BOILED POTATOES WITH BUTTER SAUCE
IRISH HAT TIMBALES
A Spinach Timbale Crown Resting on a Brim of Buttered Toast, Dipped in Minced Parsley, and a Hatband of Hard-Cooked Egg White

ENDIVE SALAD
CORNMEAL CRISPS ROQUEFORT DRESSING

GREEN PEPPERMINT ICE CREAM WITH CHOPPED ANGELICA
or
MERINGUE GLACÉE WITH GREEN-CHERRY GARNISH

COFFEE

Drawings by Weldon Bailey

"Menus for St. Patrick's Day Entertaining." Article includes luncheon and dinner suggestions. *Ladies' Home Journal*, March 1929.

Menu from the New York and Cuba Mail Steamship Company's *T.E.L. Oriente*, March 17, 1932. Menu contents include signatures of guests.

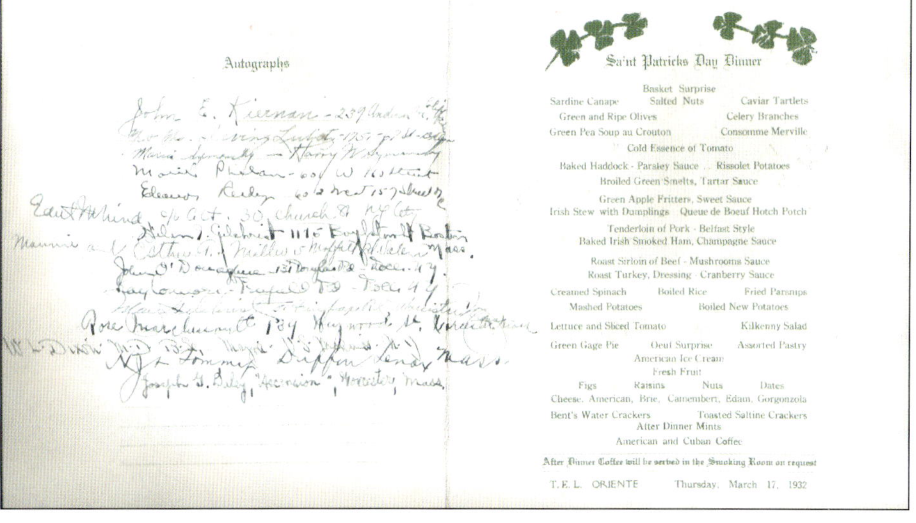

Autographs

Sa'nt Patricks Day Dinner

Basket Surprise
Sardine Canape Salted Nuts Caviar Tartlets
Green and Ripe Olives Celery Branches
Green Pea Soup au Crouton Consomme Merville
Cold Essence of Tomato
Baked Haddock - Parsley Sauce .. Rissolet Potatoes
Broiled Green Smelts, Tartar Sauce
Green Apple Fritters, Sweet Sauce
Irish Stew with Dumplings Queue de Boeuf Hotch Potch
Tenderloin of Pork - Belfast Style
Baked Irish Smoked Ham, Champagne Sauce
Roast Sirloin of Beef - Mushrooms Sauce
Roast Turkey, Dressing · Cranberry Sauce
Creamed Spinach Boiled Rice Fried Parsnips
Mashed Potatoes Boiled New Potatoes
Lettuce and Sliced Tomato Kilkenny Salad
Green Gage Pie Oeuf Surprise Assorted Pastry
American Ice Cream
Fresh Fruit
Figs Raisins Nuts Dates
Cheese. American, Brie, Camembert, Edam, Gorgonzola
Bent's Water Crackers Toasted Saltine Crackers
After Dinner Mints
American and Cuban Coffee

After Dinner Coffee will be served in the Smoking Room on request

T. E. L. ORIENTE Thursday, March 17, 1932

"Aquatic Eats." Menu from the *R.M.S. Franconia*, March 17, 1930, gives humorous names for menu offerings.

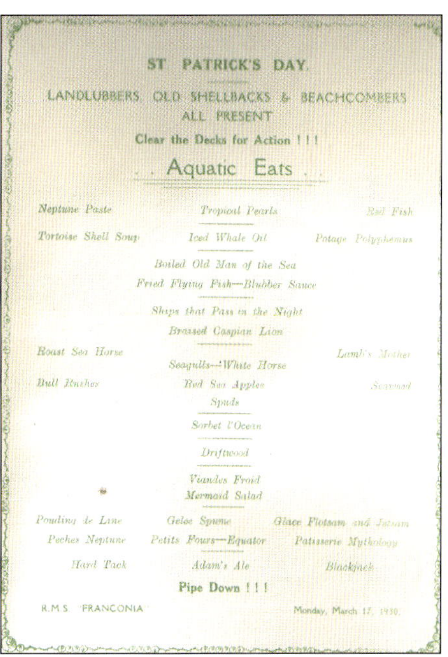

ST PATRICK'S DAY.

LANDLUBBERS, OLD SHELLBACKS & BEACHCOMBERS
ALL PRESENT

Clear the Decks for Action ! ! !

. . Aquatic Eats . . .

Neptune Paste Tropical Pearls Red Fish

Tortoise Shell Soup Iced Whale Oil Potage Polyphemus

Boiled Old Man of the Sea
Fried Flying Fish—Blubber Sauce

Ships that Pass in the Night
Brassed Caspian Lion

Roast Sea Horse Lamb's Mother
Seagulls—White Horse
Bull Rushes Red Sea Apples Seaweed
Spuds

Sorbet l'Ocean

Driftwood

Viandes Froid
Mermaid Salad

Pouding de Line Gelee Spume Glace Flotsam and Jetsam
Peches Neptune Petits Fours—Equator Patisserie Mythology

Hard Tack Adam's Ale Blackjack

Pipe Down ! ! !

R.M.S. "FRANCONIA" Monday, March 17, 1930.

Decorating the Table

The St. Patrick's Day table, like other holidays, can be set with a whole range of festive arrangements utilizing ceramic tableware, glassware, paper, figural items, salt and pepper shakers, and cloth table coverings.

St. Patrick's Day

AT SEA

HAMBURG-AMERIKA

LINIE

"Fiesta-Shamrock." Place setting of four: dinner plate, 8"d, luncheon plate, 7"d, bowl 7"d., and mug, 3.5"d. Platter, 13.5"l, and set of salt and pepper shakers, 2.25"d. The Homer Laughlin Company, Newell, West Virginia.

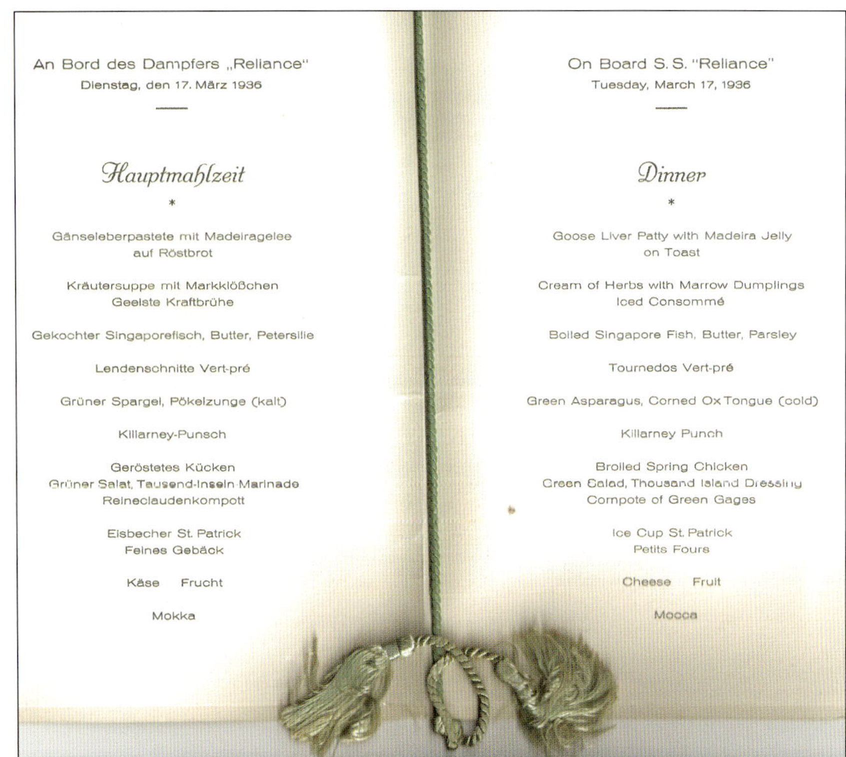

An Bord des Dampfers „Reliance"
Dienstag, den 17. März 1936

Hauptmahlzeit

*

Gänseleberpastete mit Madeiragelee
auf Röstbrot

Kräutersuppe mit Markklößchen
Geeiste Kraftbrühe

Gekochter Singaporefisch, Butter, Petersilie

Lendenschnitte Vert-pré

Grüner Spargel, Pökelzunge (kalt)

Killarney-Punsch

Geröstetes Kücken
Grüner Salat, Tausend-Inseln-Marinade
Reineclaudenkompott

Eisbecher St. Patrick
Feines Gebäck

Käse Frucht

Mokka

On Board S. S. "Reliance"
Tuesday, March 17, 1936

Dinner

*

Goose Liver Patty with Madeira Jelly
on Toast

Cream of Herbs with Marrow Dumplings
Iced Consommé

Boiled Singapore Fish, Butter, Parsley

Tournedos Vert-pré

Green Asparagus, Corned Ox Tongue (cold)

Killarney Punch

Broiled Spring Chicken
Green Salad, Thousand Island Dressing
Compote of Green Gages

Ice Cup St. Patrick
Petits Fours

Cheese Fruit

Mocca

"St. Patrick's Day At Sea." Menu from Hamburg-Amerika Linie's *S.S. Reliance*, March 17, 1936. Also written in German.

Decorative elements on this bowl include four raised shamrocks on the rim, 4"h x 8"d. "Bella Casa" by Ganz. Made in China.

"Happy St. Patrick's Day." This set of four salad plates (three shown) features two different scenes. Rosanna, Made in China. With decorative box.

This set of four plates (two shown) features two scenes: "Luck O' The Irish" and "Pot of Gold." Rosanna, Made in China.

Salt and Pepper Set. Leprechauns dancing a jig and playing a violin, 4.5"h. F(itz) & F(loyd), 1988; paper label hand-painted.

Tea Mugs, 4.6"h; dessert plates, 8"d; and pipe-smoking Irishman figural teapot, 5"h x 7.5"l. Mugs and plates set with a shamrock motif. Made in Ireland.

Glass Vase. Hand-fired, square shaped with a medium blue-green coloration, 7"h x 2.5" base. Artist: Keith Leadbetter. Jerpoint Glass Studio, Stoneyford, County Kilkenny, Ireland.

Figural Cheese/Butter Spreaders. *L-R*: Pipe with Leprechaun Head, St. Patrick, Leprechaun on a Pot of Gold, and Irish Harp. Stainless steel knives. Made by Radko. With box.

Three Vases. *L-R*: Vase, squat base, tall cylindrical neck-Dark green on White with Shamrocks, 6.50"h x 1.5"d base. Lefton China hand-painted in gold stamp and foil sticker, Lefton Japan; Vase, circular base, tall cylindrical neck. Light green with shamrocks design, 6"h x 3"d base. Homer Laughlin impressed "Fiesta" USA on base; Vase with squat base, narrow neck with lip-Ivory base with delicate light green shamrocks on neck, 5.25"h x 3"d base. Belleek, Ireland, (green stamp) on base. Reg. No. D 857.

Leprechaun with a peaked cap painted in dark green, black boots, and gloves, wearing a gold chain. Cookie jar, 12"h x 6.5"l. McCoy (Pottery) incised on a white unglazed base. Quite rare.

Nut/Candy Cups. Set of three with green ruffled crepe paper, cardboard, and die-cut Irish figures, 3" square. USA made. Background: Two water glasses with a three-color shamrock design, 6.5"h. Made in Thailand.

Leprechaun sitting on a barrel with Gold Coins. Cookie jar, 7.50"h x 5"d girth. Made in China (black stamp).

Hand-painted ceramic-three pronged tree trunk candleholder, 10.75"h x 5"d base. F(itz) & F(loyd), 1988. *Left*: Leprechaun playing violin is the front; *Right*: Leprechaun dancing the jig is the back.

Salt and Pepper Set of an Irish Boy and Girl dressed in medium green and red attire, 3"h. Blue stamp at base "Germany."

Ashtray with a Stagecoach decal design, 4"d. Irish Porcelain, Made in Ireland. Placed on 12" square cloth napkin with "Good Luck" symbols of horseshoes, stars, and wishbones.

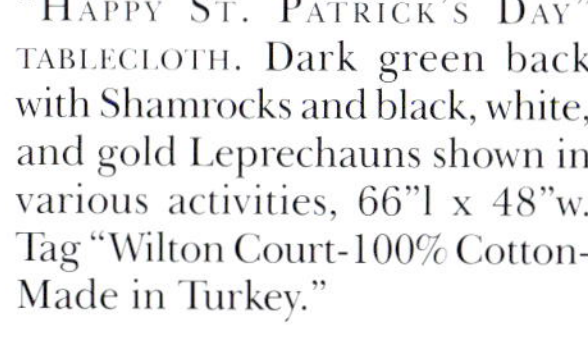

"Happy St. Patrick's Day" tablecloth. Dark green back with Shamrocks and black, white, and gold Leprechauns shown in various activities, 66"l x 48"w. Tag "Wilton Court-100% Cotton-Made in Turkey."

Salt and Pepper Shakers of a seated young Irish boy and girl, 3.25"h. No marks.

Hamm's Brewery Salt and Pepper Set. Sascha, the Hamm's Beer Bear, 4.75"h, and Pot of Gold bottle tops, 2"h. Made in Japan, 2004.

Tablecloth with white back and five main design elements, 4' square. *Center*: Green square with an ancient Triskele or triple spiral. *Bottom left, Corner (1)*: O'Connell Street Dublin; *Top left, Corner (2)*: Glendalough; *Top right, Corner (3)*: The Giants Causeway; and *Bottom right, Corner (4)*: The Rock of Cashel.

Chocolate Moulds

Chocolate moulds began to be collectible items in the early 1980s when collectors started researching and writing "bibles" on the subject. Chocolate moulds (sometimes termed "ice cream moulds") can be divided into two main classifications: Novelty Full Figure Moulds (NFFM) and Flat Moulds. The Novelty Full Figure Moulds have at least two mirror image pieces and are three-dimensional in shape. Flats are one-piece moulds used to form half-figures and simple geometric shapes.

Chocolate moulds were made out of tinplate or pewter and first manufactured in Germany in the early 1830s. By 1880, they were being made in the United States by Eppelsheimer & Co. in New York City. Due to its fine quality reputation for making detailed moulds, Eppelsheimer & Co. became the largest manufacturer of domestic moulds. Nearly one hundred years later, due to the rising cost of quality tinplate and the increasing demand for cheaper (but less detailed) plastic moulds, the firm that then owned Eppelsheimer phased out its metal chocolate mould production in 1974. Chocolate moulds are highly collectible today, and items representing St. Patrick's Day symbols are rare simply because chocolate is not associated with the celebration of that day.

Six novelty full-figure chocolate moulds made of pewter.

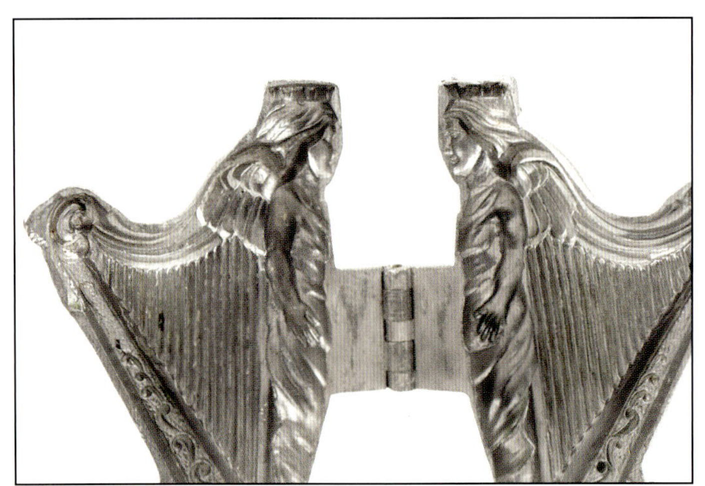

Four novelty full-figure chocolate moulds. *Top Left*: Shamrock, 7"w. Made by Eppelsheimer (E & CO N.Y.) #1191; *Top Right*: Harp, 7.25"w. Unmarked; *Bottom Left*: Harp, 7.5"w. #36; *Bottom Right*: Potato, 5.5"w. Made by E & CO N.Y. #244.

Two novelty full-figure chocolate moulds: Shamrock, 7.5"w, made by S & Co. #560, and Pipe, 11.25"w., #374.

Chapter 8

Irish-Themed Decorations

There have been many St. Patrick's Day collectibles issued that either are purely decorative in intent or have some rather superficial utilitarian value, but are still prized for their eye appeal. The latter category mainly includes coin banks and trinket boxes. For the most part collectibles in this category are considered "smalls" due their size and aesthetic appeal.

Left: Miniature Pig Planter in medium green bisque with green bow, 2.25"h x 4.5"l. No marks; *Right*: "JB" the Scottie Dog in a pink ivory blush, hand-painted with small shamrocks, 3"h x 2.5"l. Artist: Charles LaCroix. Boyd's Crystal Art Glass, Cambridge, Ohio.

Pixie Coin Bank. Smiling Head Resting on Hands, Sitting on "Barrel O'Money," 8.75"h x 4"d girth. "Marika's Original By Lefton" in relief on base (red/gold foil sticker).

Pig Coin Banks. *Left*: White with Green Shamrocks, 3"l x 2.5"w. Lefton (red/gold sticker); clear label "Lefton, China, hand-painted"; *Right*: Holiday Sitting Bear, Opal satin glass with light green paint spray decorated with medium green shamrocks and bow tie, 3.5"h. Base "Fenton Hand-painted in USA" silver foil label; "Exclusively for Collector's Showcase" black stamp. 100 sets. Artist signed: S. Van Zile.

"Good Luck from Ireland." An Irishman and his donkey, 5.25"h x 4.25"l. A Tseapain Tir A Dheanta black stamp on base.

Two Leprechauns carrying a heavy Pot of Gold on a long stick, 4.5"h x 4.5"l. Hand-painted papier-mache, handmade by Char Theurer 2006.

Angel with Green Shamrock wings holding a Dove of Peace, 8"h. Molded wood pulp. No marks.

Irish Boy (6"h) and Irish Girl (5.75"h) each holding shamrocks. Molded wood pulp. Napcoware Import Japan (red/gold sticker). M-8363 black stamp.

Figural Nut Cracker. Leprechaun, wearing a green felt hat and green felt smock, is holding a pipe and a tree of shamrocks. On the circular wood base is a Pot of Gold. 13"h. Made in China (gold foil sticker).

Irishman dressed in light green attire, sitting on a large tree stump with a hoard of gold coins at his side, 7.25"h. Hand-painted ceramic, handmade by MJH 1984.

A Leprechaun/Gnome Doorstop, 10.5"h. Painted Cast Iron, c. late 1920s to late 1930s. American made probably by Hubley Manufacturing Company, Lancaster, PA, the foremost cast iron doorstop manufacturer in the United States.

Three young girls in various poses holding a shamrock, 3.75"h. Lefton, Japan #403 (red/gold label).

Trinket Boxes. *Left and Right*: Leprechaun sitting on Pot of Gold, being the cover for the hinged circular, porcelain box, 2.75"h. Comes with a green shamrock inside. Made in China (gold foil sticker). *Middle*: Leprechaun Head on heart-shaped lid, 3.75"h x 3.25"w. Celtic Collection-Possible Dreams, 2002 paper label. Made in China (gold foil label).

Three young girls in various poses, 3.5" to 4"h. Lefton, Japan #8149 (red/gold label).

Four Leprechauns standing and lying down in various poses. Sizes range from 4.25"h to 3.75"l. Designed by: Marika. Lefton, Japan #3522 (red/gold label).

Left: Winged Irish Girl "March" holding a jeweled shamrock and jewels in her skirt, 4.75"h. Lefton, Japan #1987J-1957 (red/silver label). *Right*: Irish Boy "March" holding a shamrock decorated kite, 5"h. Black stamp #2300.

Left: Two Smiling Young Leprechauns/Elves sitting on a toadstool, 3.25"h. No marks. *Right*: Young Leprechauns, one holding a bottle and one with empty pockets, 3"h. Lefton, Japan #954 (red/gold label).

Left: Smiling Irish Boy holding a pipe, 3.5"h. Lefton, Japan (red/gold label); *Right*: Young Irish boy blowing a horn while stepping over two mushrooms, 4.5"h. Lefton, Japan (red/gold label).

Decorative glass plate featuring "Snoopy/ Woodstock St. Patrick's Day" designs on cloth applied to the glass, 10"d. Handmade.

"St. Patrick's Day 1976 – Third Lock on the Logan Belfast" decorative porcelain plate, 7.5"d. Kilkelly by Seltman Weiden, Konigl. Pr. Tettau West Germany. Ltd. Edition of 3,000 pieces.

"Shamrock Valencias" decorative porcelain plate, 7.75"d. Reproduction of a citrus crate label. Oneida-Vintage Label Collection. China.

"Happy St. Patrick's Day" in black script on a decorative porcelain plate, 11" square. Decorated with shamrocks in greenish-blue color shadings. Rosanna. Made in China.

Ceramic and Pottery Planters

Due to their wide array of shapes, colors, and glazes, ceramic and pottery planters are a specialized collecting entity in of itself. There are three types of planters: head types, wall pockets, and figural. For the most part St. Patrick's Day and Irish images fit into the third category. Typically St. Patrick's Day planters are decorated with happy faced children, whimsical leprechauns, and symbols such as shamrocks and top hats. As defined, planters and related pieces are rather small, shallow objects that you would normally "pot" live plants or flowers. The vast majority of these floral planters were made in Japan, though some of the early pottery was also crafted in the United States and Europe.

However, since the 1960s, due to the simplicity of most planter molds, production was established in low-wage cost countries such as Japan. Many planters were unmarked while others are stamped "Made in Japan." Most of these also had foil or paper labels signifying the United States importer/designer such as "Enesco," "Inarco," "Lefton," "Napco," and "Relpo." Eventually, production over the past twenty years has shifted to Taiwan and China. In order to provide the colorful niceties as a way of dressing up the St. Patrick's Day table or its surrounding area, colorful figural planters, often given as "thank-you" gifts, were the answer.

Little Boy and Little Girl Dancing Planters. Boy planter, 5.75"h x 4.5"l x 3"w. Relpo K1760 (black stamp), black/gold foil, Chicago, Illinois. Girl planter, 5.50"h x 4.5"l x 3.50"w. Relpo Japan K1760 black stamp, (black/gold foil).

Planters of a green hat-wearing little boy seated on Pot of Gold, holding a Shamrock, 6"h x 4.5"l x 4.75"w. Lefton (red/gold sticker), "Exclusives Japan" incised 6251, and a bearded Leprechaun with a green hat and Shamrocks décor, 6"h x 5.5"l x 4"w. No marks.

Planter of a red-bearded Irishman sitting on a gold polka-dotted mushroom, with pipe in hand, playing the mandolin, 6.25"h x 4.5"l x 3.5"w. #816, no marks.

Planter of little boy and girl dancing, 5.50"h x 4.5"l x 3.75"w. Lefton (red/gold foil sticker), "Exclusives Japan."

Planters of bearded Leprechaun wearing a green hat and outfit and holding a shillelagh, 5.50"h x 4.0"l x 2.50"w. Incised encircled Japan 6104, Rubens Originals. Los Angeles. Made in Japan (red/gold foil sticker), and an Elf with peaked cap sitting by a tree trunk, 3.25"h x 6.5"l x 4"w. Lefton (red/gold foil sticker), "Exclusives Japan."

Planters of two bearded Leprechauns, one wearing a black hat and standing next to a large mug with a Shamrock motif, 5"h x 5.5"l x 3.5"w.; the other also wearing a black hat, but standing behind Large Shamrock, 4"h x 4.5"l x 2.75"w. Both with black stamp "Hand Decorated Stafford Japan."

Planters. *Left*: Little Girl, wearing a green hair bow and holding hat full of Shamrocks, 6" h x 4.25" l x 3.75" w. Relpo A-1992 black stamp with blue/gold foil. *Right*: Little Boy Dancing, 5.75"h x 4.5"l x 3"w. Relpo K1760 black stamp with black/gold foil. Relpo Chicago, IL; Made in Japan.

Three Top Hat Planters. *Left*: Irish Hat with gold buckle, violin, and white flowers, 4.50"h x 4.5"l x 3.25"w. Relpo C-1529 blue stamp; *Middle*: Irish Hat, dark green with yellow buckle and a light green Shamrock, 4.25"h x 4"d x 4.50"w. Lefton red/gold foil sticker, "Exclusives Japan" 4515 black stamp; *Right*: Medium green Irish Hat shaped with brim, 3.50"h x 5"d brim. Haeger 383 U.S.A. Raised letters on base.

IDENTICAL SHAMROCK PLANTERS WITH TIED BOW OVER PIPE, 5.75"H X 5"L X 2.50"W. The one on the left is black stamped "Japan #57985" while the one on the right is black stamped "Japan #62985." Both have "A Fine Quality" Japan blue and gold foil sticker.

Treasure-Craft was founded in Gardena, California, in 1945 by Andrew Levin. He began his business by selling items from local pottery makers. By the late 1940s Treasure Craft began manufacturing its own ceramics at South Gate. One of their early lines was "The Lucky California Sprite," which was a series of planters with leprechauns or elves staged with the planters or shown alone.

"LEPRECHAUN CRYING SEATED ON LOG." Ceramic planter in dark green gloss, 5.5"h x 7.5"l. Paper label reads "Treasure-Craft, South Gate, California." *Front*: LEPRECHAUN RECLINING, ceramic in green gloss, 4.5"l, and LEPRECHAUN PLAYING VIOLIN, 3.75"l.

"LEPRECHAUN LEANING ON WELL" ceramic planter in dark green gloss, 5"h x 5.5"l, and LEPRECHAUN RECLINING "DREAMY" in dark green gloss, 3.5"l, with "The Lucky California Sprite-1949" box. Treasure-Craft, South Gate, California.

Ornaments

The Shiny-Brite Company

With four factories in New Jersey and a showroom in New York, the Shiny-Brite Company produced the most popular Christmas tree ornaments in the United States throughout the 1940s and 1950s.

In 1937, Max Eckardt established Shiny-Brite ornaments, working with the Corning Glass Company to mass produce glass Christmas ornaments. Eckardt had been importing hand-blown glass balls from Germany since around 1907, but had the foresight to anticipate a disruption in his supply from the upcoming war. Corning adapted their process for making light bulbs to making clear glass ornaments, which were then shipped to Eckardt's factories to be decorated by hand. The fact that Shiny-Brite ornaments were an American-made product was stressed as a selling point during World War II, but glass ornaments were fragile — drop one and you lost a keepsake forever.

Following the war, Shiny-Brite introduced a line of ornaments with a newly designed metal hook that provided the user with two lengths of hanger. The long hook traveled through the center of the ornament and exited the bottom, where it attached to the foot of the ornament. This provided the "short" hanger. Unlatched from the bottom, the entire length of the hook was available, allowing the ornament to dangle at a greater distance from the tree limb to which it was attached. This arrangement was designed to allow the ornament to fill sparsely limbed areas of a natural tree, but due to the increase in cost of buying a natural tree that usually lasted only two to three weeks (and flammable when dried out), cheaper artificial aluminum Christmas trees (with no gaps) were first manufactured in 1958.

Shortly thereafter the newer plastic ornaments became quite popular due to their low cost and durability. This forced Shiny-Brite to close its doors in 1962. Shiny-Brite's most popular ornaments — bells, reflectors, and finial tree-toppers — have been reissued by Christopher Radko since 2001.

Christopher Radko

The demand for specialized, "Old World" ornaments for most holidays, including Christmas, has expanded exponentially since the late 1980s. The honor for this somewhat recent phenomenon belongs to Christopher Radko. While on a trip to visit relatives in Poland in 1985, he was able to convince some former Polish glass blowers to revive their art of blowing decorative glass ornaments. Since that year, Radko has been designing and producing holiday decorations of the highest quality. While he has concentrated his efforts on traditional Christmas ornaments, Radko has also produced specific themed ornaments for every major American holiday.

During his twenty-five years of exporting ornaments to America from Poland, the Czech Republic, Germany, and Italy, he has sold more than 18 million ornaments comprising nearly 7,000 designs. Success breeds healthy competition and, today, there are many other boutique firms designing and exporting ornaments for resale into an increasingly surfeit marketplace. For certain limited/special edition ornaments, there is a rather healthy secondary market.

While the most exquisite ornaments still are produced overseas in Eastern Europe by utilizing hand-blown glass and painting methods, cheaper competition is rising its head from mainland China. Specialized ornaments like the Radko collection are not inexpensive, with the average cost being upwards of $40 or more, whilst the Chinese counterparts are a fraction of that amount. Time will tell whether quality trumps cost.

Shiny Brite ornaments featuring "Dancing Irish Boys," 7"d. Set of eight round "plastic" orbs with two design features. Made in USA, c. 1950s, Max Eckardt & Sons, New York.

"Faith of Old." Traditional High Cross, green and gold glitter with blue jewels, 7.5"h. Christopher Radko, 2004. Made in Poland.

"Saint Paddy's Way." Patrick holding a harp and crozier with Pot of Gold at his feet, 7.25"h. Christopher Radko, 2004. No. 1010829, Made in Poland.

"Snow Lucky-Ireland." Rotund Snowman with pipe dressed in Irish apparel with a chest of gold at his feet, 6.75"h. Part of the Radko "Snowmen Around the World Collection." No. 1011289. Christopher Radko, 2004. Made in Poland.

"Scotch Whiskers." Scotch/Irish Bagpiper, 7.5"h. No. 98-168-0. Christopher Radko, 1996. Made in Poland.

"Golden Clover." Leprechaun behind Gold 4-leaf Clover, 5"h. No. 00-182-A. Slavic Treasures 1997-2000. Made in Poland.

"Emerald Blessings." St. Patrick as Bishop with toys at his feet, 6.75"h. No. 3010540. Christopher Radko, 2003. Made in Poland.

"Angel of Erin." Red-haired Irish Angel dressed in turquoise and pinkish-purple gown with gold glitter, 6.5"h. No. 01-0199-0. Christopher Radko, 2000. Made in Poland.

Left: "Rollin' O'Reilly." Rotund Irish Leprechaun, 4"h. No. 1010054. Christopher Radko, 2002. Made in Poland. *Right*: "Shamrock Showers." Leprechaun with Shamrocks falling, 4.75"h. No. 1010744. Radko, 2004. Made in Poland.

"Pot Lucky." Pot of Gold surrounded by a Rainbow and Shamrocks, 5.5"h. No. 1012209. Radko, 2004. Made in Poland.

"Top O' The Tree" finial or tree-topper. Dancing Leprechaun holding a Shamrock on top of a reflective glitter ornament, 9" h. No. 00-190-0. Radko, 2000. Made in Poland.

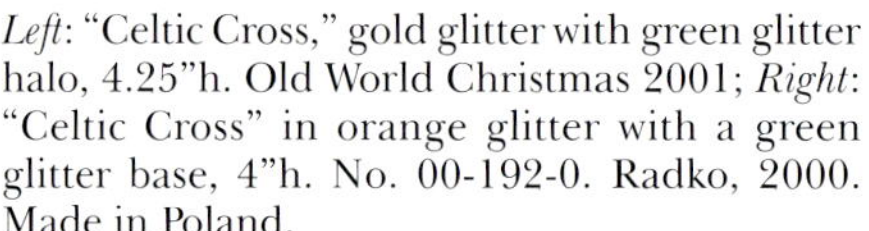

Left: "Celtic Cross," gold glitter with green glitter halo, 4.25"h. Old World Christmas 2001; *Right*: "Celtic Cross" in orange glitter with a green glitter base, 4"h. No. 00-192-0. Radko, 2000. Made in Poland.

"Happy St.Patrick's Day." *Front*: Leprechaun with Rainbow ending at Pot of Gold and Shamrocks. *Back*: Divided Back Postcard. 5"l x 3"h. Radko, 2000. Made in Poland.

Set of 12 painted, wooden, whimsical Irish and St. Patrick's Day mini-ornaments, 1.75"h to 3.5"h. No. J3011. With display box. Made in China, 2005.

Candy Containers

In the mid to late nineteenth century, in the area of Sonneberg, Thuringia, Germany, there emerged a toy-making industry that, for the most part, was made up of family-based businesses. One aspect of this embryonic industry was the making of candy containers from four types of materials: paper mache, pressed cardboard, Plaster of Paris (chalkware), and composition of various materials like sawdust, clay, flour, and glue. The first containers to be exported to the United States after the American Civil War were Easter bunnies followed by Father Christmas shown usually holding an evergreen branch. When other holidays started to became popular in their own right (i.e. Halloween and Thanksgiving), the appropriate images were also made into candy containers. Finally when St. Patrick's Day became widely celebrated, the German candy container manufacturers were quick to respond with containers that exemplified the symbols of St. Patrick.

Prior to World War I, containers from Thuringia and Saxony were marked "Germany." From the 1920s to the late 1930s, similar containers were marked "Made in Germany." In the period directly after World War II, pieces from Germany were marked "Made in U.S. Zone Germany" or "Container Made in Western Zone Germany." In the 1930s, Japan entered the market with look-alike containers, but not as finely detailed. They were marked "Made in Japan" and, for several years right after World War II, "Made in Occupied Japan." Japan also introduced the use of celluloid and plastic (distinguished by being hard and brittle) for the production of whimsical small holiday items. In the marketplace, there is a premium for handcrafted candy containers made prior to World War I and these represent the most expensive and sought after of any St. Patrick's Day collectibles due to their rarity.

These cute "Pig" candy containers are made of pressed cardboard with light green flocked coating, 4.25"h x 5.75"l. The pig's head ends in a wire spring that will jiggle when the pig is moved. Prior to World War II the German firm of Emil Stauch made this type of wired container. "Made in Western Germany" is lithographed inside the container.

Left: Large pig, dark green pressed cardboard, candy container. Body separates. 4"h x 4.75"l. Marked "Germany" with a black stamp on underside; *Middle and Right*: Two smaller pigs made with composition material. Their medium green flocked coating is set off with a pink nose. Head is removable. 2.5"h x 4.25"l. No marks, but German in style.

Left: Top Hat candy container, light green metallic covering over cardboard with a triple Shamrock decoration, 3.25"h x 3.75"l. Purple ink oval stamp "Made in Japan" on base; *Back*: Two Derby Hats made of Kelly green felt with gold ribbon band, green feather, and white cardboard container. 3"h x 6"l. No Marks. *Front right*: Top Hat with Die Cut "Little Irish Lass" décor, green painted crepe over pressed cardboard, 2.25"h x 2.25"l base. Marked "Germany" with a black stamp inside the hat rim. *Below*: Close-up of the hat candy container.

Candy Containers. *Far Left*: Irish Man with Top Hat standing on circular green container base and wearing medium green frock coat and hat with gold britches, 4.25"h x 1.88"d base. Papier-mache. Marked "Germany" with black stamp on base. *Near Left*: Irish Woman with Kelly green bonnet standing on circular green container base, white ruffled dress, green scarf and shoes, 4"h x 1.88"d base. Papier-mache. Marked "Germany" with black stamp on base. *Center*: Irish Man with ivory Top Hat standing on a circular light green container base, holding a Shamrock, wearing a pea green frock coat and britches, 4.75"h x 1.5"d base. Composition. No marks, but German in style. *Near Right*: Irish Boy seated on container base with grey Fez hat, Kelly green coat, red vest, blue stockings, 2.50"h x 0.88"d base. Composition. No marks, but German in style. *Far Right*: Irish Man with black Top Hat standing on a circular light green container base, Kelly green coat, Light Green pants, black shoes, 3.5"h x 1.25"d base. Composition. No marks, but German in style. *Front*: Brown Potato with green Shamrock tied by a gold Ribbon decoration, 1.75"h x 3.5"l. Papier-mache. Marked with "Germany" brown stamp on removable container base.

CANDY CONTAINERS. *Left*: Irish Girl holding Shamrock standing on removable container base, wearing dark green hat, white bow, and white dress, 6.50"h x 3"d base. Base has green glitter and metallic angel hair. *Right*: Irish Boy holding Shamrock and Pipe standing on removable container base and wearing dark green hat and frock coat with white britches, 6.75"h x 3"d base. Base has green glitter and metallic angle hair. Composition. K. D. Vintage #STP 4 & 5 (new).

FIVE SEPARATE NODDER FIGURES ALL HOLDING AN IRISH SYMBOL. Sizes range from 3" to 3.25"h. Painted bisque construction. All of them are incised on the back with a "Germany" stamp; they date from the early twentieth century after World War I. Rare.

Nodders

In Thuringia, Germany, the same location where candy containers were made for export, similar Germany artisans in the nineteenth century manufactured many types of nodders for export. While nodders are known by many names, including nodding figures, pagods, or head hangers, the mechanism to effect movement is the same. Typically nodders consist of two or more internal components, balanced counterweights, attached by a string to produce movement of the head. If the nodder's string is detached or broken in any way, it is almost impossible to affect a repair that will produce the same desired original effect. Materials used to produce these whimsical playthings and decorations were bisque and porcelain, paper mache, pressed cardboard, and celluloid and early plastics. As export items, nodders were used as giveaways or in prizes at games of chance at the circus and fairs during the early twentieth century. Today, a different type of nodder is being produced — bobbin' heads or bobbleheads — to represent the facial characteristics of famous sports people and celebrities.

LEPRECHAUN BOBBLEHEAD DANCING A JIG ON A FIELD OF SHAMROCKS WITH A POT OF GOLD NEARBY, 7.5"H x 2.5"D. Painted molded resin composition. Wire spring loaded mechanism for the head movement. Made in China.

SEATED GOLDEN BOBBLE BEAR DRESSED IN IRISH ATTIRE HOLDING AN IRISH FLAG, 5"H x 3"D. The Bobble Bear is seated on top of a spring mechanism leading to a field of shamrocks. Painted molded resin composition. "St. Patrick's Collection." Made in China.

Celluloid and Plastic Figures

Celluloid was the first "thermoplastic." It was produced as early as the 1890s until the early 1950s. Celluloid is made from cotton dissolved by nitric acid producing a "pulp" that is mixed with camphor gum, formed in sheets, and then molded using heat into various shapes and figures. The problem with celluloid is that it is flammable and will decompose over time. The Japanese used this material to produce many of their toy figures from the mid-1920s to the mid-1930s. With new technology emerging in the late 1940s and early 1950s, the invention of many types of plastic began to supplement celluloid due to low costs of manufacture, flexibility, durability, and being chemically resistant. The injection mold process could allow the manufacture of thousands of like items in a short period of time.

Leprechaun with Pipe and Green foil hat, 5"h. Cotton and felt clothing, Cotton beard. Hand-painted features on celluloid. Moveable arms and head for posing. Stamp at bottom of foot reads: "Japan."

Series of six green Irish Leprechaun plastic figures with different painted faces and vests, 3.25"h. They were produced with different color pipes and canes. Both arms were movable and worked by a series of rubber-like bands, which, if broken, cannot be repaired due to the units being sealed at the factory. These c. early 1950s items are fragile. Raised wording on the back of the legs: "Made in Hong Kong."

Chapter 9
Dolls and Toys

One of the largest traditional toy categories in terms of unit value is dolls. As opposed to Action Figures and Accessories, which appeal almost exclusively to males, Dolls (handmade and mass produced) have the same strong attraction for females. While Dolls have been popular from the beginning of history, each generation has had its favorites, inspiring fads and crazes yielding to a varied range of collectible dolls. The Cabbage Patch Doll is an example of this craze that fizzled out in the late 1980s with little interest today.

Another well-known company, Ty, Inc., has enjoyed popularity from its inception in 1986 making conventional plush animals, but, with the introduction of Beanie Babies (palm-held plush animals filled with pellets) in 1993, the company's reputation exploded and another fad was born. Today, Ty Inc., to its credit, is still reinventing itself by continually introducing new plush toys. Dolls, typically, were either made to be played with as a childhood favorite or, in many instances, displayed with many outfits and accessories. Unfortunately these fads led many collectors to believe that the accumulation of said items was worthy of an investment. Hopefully today collectors have realized that faddish and "have-to-have" items have a rather quick burnout rate and that collectibles sold as Limited Edition ______ (fill in the blank) are just that — limited marketability!

Musical Dolls of All Nations' "Little Miss Ireland," 16"h. A Connoisseur Collection Doll with Stand; features hand-painted porcelain head, arms, and legs and hand-finished costume. Each doll has a 16-note windup musical movement. 1999. Seymour Mann, Dallas, Texas.

"Leprechaun" Plush Doll, 15"h. Black-bearded face with pipe. With tag. Sugarloaf Creations, Boulder, Colorado.

Handmade Dolls

The Handmade Doll industry is probably one of the largest vibrant "cottage" industries in America. Today there are a myriad of home-based creative doll designers who make one-of-a-kind (OOAK) handmade primitive, rag, cloth, polymer clay, and porcelain dolls for sale. Since 2005 designers and makers of a wide range of handmade items (not just dolls) have a dedicated e-commerce website, ETSY, to sell vintage (items must be older than twenty years) and handmade items, as well as art and art supplies. At any one time this website has more than 85,000 dolls and doll-making supplies in eighteen categories for sale at very reasonable prices. Pursuant to the overall doll "industry," there are at least ten doll organizations one can join and fifteen or more doll magazines to purchase. In many respects handmade dolls remains one of the last bastions of Americana creative design.

While the authors are not doll collectors, we searched for and found several home-based doll designers and makers who were selling OOAK primitive and cloth/rag dolls for St. Patrick's Day. These unique, hand-embroidered dolls are full of personality with imaginative and creative interpretations of Irish folk and leprechauns. Handmade Raggedy Ann and Andy dolls are a favorite theme of doll makers as the traditional red hair of the dolls no doubt evoked their "Irishness." We are glad to share some of our unique dolls with our readers. We could not find a doll with a representation of St. Patrick, but perhaps this book will be an inspiration to some designer to produce something of good taste that is fondly evocative of the good Saint.

Handmade Primitive Irish Leprechaun, 23"h. Face and ears are hand-sculpted, eyes are hand-drawn, and the auburn hair is sewn to the head. Material is muslin and tea-dyed and the outfit is in green-toned shades. Artist: Gayle Garcia, Goose 'N Berry Corners, Michigan.

Handmade Primitive Howling Hag, 22"h. Face is hand-sculpted with dark brown hair sewn to the head. Outfit made of light green felt material with glitter, argyle pattern shirt, and holding in the left hand a dark green shamrock and in the right hand a boot filled with evergreen branches and shamrocks. Artist: Sandra Dalen, Surrey, British Columbia.

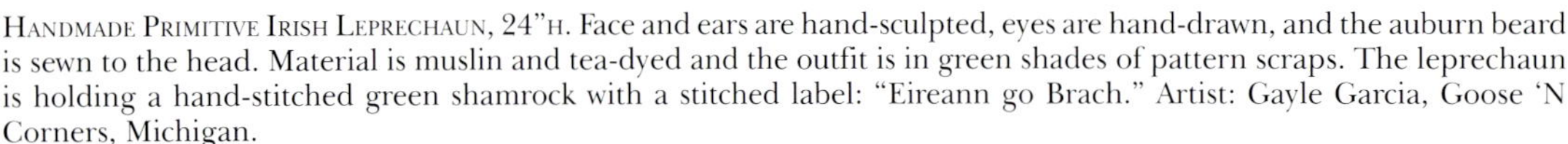

Handmade Primitive Irish Leprechaun, 24"h. Face and ears are hand-sculpted, eyes are hand-drawn, and the auburn beard is sewn to the head. Material is muslin and tea-dyed and the outfit is in green shades of pattern scraps. The leprechaun is holding a hand-stitched green shamrock with a stitched label: "Eireann go Brach." Artist: Gayle Garcia, Goose 'N Corners, Michigan.

Handmade Primitive Irish Raggedy Ann Rag Doll, 14"h. Hand-stitched face with reddish-brown yarn hair. Dressed with a slightly grunged white felt jacket, a Shamrock pattern skirt, and a tea-dyed petticoat. Hang tag. Comes with a green bottle of "Magic Dust." Artist: Connie O'Hanlon, New England.

Handmade Primitive Irish Leprechaun, 23"h. Kelly green felt hat, mustard felt vest with coins, dark green pattern pants, and auburn hair and beard with a Pot 'O Gold. Artist: Rebecca A. Heaberlin, Raggedy Hugs and Primitive Stitches, Pennsylvania.

"Lucky," handmade Primitive Irish Leprechaun, 26"h. Hand-stitched tea dyed muslin face, bells for eyes, and dark brown hair and beard on a balding head. Kelly green vest with tea-dyed muslin shirt and pants decorated with small red stars. He is carrying three hand-stitched shamrocks covered with different shamrock cloth patterns. Artist: Kelly Mallory-Redding, Pennsylvania.

HANDMADE PRIMITIVE LEPRECHAUN, 10.5"H. Hand-painted face with scruffy brownish-red hair and beard and hand-painted muslin clothed body with disjointed painted wooden arms and legs. Hang tag: "May the Leprechauns be near you to spread luck along your way/And may Irish Angels smile upon you This St. Patrick's Day." Artist: Sunny Bach, Pennsylvania.

HANDMADE IRISH RAGGEDY ANNIE RAG DOLL, 20"H. Face is hand-painted with dark brownish-red yarn hair and dressed in a shamrock pattern cloth skirt and a green gingham blouse and long dress. There is an assortment of decorative add-ons like bottle caps, buttons, and wooden shamrocks. Artist: Alexa, Oregon.

HANDMADE PRIMITIVE LEPRECHAUN, 22"H. Face is hand-sculpted and the eyes are drawn and painted. The auburn hair and beard are sewn to the head, and he is wearing a plaid pattern long frock coat, shamrock vest, and green striped pants. His left hand is holding a corncob pipe and his right hand is holding a shamrock. Artist: Gayle Garcia, Goose 'N Corners, Michigan.

"Rosie," handmade Raggedy Ann Rag Doll, 18"h. Face is hand-painted and set off by red yarn for hair. Green toned dress with "Luck of the Irish" wording. Black and green shamrock bloomers. Comes with a green shamrock on black cloth pillow with an appliqué panel of an embroidered "Luck of the Irish" sign. Pillow 9"l. Artist: Gayle Garcia, Goose 'N Corners, Michigan.

Handmade Raggedy Ann and Raggedy Andy Rag Dolls. Ann has a hand-painted, stitched button eyes face with dark red yarn for hair. White cotton sweater and St. Patrick's Day pattern green and yellow skirt and green bloomers, 17"h; Andy has a Kelly green felt cap and a hand-painted, stitched button eyes face with dark red yarn for hair. He has a green and yellow St. Patrick's Day pattern shirt and green pants. 18"h. Artist: Rebecca A. Heaberlin, Raggedy Hugs and Primitive Stitches, Pennsylvania.

Handmade Primitive Folk Art, 5"h x 5"l. Set of four "Ornies" or shamrock ornaments made with tea-dyed green plaid pattern muslin material. Sewn-in face with pipe image. Can be hung or placed around other items as focal points. Artist: Linda Great.

Handmade Papier-mache Doll, 9.5"h. Irish Girl holding large green shamrock with glitter. Painted (white dress and green shamrocks), molded, and stained papier-mache. Artist: Julie Karanik, Texas.

Doll Manufacturers

St. Patrick's Day dolls are usually represented by either a leprechaun or "poseable" male and female Irish figures. These dolls were static display items more in keeping with their historic perspective of the holiday. Some of America's most loved and best-known doll manufacturers, such as Mattel, the (Madame) Alexander Doll Company, and the Annalee Mobilitee Doll Company, have had offerings for St. Patrick's Day. While Mattel's "Barbie" dolls and Madame Alexander's "Wendy" dolls are feverishly collected, it is the Annalee Mobilitee Doll Company that has distinguished itself with the range and depth of St. Patrick's Day doll offerings.

Madame Alexander "Wendy Go Bragh!" Doll, 8"h. She's wearing a white satin gown decorated with green shamrocks and has green filigree wings.

Madame Alexander "Celtic Dancer" Doll, 8"h. Her purple dress is decorated with Celtic symbols. With tags. 2002.

Dolls of the World Barbie "Princess of Ireland" Doll, 12"h. This doll reflects the rich green color of Ireland draped in a shimmering green gown that features a regal pattern inspired by ancient Celtic colors and designs. At her waist she wears a half-belt with three "medallions" imprinted with Celtic inspired art topped with a golden crown on her head. With box. Mattel Inc., El Segundo, California.

Madame Alexander "Luck of the Irish" Doll, 8"h. Irish girl dressed in white sweater and green pleated shirt. Her "Young Leprechaun" companion has a Pot of Gold. With box and tags. 2004.

Madame Alexander "Sweet Irish Wendy" Doll, 8"h. Decorated Irish dancer dress in shades of green. With box and tags. 2003.

Annalee Mobilitee Doll Company

Barbara Annalee Thorndike nee Davis (1915-2002) started a small, home-based craft industry making cotton cloth dolls and puppets in 1934 in Concord, New Hampshire. Over the next thirty years Annalee and her husband perfected the manufacturing of wool-based felt dolls. For instance, unlike other crude cloth dolls of the early twentieth century, Annalee wanted her dolls to tell a story through expression, detailed clothing, and proper positioning. Her dolls were famous for their creative painted felt faces portraying sunny dispositions. Wire frames designed by Annalee's husband provided the internal support to allow the finished dolls to be positioned into poseable or "Mobilitee" figures according to the desired motif.

When the doll company incorporated in 1955, it was called Annalee Mobilitee Dolls in recognition of this very unusual feature. By the mid-1960s Annalee's dolls were marketed nationwide. The growth of Annalee became so great that local production could not keep up with sales trends. By 2001 all production was sent overseas to Hong Kong. However, due to some intra-family wrangling, Annalee was sold in 2008 after seventy-four years in business. Today, just thirty people, including designers and sales and marketing, occupy the corporate offices in Meredith, New Hampshire.

Annalee Mobilitee Leprechaun Doll, 17"h. With tag. Designed in Meredith, New Hampshire, 2005.

Annalee Mobilitee Dolls. *Top*: "Toast to the Irish Leprechaun," 10"h, 2007. *Bottom*: "Leprechaun Head Pin," 3"h, 2008. With tags.

Annalee Mobilitee Dolls. *Left*: Fully bearded Leprechaun with mug on mushroom pad, 8"h, 1997. *Middle*: Fully bearded leprechaun wearing Irish cap with mug "Toast to the Irish Leprechaun," 10"h, 2007. *Right*: Bearded leprechaun holding gold coins "Lucky the Leprechaun," 7"h, 1999. All have cloth tags.

Annalee Mobilitee Dolls. *Left*: Small Seated Medium green Leprechaun/Elf, 4.5"h x 5"l, 1991. *Right*: Small Seated Kelly green Leprechaun, 4"h x 3.5"l, 1990. With tags.

Annalee Mobilitee, Irishman Doll, standing bearded leprechaun with hat standing on rock with pipe, 9"h. With tag. 1998.

Annalee Mobilitee Irishmen Dolls,7.75"h. Both are standing and bearded; one is holding a large green mug, the other a "Happy St. Patrick's Day" sign. With tags. Both early 1980s.

Seated Annalee Mobilitee Irishman Doll, wearing a Kelly green frock coat, and holding gold coins, 15"h. With tag. Early 1980s.

Standing Annalee Mobilitee Irishman Doll playing the fiddle, 15"h. Next to him is a box of Lucky Stout. With tag. 2006.

Annalee Mobilitee Dolls. *Left*: "St. Patrick's Day Girl" gathering Shamrocks, 7"h, 1997. *Right*: Elderly Irish Gentleman holding a Silver Box and a Shamrock, 9.5"h, 1999. With tags.

Annalee Mobilitee Dolls. *Left*: Concertina Playing "St. Patrick's Day Boy," 7"h, 1997. *Middle*: Seated Leprechaun with long tailing cap, 4"h x 4"l, 1991. *Right*: Concertina Playing Irish Boy with green Shamrock at feet, 8"h. 1996. With tags.

Annalee Mobilitee Mouse Dolls, all 7"h. *L-R*: The seated "Katie O' Mouse," 1999; Placid Male Mouse holding Mug of Beer, 1993; and the flower-smelling "Katie O' Mouse," 1999. With tags.

Annalee Mobilitee Dolls. *Left*: Ale Drinking Irishman with Mug, 11"h, 2005. *Right*: Beer Drinking "Leprechaun" with mug, 8"h, 2005.

Byers' Choice

A Pennsylvania–based company, Byers' Choice Ltd. is best known for their Carolers line of figural dolls. While there are hundreds of dolls dressed specifically for certain holidays (mainly Christmas), representing different groups, or for special events, each Caroler is posed in a singing mode. While the firm got its start in 1978 as a home-based business designing Christmas carolers, it has expanded its lines to include a myriad of "caroling" situations. Today Byers' Choice is still producing hand-crafted American-made figurines for a traditional Christmas employing 180 artisans. Another line of Byers' is called Kindles. These figurines are smaller than the Carolers and seem to be "helpers" to the Carolers in various vignettes. The exception is that the Kindles are not "singers."

Byers' Choice Ltd. "Carolers," 9.25" h. A harp-playing Irish girl wearing a shamrock decorated skirt and a bearded Irishman, holding a sprig of shamrocks, in green felt jacket and black pants. 2006.

Plush and Cloth Animals

Another childhood favorite is the Plush Animal. This category is more cross-gender due to the everlasting popularity of the American teddy bear. As opposed to dolls, Plush animals are much more "user friendly" and can withstand a fair amount of playful abuse. While stuffed toys probably originated with Steif in Germany, American stuffed toys have enjoyed over one hundred years of popularity. This category is also subject to fads as witnessed by the Beanie Baby phenomenon, which reached a crescendo in the late 1990s and early 2000s.

Needless to say the Plush-area of collecting is very emotionally charged due to the on-going desirability of stuffed bears, animals, and licensed character dolls. With the use of cheaper synthetic acrylic plush, as opposed to natural mohair, Far Eastern manufacturers have flooded the Plush animal market over the past several decades with items that have very little collector value, but to children these "warm fuzzies" can still give hours and hours of safe and secure contentment.

Byers' Choice Ltd. Bendable Ornaments. "Kindles – Hops, Charm, Rich, Jig." "Hops" with a large beer mug, 4.5"h; "Charm," green outfit, with a pipe, 7"h; "Rich" with his Pot of Gold, 5.5"h; "Jig," green outfit, with a fiddle, 7"h.

"Dublin, the Beanie Buddy" Plush Bear, 14"h. "Buddies" are larger variations of "Beanie Babies." With ear tag. Ty, Inc., 2003.

"O' Lucky, Beanie Baby" Plush Bear, 9"h. With ear tag. Ty, Inc., 2006.

Beanie Babies Plush Bears, 8"h. *Left*: "Killarney" with Pot of Gold/Rainbow crest, 2003. *Middle*: "Lucky" with shamrock bow, 2002. *Right*: "Erin" with white shamrock crest, 1997. With ear tags. Ty, Inc.

Plush Bears. *Left*: "McWooly," variegated green with shamrock bow, 8" h, 2004. *Middle*: "Lucky O' Day," wooly brown with light green shamrock tie, and green hat, 9"h, 2005. Beanie babies, with ear tags. Ty, Inc. *Right*: "Sean," with green and black velour jacket and pants, green hat, and shamrock vest, 8"h, 2006. Made in Ireland by Traditional Craft Limited. With tag.

Beanie Babies Plush Animals. *Left/Right*: "Clover," white plush with green shamrocks and matching bow, 7.5"h, 2001. *Middle*: "Blarn-e," white plush dog with green shamrocks, 8.5"l, 2003. With ear tags. Ty, Inc.

Toys

Outside of dolls that bear a resemblance to leprechauns and other primitive Irish figures or plush animals, St. Patrick's Day items are barely represented in the toy category. There are some musical toys that play songs, noisemakers, puzzles, and nesting dolls, but little else has ever been offered. For the most part, St. Patrick's Day, except for the parades, holds little interest for young children, so toy manufacturers have responded accordingly.

Plush Animals. *Left*: "Snoopy," white plush with green felt hat and shiny green bow tie, 8.5"h, 2003. *Right*: "Woodstock," yellow plush with green felt hat holding a green shamrock, 8"h, 2003. Hallmark Cards, Missouri.

Cloth Snoopy's, 6.5"h. "Kiss Me, I'm Irish!"; "Blarney Beagle!"; "Joe Shamrock." Lithographed artwork on white cloth. Determined Productions, Inc., San Francisco, California, c. early 1990s.

"Irish Jig Leprechaun" Musical Toy, 9"h. Text: "Faith an' begorrah! This little fella's got his pot o' gold and walking stick ready to move and shake to a festive Irish tune! Happy St. Patty's Day!" Sings and dances to "Come On Eileen." Takes three AA batteries. With box. Gemmy Industries Corp., Texas, 2004. Made in China.

"Doolin' Singing Leprechaun" Musical Toy, 14"h. Attired in a green outfit, beard-molded face, and playing the fiddle. Plays "When Irish Eyes Are Smiling." Takes three AA batteries. With box. 2005. Made in China.

"Leprechaun's Luck" Puzzle, 15" square. Text: "World's Most Difficult Puzzle." This jigsaw puzzle has a picture on both sides, rotated ninety degrees from each other. Expert Edition. 500 pieces. Buffalo Games, Inc., 1987.

Noisemakers. *Left*: Smiling Girl's face painted on a circular noise box attached to a shaker stick. Green crepe paper decoration, 13"h, c. 1930s. Made in the USA by C. A. Reed Company, Williamsport, Pennsylvania; *Right*: Noise Rotating Clicker with lithographed scene of tipsy Irishman leaning against a lamp post, 4.5"l. Made in USA by Kirchhof 'Life of the Party' Products.

Nesting Dolls. Smiling and bearded Leprechaun holding pocket watch painted in green and yellow. Series of five ranging from 4" to 1.5"h. Painted. Made in China.

"Smiling Leprechaun holding Hat" Wind Up Toy, 3"h. This plastic action figure bounces along. HMK Cos., c. early 1990s. Made in Hong Kong.

Nesting Dolls. Series of seven images (left to right): Irish Man holding fiddle, Irish Lady, Irish Girl holding harp, Irish Boy dancing, Irish Harp, Irish Beer, and Shamrock. Painted. Made in Russia.

Chapter 10
Irish-American Music and Dance

The rich pantheon of what constitutes Celtic Music is both wide and varied. During the first wave of Irish immigration prior to the Great Diaspora, the majority were Scots-Irish Presbyterians and the Welsh. When reaching the shores of America, many of them were drawn to the mountainous parts of some of the Southern states. In those remote areas, the traditional Scottish, English, and Scots-Irish music took on an American flavor and, intermixed with some Negro gospel rhythms, became what is known today as "country music."

During the times of the Great Diaspora and its aftermath, when millions of Irish-Catholics came to America, they brought with them what is called Irish Traditional Music and the love of dance. Certain music genres require the use of instruments that bring out what is considered to be evocative of that style. When you go to an Irish pub either here or abroad, you know that you will get an earful of great Irish music by the instruments at hand — mandolins, banjos, accordions, fiddles, flutes, uilleann pipes, tin whistles, and the brodhran.

In the United States, Irish Traditional music was popularized by three groups with decades of music in their repertoires. The first group, the four Clancy Brothers, emigrated from County Tipperary and started performing in 1955. They are widely credited for popularizing Irish Traditional music. The second group, The Chieftains from Dublin, Ireland, started performing in 1962. This multiple Grammy award-winning group also was considered instrumental as one of the first bands to make Irish Traditional music popular. The third group, The Irish Rovers, is a Canadian-Irish group. From their start in 1963, they have been well-known for their Irish folk and many renditions of Irish drinking songs.

Ceili

If there is singing, then there is sure to be dancing and that would be called a "ceili," a social gathering featuring Irish music and dance. There is Irish social dancing comprised of set (danced by four couples in a square) or ceili (danced by two to sixteen people). There is also performance dancing of which the most popular form worldwide is the stepdance; this was made popular by Michael Faltley in 1994 through his theatrical performance of *Riverdance*. In this form, stepdancing is characterized by rapid leg and foot movements using a hard shoe for percussion sounds and keeping the upper body and both arms fairly rigid and stationary. As portrayed, *Riverdance* is the story of the Irish culture and the Irish immigration to America. In 2011, *Riverdance* was in the midst of its farewell tour.

Artist signed HBG (H. B. Griggs); it offers a stylized St. Patrick's Day Greetings accompanied by a score of music. Published by L & E (Leubrie and Elkins), Series 2253.

The lyrics "Come back to Erin" accompany the Maid of Erin. Published by M. W. Taggart, Series N 807.

"The Irish Emigrant." A song that expresses sorrow over the loss of his wife at childbirth whose grave he must leave forever as he is emigrating from Ireland. Publisher Unknown.

New York Herald, March 14, 1915. A full-color, full-page section of the newspaper illustrating a new dance: the "Dolly Dip-A touch of Tango makes the whole world spin." The text says: "Oh, just listen to that dandy One Step": *"St. Patrick's Day" ... St. Patrick's Day is joy day/ The colleens all turn out/ To see the boys go marching/ To music, and to shout.*

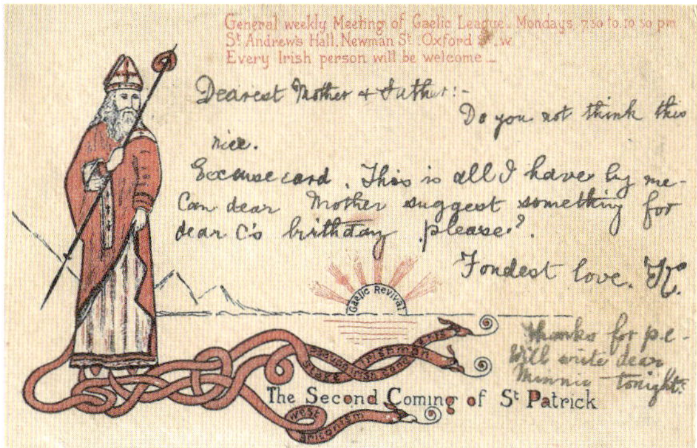

These two postcards carry a message to the recipient. One is an invitation to the "Irish Musical Festival in Queen's Hall, St. Patrick's Day, 1904," the other to a "General weekly Meeting of Gaelic League…Every Irish person will be welcome."

"A true Irishman can jig a bit and sing 'the wearing of the green.'" The dancing Irishman with his sweet Colleen, both fancily dressed, dance to the music. Publisher unknown, St. Patrick Series No. 4.

"Our hearts are gay on St. Patrick's Day." An Irishman with his pipe and carrying his shillelagh dances with his Irish lass. Publisher unknown.

Irish Melodies

By the end of the nineteenth century to the start of the twentieth century, the only way one could hear Irish music was either at an Irish pub, a Festival Hall, or at a Catholic Church, which would sponsor Irish dancing in the parish hall. In a few short years, "talking machines" would be available to use wax cylinders and hard vinyl records to listen to recorded music and, by 1925, wireless radio was available for the beginning of a wide range of musical programming. During this era, traditional Irish music began a transformation into light Irish melodies associated with popular song lyrics. Many of these lyrics, written by songwriters or adapted to meet the need of the market, were published by publishers who set up shop in New York's Tin Pan Alley. These popular lyrics found their way into graphically inspired sheet music, which are collector items today.

"Dancing the Irish Breakdown." Published by M. W. Taggart, New York, Series N 802.

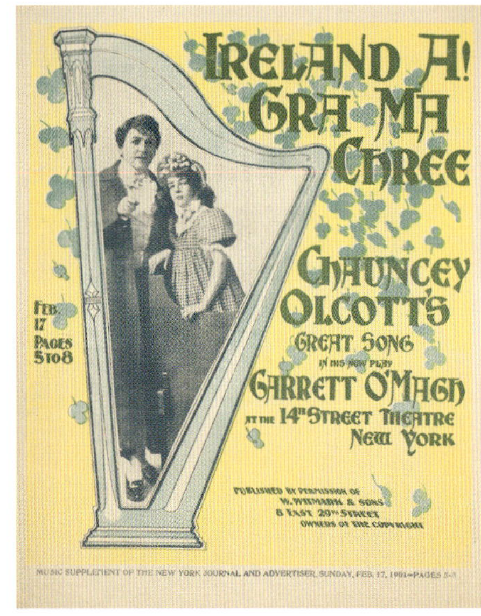

"Ireland A! Gra Ma Chree!" Sheet music by Chauncey Olcott, 1901.

"It's St. Patrick's Day." Greeting card with Snoopy and Woodstock.

"The Hinkey Dee" sheet music. This Fox Trot song was part of George M. Cohan's musical "Little Nellie Kelly," 1922.

"Dancing An Irish Jig." Set of two items showing an Irish girl dancing a jIg accompanied by a Fiddler and a Brodhran player. The Heritage Village Collection, Department 56, Eden Prairie, Minnesota.

"Molly O (I Love You)." Sheet music by Emery (lyrics) and McNeil (music), 1921.

"Somewhere in Ireland." Sheet music by Brennan and Ball, 1917; sung by Maud Lambert.

"For Killarney and You." Sheet music by Walsh and Teasdale, 1910; sung by Blanche Andrews.

"If I Knock The 'L' Out Of Kelly (It would still be Kelly to me)." Sheet music by Lewis/Young and Grant, 1916; sung by Nellie V. Nichols.

"Tip-Top Tipperary Mary." Sheet music by MacDonald and Carroll, 1914.

"St. Patrick's Day is a Bad Day for Coons." Sheet music for the humorous race song from the "Mammouth Minstrels," 1901. Composed by Irving Jones, sung by Lew Doakstader.

"Airs of Old Erin." Song book, c. 1806-1807. An Album of the best loved Thomas Moore (Irish poet) and other Irish songs with an excerpt from "Erin! The tear and the smile" by Moore.

"Pick A Little Four Leaf Clover (And Send It Over To Me)." Sheet music by Reisner/Rose and Olman, 1918.

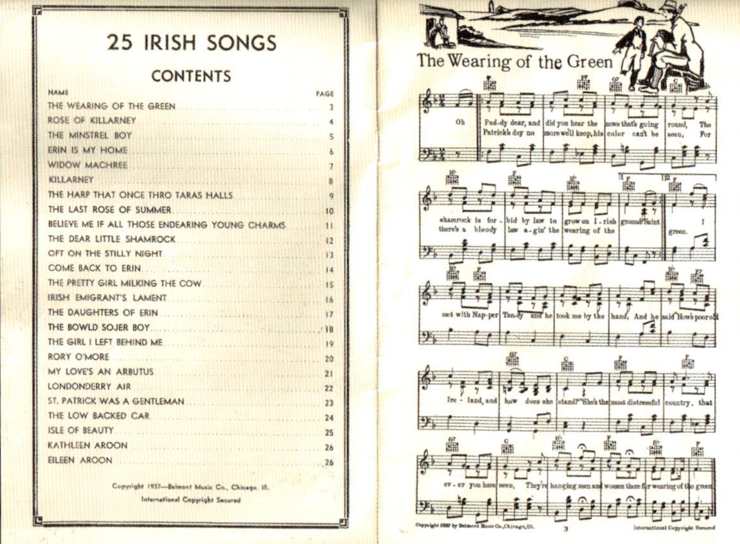

25 IRISH SONGS

CONTENTS

NAME	PAGE
THE WEARING OF THE GREEN	3
ROSE OF KILLARNEY	4
THE MINSTREL BOY	5
ERIN IS MY HOME	6
WIDOW MACHREE	7
KILLARNEY	8
THE HARP THAT ONCE THRO TARAS HALLS	9
THE LAST ROSE OF SUMMER	10
BELIEVE ME IF ALL THOSE ENDEARING YOUNG CHARMS	11
THE DEAR LITTLE SHAMROCK	12
OFT ON THE STILLY NIGHT	13
COME BACK TO ERIN	14
THE PRETTY GIRL MILKING THE COW	15
IRISH EMIGRANT'S LAMENT	16
THE DAUGHTERS OF ERIN	17
THE BOWLD SOJER BOY	18
THE GIRL I LEFT BEHIND ME	19
RORY O'MORE	20
MY LOVE'S AN ARBUTUS	21
LONDONDERRY AIR	22
ST. PATRICK WAS A GENTLEMAN	23
THE LOW BACKED CAR	24
ISLE OF BEAUTY	25
KATHLEEN AROON	26
EILEEN AROON	26

Copyright 1937—Belmont Music Co., Chicago, Ill.
International Copyright Secured

"Irish Songs." Song book from the Belmont Music Company, Chicago, IL, 1937. Inside cover shows a listing of 25 popular Irish songs.

Sheet Music. *Left*: "Smiling Irish Eyes" by Ruby and Perkins, 1929. Song is from the Vitaphone Picture *Smiling Irish Eyes* and was sung by Colleen Moore. *Right*: "Pretty Kitty Kelly" by Pease and Nelson, 1920.

SHEET MUSIC. *Top to Bottom, L-R*: "St. Patrick's Day Parade," sung by Dennis Day, 1951; "Johnny Doughboy found a Rose in Ireland," sung by Kate Smith, 1947; *Finian's Rainbow*, a 1947 Broadway play that ran for 725 performances; "I'm Lookin Over A Four Leaf Clover," sung by Larry Fotine, 1927; "Mother Machree," by Young and Olcott/Ball, 1910; "Too-Ra-Loo-Ra-Loo-Ral That's An Irish Lullaby," sung by Bing Crosby from the Paramount Picture *Going My Way*, 1944.

"IRISH KEWPIE CHILDREN." Music box plays "When Irish Eyes are Smiling." Bisque, 5.75"h x 4"d base. Geo. Z. Lefton 1986 #05493 (gold stamp). Lefton (red/gold sticker Exclusives Taiwan). 1986.

Music Boxes

Besides sheet music, figural music boxes that play well-known Irish tunes are popular collector items. Associated with these boxes are the musician-playing leprechauns and other figural and ephemera items to please the senses.

"IRISH BOY & GIRL STANDING ON GREEN COATED BASE." Bisque music box, 5"h x 4"d base. Lefton, (red/gold sticker "Exclusives Taiwan"). Lefton, China, hand-painted gold stamp 00124.

PORCELAIN MUSIC BOXES. *Left*: "Irish Woman Dancing" with circular base, 8"h x 4.5"d. *Right*: "Irish Man holding Shillelagh" with circular base, 8.5"h x 4.5"d. From Schmid Bros. with "Made in Japan" brown/gold stickers.

"IRISH BOY DANCER AND LEPRECHAUN PLAYING FIDDLE ON BROWN TREE STUMP." Ceramic music box, 6"h x 4"d. Plays "My Wild Irish Rose." Lefton, (red/gold sticker "Exclusives Japan").

"Irish Girl Dancer holding a basket of shamrocks decorated with green jewels." Porcelain music box, 6"h x 4"d. Plays "When Irish Eyes are Smiling." Lefton/Sankyo. Made in Japan.

"Irish Boy & Girl Dancers." Ceramic music box on a shamrock-decorated, green covered base, wearing peaked caps, 6"h. Gorham blue/silver foil sticker. Made in Japan.

"Irish Boy & Girl Dancers." Bisque music box on green covered base, 6.5"h x 3.5"d base. Plays "When Irish Eyes are Smiling." Lefton, China. Hand-painted gold stamp "04370." 1984.

"Irish Girl with large green bonnet and white apron carrying a basket of shamrocks." Ceramic music box, 6"h x 4.5"d base. Lefton, (red/gold sticker Exclusives Japan). #1432 black stamp.

Musical Snow Glass Globe. Irish Sheep Herder with brown backpack walking on green shamrocks surrounded by three lambs on white porcelain base, 5"h x 3.5"d base. No marks.

Irish Musicians, 8"h. Set of three: Brodhran Drum player, Tin Whistle player, and Flute Player. Molded painted wood resin. David Enterprises Ltd., Made in China.

Irish Musicians, 4"h to 4.5"h. Ceramic set of three: Horn player; Small Horn player; and Flute player. Lefton, (red/gold sticker Exclusives Japan). #6203.

Irish Musicians and Dancers, 4"h. Ceramic set of five (L-R): Dancer; Fiddle player, Life of the Party, Dancer, and Fiddle player. Lefton, (red/gold sticker "Exclusives Japan").

Irish Crooners

When electric phonographs became widely available, 78 rpm, 45 rpm, and 33 rpm vinyl records containing popular Irish songs sung by famous crooners such as Bing Crosby and Dennis Day were sure sellers.

"St. Patrick's Day" record albums by Bing Crosby, 1946-1949. *Left*: Set of four 45 rpm Decca Records 9-31. *Middle*: Long Play 33 1/3 rpm Record DL 5037. *Right*: Set of Five 78 rpm. Decca Records A-495.

"Shamrock Melodies." Sung by Dennis Day; four records, 78 rpm. RCA Victor P-153.

"The Smiling Irish Voice of Denis Delaney-Lyric Tenor of Boston's Famed Clover Club." Three records; they were sold for the Benefit of Archbishop Cushing Charity Fund, Inc.

"St. Patrick's Day in Dublin." Record album. Sonologue, USA. 1968.

"Shillelaghs and Shamrocks" record album. Twelve popular Irish melodies sung by Bing Crosby. Long play 33 1/3 rpm. Decca Records DL-78207.

Chapter 11
Paper Decorations

A very important category of traditional St. Patrick's Day decorations is Paper Decorations encompassing a wide range of items including tableware accessories, party magazines and booklets, banners, honeycomb tissue centerpieces, invitations, place markers, bridge tallies, crepe paper items, and cardboard cutouts. As the twentieth century progressed, each of these items ebbed and flowed in popularity. Today the St. Patrick's Day table still feature these timeless paper decorations, even though many of the new items sold are now plastic.

Vintage paper decorations rarely escape the ravages of time gently. The continual opening and closing of the honeycomb centerpieces usually results in the delicate tissue paper being ripped or the small metal flange to keep the unit open breaking. Accordingly, the flat cut-out items are hard to find in very good to excellent condition, as they were usually stuck to a vertical surface with tape or a thumb tack. Missing paper, creased cardboard, or pin holes accompany many of these decorations today. When originally issued, these colorfully contrived items were meant to be used and eventually discarded — not to be saved for future posterity.

Some firms today try to capitalize on the nostalgia of yesteryear by issuing digital collage sheets meant to resemble some of the vintage postcards of the early twentieth century. For instance, these attractive dome tags, by means of a digital file on a CD, can be printed on paper, transparencies, or fabric to be used for a variety of decorative ideas. Many doll designers use these faux-vintage dome cards and attach them to dolls to give a vintage look.

Digital Collage Sheet of reproduced vintage St. Patrick's Day postcards fitted on cut-out hanging dome cards suitable for gifts, 2004.

Manufacturers

The leaders in the design and production of popular paper decorations were the Dennison Manufacturing Company of Framingham, Maine; the Beistle Company of Shippensburg, Pennsylvania; and the C. A. Reed Company of Williamsport, Pennsylvania. Of the three, only the Beistle Company, founded in 1900 in Pittsburgh, Pennsylvania, by M. L. Beistle, is still in operation today. Their current webpage states that they are "the oldest and largest manufacturer of theme decorations and party goods."

Beistle's online seasonal goods catalog for St. Patrick's Day lists 239 products, many of which are detailed paper die-cuts of shamrocks, leprechauns, green top hats, and Erin-go-Bragh banners — the same timeless designs that have been produced almost continuously (except World War

II) since the early 1900s. In 1910, the Beistle Company was the first American firm to produce honeycombed tissue decorations and incorporate that complex paper forming technology into new lines of paper decorations. Despite the usual competition from the Orient, the Beistle Company continues to thrive in today's environment, producing celebratory items for a whole host of notable events.

Dennison Manufacturing Company

Founded in 1844 by Andrew Dennison, the Dennison Manufacturing Company initially made jewelry boxes, but the firm soon expanded into the production of tags, labels, and tissue paper. They, too, segued into the die-cut and party supplies line after the turn-of-the-twentieth century and were best-known for their extensive line of Halloween products. Unlike Beistle, Dennison was unable to compete successfully against foreign competition in holiday decorations in spite of having other business lines, such as printing and packaging equipment.

In 1990, Avery International Corporation of Pasadena, California, brought about a strategic merger of interests with Dennison. The resultant company today is the Avery Dennison Corporation, a multi-billion dollar global leader in the production of pressure-sensitive adhesives and materials. Alas, no decorations are being produced by this firm today.

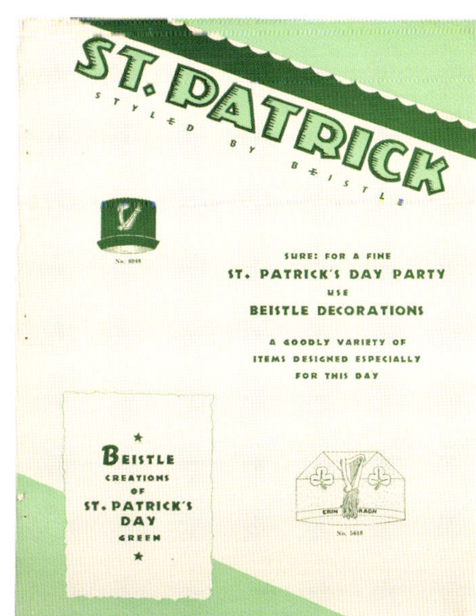

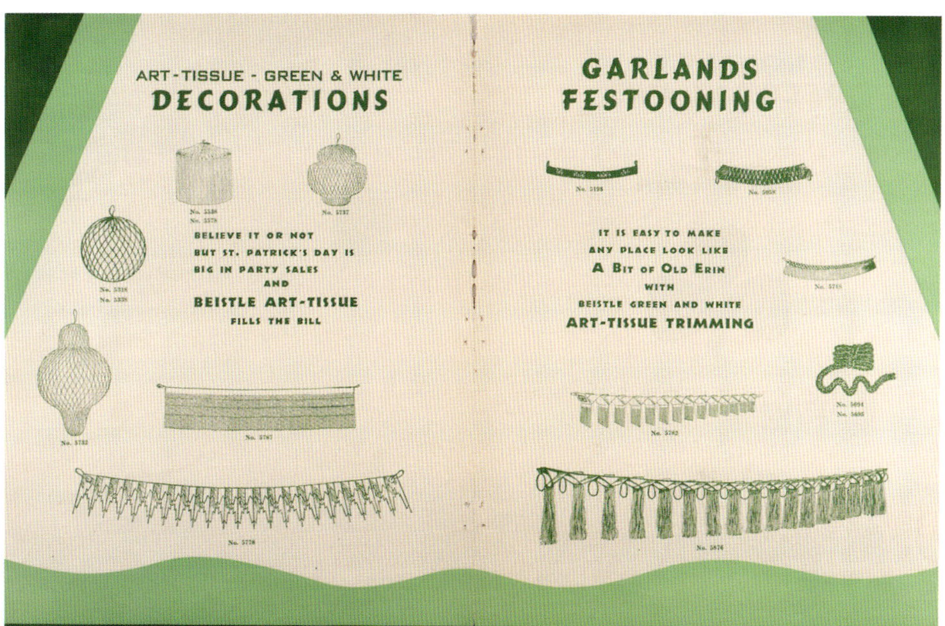

"St. Patrick Styled By Beistle-Beistle Creations of St. Patrick's Day Green." A 1939 four-page catalogue, with price list, emphasizing Art Tissue decorations, Garlands, and Novelty Decorations.

1939 PRICE LIST

All Prices Per Gross Unless Otherwise Specified

Prices subject to change without notice.

No.	Description	D'gn	Pack Doz.	Wt. Per Box	Price Per Gr.
5058	Green & White Square Garland	1	2	1½	6.00
*5198	Green & White Oval Garland	1	4	2	3.33
*5318	Green & White 19" Tissue Ball	1	½	3½	33.33
5338	Green & White Tissue Ball 11½"	1	1	2½	12.00
5538	Green & White Small Hanging Dec.	1	1	1¾	12.00
*5578	Green and White Hanging Dec.	1	½	3	26.67
*5617	St. Patrick Crepe Hat	6	12	3¼	3.33
*5618	St. Patrick Crepe Hat, w plume	6	12	4⅜	3.75
5694	Green & White Solid Festooning	1	6	24	30.00
5695	Green & White Mixed Festooning	1	6	24	30.00
5718	Green & White Fringe Garland	1	1	1½	12.00
*5732	Green & White 24" Nov. Tis. Dec.	1	½	3½	33.33
5737	Gr. & Wh. 11½" Nov. Ball Dec.	4	1	2	12.00
*5778	Green & White Border Decoration	1	2	1½	6.00
5782	Gr. & Wh. Stringless Garland	1	1	2¼	12.00
*5787	Gr. & Wh. Fringe Drapery	1	1	5	33.33
*5807	Shamrock Cut Out, 13"	1	3	1⅞	3.33
*5876	Gr. & Wh. Fringe Garland, 20'	1	1	3	24.00
*5967	Erin Go Bragh Sign	1	1	3½	33.33
*6940	St. Patrick Sign	1	1	2	13.33
*6945	St. Patrick Centerpiece	1	3	3	13.33
6946	St. Patrick High Hat	4	3	3⅝	6.00

"Lucky the Jointed Leprechaun." A Beistle Company Creation, 30" long; original unopened packaging. A very large party decoration made by joining individually printed cutouts together. Early 1970s.

St. Patrick's Day Favors
that you can make easily

With the Pictures on the Preceding Page to Follow It Will Not Be Work to Make Them But Real Fun

By Frances A. Carleton

On St. Patrick's Day the favors and prizes for a bridge party should be daintily crisp and green, suggesting the gay little shamrock, emblem of the Emerald Isle. Other appropriate emblems, too, can be worked in to help create a real "Irish atmosphere."

You can decorate the living room where the game is to be played or not, just as you please, but the tables should be numbered in some way that suggests the day, and the score cards may help to carry out the chosen scheme.

Table Markers

Irish Hat. An Irish hat standing in the center of each table is quite an unusual way to mark it. To make one, cut a strip of emerald green crepe paper 15 inches long and 20 inches wide. Crease sharply through the middle *across the grain*, making a double piece 15 by 10 inches. Paste the two short double ends together. Gather the raw edges together tightly and fasten with spool wire. Place the folded edge on the table and stretch carefully until a brim about one and one-half inches wide is formed. Make a sharp crease all around the hat two inches from the center. Cut a circle of crepe paper four inches in diameter and paste to the top of the hat. Add a band of black crepe paper with a flat bow and the required numeral cut from gold paper.

When the hat is set aside at the beginning of the playing a dish of green mints may be revealed all snugly hidden beneath it.

Shamrock Table Number. Wrap a piece of No. 7 Wire 24 inches long with a strip of emerald green crepe paper. Cut a numeral from cardboard and cover it with gold metallics. Glue the wire to the back of the numeral, allowing about 20 inches to extend below it. Eight inches below the bottom of the numeral bend the wire into a flat spiral stand. Glue three cardboard shamrocks around this base and two more back to back on the upstanding piece of wire. Cut-outs S 571 are the best size to use. Finish with a gauze ribbon bow or a rosette of tinsel threads.

Shamrock Score Card. Wrap a piece of small flag stick about 10 inches long with a narrow strip of emerald green crepe paper. Cut a sheet from a regular printed score pad in three pieces. Paste the "count" on the upper leaf of a green cardboard shamrock, the "honor score" on one side leaf and the "tricks" on the other. Punch two small holes in the shamrock near the stem and tie the stick in place firmly with a narrow green ribbon. Leave one end long enough to attach a score pencil. A bow of fluffy gauze ribbon or maline will add a dainty touch but is not absolutely necessary.

Harp Score Card. Score and fold a piece of green mounting board to 6 by 11 inches in size. Round off the top and bottom as illustrated. Paste a plain printed score pad in the inside. Decorate the front cover with a printed harp cut-out and finish by tying a tiny score pencil to the upper right corner with narrow ribbon.

Prizes

Few people care to receive strictly holiday novelties as bridge prizes, but really useful articles may be cleverly disguised and thus be made particularly suitable for some special occasion.

For St. Patrick's Day, the prizes may be arranged as shown on the previous page. Any articles that you have chosen can be similarly arranged.

"Eversharp" Pencil or Fountain Pen. A spray of shamrocks is made by pasting several shamrocks back to back with pieces of green covered wire about four inches long between them. They are gathered together in a bunch and tied to the pencil with a ribbon bow.

Irish Tea Bouquet. Fasten pieces of wire about six inches long to about a dozen small bags of tea. Group together in a bunch and surround with emerald green crepe paper petals that have been twisted across the top so that they resemble shamrock leaves. Wrap the stem with silver tin foil and tie with green ribbons with long fluttering ends.

Irish Colleen Perfume Bottle. Mount a girl's head and shoulders cut from a fashion sheet or magazine on cardboard and cut out. Fasten to the top of a bottle of perfume or talcum powder. Make wire arms the same way as described for the other dolls. Fasten across the doll's shoulders. Make a skirt of light green crepe paper and over it arrange a deep pointed frill of emerald green. A straight band will form the waist and a frill made of light green, gathered a little off center, will form a neck ruff as well as sleeves. A spray of "shamrocks" made the same way as those that decorate the pencil should be put in the doll's hand.

Irish Girl Compact. Bend both ends of a piece of No. 9 Wire 16 inches long down one-half inch to form loops. Wrap with a strip of apricot crepe paper. Fasten to the bottom of the compact with gummed tape. Draw a face on a cardboard disk with India ink two inches in diameter. Cut four pieces of wire about two and one-half inches long and fasten to the back of the disk in a group with gummed tape. Allow an inch and a half to extend below the cardboard. Bend these wires at right angles one inch from the end *Continued on page 36*

8 DENNISON'S PARTY MAGAZINE

An Irish Shenanigan
Full of Wit and Humor for March 17th

By Kathleen Webster

Irishmen are famous the world over for their ability to make and take jokes; so what could be a better way to entertain your friends on St. Patrick's Day than by giving a real old-fashioned Irish Shenanigan, with jokes, tomfoolery and fun?

The invitations will supply the keynote to the evening's fun, if they are written on note size correspondence paper with green ink, rolled up and wrapped in pieces of green paper, fringed on the ends, and decorated with shamrock or T D pipe seals so that they look like the cracker mottoes with paper caps. On the outside, paste slips of white paper with "Crack this one" written on it with green ink. The invitation should be worded in the form of the usual "Mike" and "Pat" joke.

Pat: "All joking aside, did yez ever hear of a Shenanigan?"
Mike: "Shure, then, and phat is it?"
Pat: "It's something for St. Patrick's avenin'."
Mike: "And even at that, phat is it?"
Pat: "Yez better cum ter ——'s house and find out. Shure they'll change all yer blues to green."

When the guests have all arrived, pass around little Irish "Green Books," travesties on the famous English Blue Book, made of folded squares of green cardboard. On the outside write the title, "WHO'S WHO IN JOKELAND." All about the living room have little figures cut from the comic strips of the Sunday papers. Glue them to stiff cardboard, with a piece left on at the bottom which can be folded back allowing the figures to stand erect. Maggie will be there, of course, as will Jiggs, Buster Brown, little Skeezicks, Min and Andy Gump, and all the rest of the familiar inhabitants of Funnyland. Each one should be numbered, and a certain time given for the crowd to identify those they know, and to write down their names in their "Green Books." A little green leather address or note book would make a very appropriate prize for the most successful guesser.

Practical Jokes

Pass around a basket filled with all sorts of "practical" little objects in it; a hairpin, a safety pin, a needle and thread, a pencil, a cork, a pair of tweezers and so on, letting each one select something. He must play a "practical joke" on someone during the evening, using the article he has chosen. At the end of the evening, everyone who has not been able to perpetrate a joke must pay a forfeit.

Monkeyshines

Cutting monkeyshines is a game that takes the form of a relay race. Divide the crowd into two sides: the Killarneyites and the Tipperaryites. Stand the teams in two lines, facing each other. Give lists of numbered stunts, exactly alike, to the captain of each line. These lists should contain as many stunts as there are people in each line. The captains read stunt or "monkeyshine" number one and simultaneously proceed to do it. When they have completed it, they pass the slips along to the next in line, who proceeds to do "monkeyshine" number two, and so on down the line. Of course, the side that goes through the list first is the victorious team, but each side will be much handicapped by the players wanting to watch the other side, and not miss anything. All sorts of Irish stunts can be included, such as: Kiss the Blarney Stone; Dance an Irish Jig; Smoke a T D Pipe; Stage a Kilkenny Cat Fight; Play a Tune on the Irish Harp; Sing the First Verse of "The Wearing of the Green"; and so on.

Kissing the Blarney Stone

Blindfold each player in turn, and let him walk to a table, which should be five or six good steps away, pick up the first "stone" that he touches, and kiss it. As soon as this is done, the blindfold is removed, and he is allowed to read the "blarney" that is written on the bottom of the "stone." If possible, use real stones, or make them of cotton batting or crushed-up tissue paper covered with gray crepe paper, stretched over the foundation, and pasted neatly. The "blarney" may be on round or oval pieces of writing paper pasted to the "stones."

Limericks

Another very entertaining stunt is finishing up limericks. This is a particularly timely game for St. Patrick's Day. Pass around shamrocks cut from green cardboard, with the first three lines of the following

4 DENNISON'S PARTY MAGAZINE

St. Patrick's Day Favors

Continued from page 8

and fasten to the top of the box with the tape. Make a pointed frill of green crepe paper and paste to the head as shown in the illustration. Then make a three tiered ruffled skirt and tie around the neck. Add wire arms made in the same way as the legs and twist them around the neck and then bend into correct position. Finish with a bow of ribbon tied under the chin.

Serving Cups and Favors

Whether the refreshments are served at the card tables or in the dining room, there is often need of dainty serving cups or favors. Favors made of candy are always a delight to the recipient.

Shamrock Cup. Wrap a piece of wire about 20 inches long with a strip of green crepe paper. Fasten to the sides of a crinkled paper foundation cup with pieces of gummed tape. Cut a piece of both Nile and emerald green crepe paper two inches wider than the depth of the foundation cup and about one and one-fourth times the circumference. Cut one edge into rows of rounded petals three-fourths inch wide and one and one-half inches deep. Twist each petal division across the top. Gather and paste around the foundation, putting the lighter color on the inside. Shape the wire handle into a shamrock shape.

Pipe Serving Cup. Cut a strip of green crepe paper four inches by six inches, the grain the four-inch way. Roll it *with the grain* tightly around two pieces of wire five inches long, allowing the ends of the wire to extend one inch beyond one end of the roll. Bend the wires at right angles and attach to the side of a white foundation cup. Cover the cup with a piece of a "tucked streamer" and decorate with gummed shamrock seals.

Irish Boy "Life Saver." Make wire arms and legs as described for the "Irish Girl Compact," using one piece of 18-inch wire for one arm and one leg. Wrap with green crepe paper. Wrap the upper half of the candy package with apricot and the lower half with green, at the same time wrapping in the arms and legs. Draw features with India ink and make the "hair" of bright orange crepe paper clipped into a fine fringe. Finish with a bow tie. The end of this ribbon may be left long enough to attach a small name card.

Shamrock Serving Plate Cup. Make and attach the handle, first using a piece of firm wire and attaching it to the foundation cup just as described for the "Shamrock Serving Cup." Cover the cup with white crepe paper and stand in a paper plate that has been covered with a lace paper doily. Fasten the cup to the plate with two or three small paper fasteners. Trim with shamrocks as pictured.

Shamrock Plant. Wrap several wires each about nine inches long with strips of emerald green crepe paper and paste cardboard shamrocks to the ends. Make spiral by twisting loosely around a pencil. Draw faces with India ink on circles of white paper and paste in the center of each shamrock. Form in a cluster and wrap the stem thus formed with tin foil. Thrust into the center of a small chocolate frosted cup cake. Finish with a green gauze ribbon bow.

DENNISON'S PARTY MAGAZINE

Dennison's Party Magazine, March-April 1928. Articles featured were "St. Patrick's Day Favors That You Can Make Easily" and "An Irish Shenanigan, Full of Wit and Humor for March 17th." Party magazines such as *Dennison's* were full of do-it-yourself ideas on how to decorate and stage a party based on a season or event.

Smiling Bearded Leprechaun holding a Shillelagh. Large Cut-Out, 16"h.

Two Young Irish Girls Dancing surrounded by Shamrocks. Cut-Outs, 7"h.

The Dennison Company, as part of its extensive St. Patrick's Day decorations line, produced many cardboard cut-outs representing leprechauns in various guises as well as bridge tallies and party place cards. It is a small wonder that some still survive today after seventy-five years from issuance.

BRIDGE TALLIES AND PLACE CARDS CUT-OUTS.

HONEYCOMB CENTERPIECES. A Top Hat, 10"h, H. E. Luhrs, and "Erin go Bragh" superimposed over a Harp, 8.75"h.

"ERIN GO BRAGH" HONEYCOMB CENTERPIECE. A rather intricate centerpiece constructed to resemble a shamrock, 9"h. The Beistle Company.

The Beistle Company

The Beistle Company, due to their acquisition of European machinery to produce honeycombed tissue paper in early twentieth century, became the leaders in producing honeycomb centerpieces and art tissue items, such as garlands and hanging tissue balls. In the 1980s, Beistle began to experience some foreign competition in party decorations based on cost, usually from the Orient but in this case from Denmark.

HONEYCOMB CENTERPIECES. *Left*: Leprechaun/Elf sitting on a Honeycomb hat, 5.25"h. *Center*: Smiling Young Leprechaun sitting on a Honeycomb Pot of Gold, 11.5"h. *Right*: Pipe smoking leprechaun with a honeycomb Pot of Gold, 5.25"h. The Beistle Company, c. 1980s.

Left: Pipe-smoking Leprechaun sitting on a honeycomb toadstool, 11.5"h. *Right*: Fiddle-playing Leprechaun sitting on a honeycomb toadstool, 12"h. The Beistle Company, c. 1980s.

"Irish Hat." Hallmark Centerpiece with original package. Large honeycomb Top Hat with musical leprechauns used as a hat band, 12.5"h including top decoration. The Beistle Company, c. 1980s.

Top Hat with leprechauns placing shamrock cut-outs on the hat. Honeycomb, 11"h. The Beistle Company.

Top Hat with a gold foil buckle and black band. Honeycomb, 9.5"h. Made in Denmark.

Die-Cuts

Some of the most visually attractive holiday collectibles are die-cuts. The term die-cut refers to a repetitive decoration cut-out from heavy stock paper. Once an image is printed onto a large sheet of card stock, it is cut out by a "die," a very sharp and precise cutting tool. Many of the early die-cuts were also embossed. Embossing refers to stamping a raised image onto the piece, which embellishes it on coated stock.

Die-cut decorations came into the mainstream after World War I when equipment became available for large-scale use. In the United States, the two major manufacturers were Dennison and the Beistle Company, which produced die-cuts from the 1920s to the 1940s. However, the *ne plus ultra* of die-cut production and artistic design came from Germany for export to the United States. The German die-cut pieces were produced on glossy coated card stock and heavily embossed to bring out the tiniest of details. Die-cuts, regardless of the manufacturer, were used for various items including table decorations such as nut cups and place cards. German die-cuts in excellent shape are rare and expensive.

Left: Die-Cut of Young Girl wearing Shamrocks, 72 (6 x 12) images. *Center*: Die-Cut of Young Girl superimposed on a Shamrock, 48 (8 x 6) images. *Right*: Die-Cut of Young Boy wearing a Top Hat with a Pipe, 42 (6 x 7) images. K & L #33209, #33208, and #33207 respectively. Printed in Germany. 1930s.

The Peanuts Gang Cut-Outs. Snoopy, Sally, and Woodstock show their "green."

Chapter 12
Ephemera

Illustrated Postcards

At the turn-of-the-twentieth century, in a time when most people did not have a telephone, when there were often two or even three mail deliveries per day, when it took only a penny or two to mail, a new means of communication was born — the postcard. The picture postcard became the standard means of communication and the automatic choice for a quick hello, birthday greeting, or holiday message. Receiving a postcard from a friend or loved one made the day a special one. The phrase "Drop me a line" was prevalent until telephone service replaced it with "Call me." The number of postcards sent and collected reached amazing proportions during this time. An advertisement in a 1905 *Comfort* magazine proclaimed: "The Postcard craze has spread all over the world, and nearly everyone in the country gets from one to a hundred through the mail each month."

"ERIN GO BRAGH," the all so familiar greeting often translated as "Ireland's My Homeland" or "Ireland Forever" — words that offered one's allegiance and love for Ireland — became a common phrase on thousands of St. Patrick's Day postcards mailed to friends and family. Many of these postcards were sent from one Irish-American to another. Most cards were a nostalgic reminder of the old country and honored the land of their ancestors. The postcards were highly decorated with the typical Irish symbols: the Irish Colleen, the golden harp of Tara, the simian looking Irishman smoking a pipe, delicate shamrocks, golden pigs, and, of course, all "wearing the green."

In order to understand the phenomenal growth of sending and receiving postcards, a historical timeline is presented to show and identify how the postcard came of age from an American perspective.

Chronological Timeline

1861: The first copyright for a postcard was issued.

1873: The first U. S. Government pre-stamped postal card was introduced.

1893-1898: *Pioneer Era*. Postcards have undivided backs used for addresses only.

1898-1901: *Private Mailing Card Era*. In the United States private printers and publishers were given governmental approval to print and sell postcards beginning on July 1, 1898.

1901-1907: *Undivided Back Era*. While publishers could now use the notation "Post Card" on the postcard back, it was not until 1902 that all postcards had to comply with postal regulations that mandated that only the address would appear on the non-illustrated side.

1907-1915: *Divided Back Era*. In March 1907 the United States Government gave approval to publishers to produce postcards with a divided back with space for an address and a message.

1915-1930: *White Border Era*. These are Illustrated or Real Photo cards with a one-quarter inch white border encircling that illustration.

1930-1945: *Linen Era*. Postcards with a high rag content (i.e. "linen") were published associated with cheap inks marginalizing the illustration quality.

1939-Present: *Photochrome Era*. Color photographic images from any locale... Greeting cards.

Rates for Privately Manufacturer Cards Postcards

Dating postcards can be accomplished by knowing the postal rates in use during certain eras.

Effective Date	Postage (in Cents)
May 12, 1873	same as 1-oz. letter rate
July 1, 1898	1¢
November 2, 1917	2¢ (war tax)
July 1, 1919	1¢
April 15, 1925	2¢
July 1, 1928	1¢
January 1, 1952	2¢
May 11, 2009	28¢
April 17, 2011	29¢
January 22, 2012	32¢

Artist Signed Postcards

The artist-signed postcard is overwhelmingly the favorite of the entire postcard field. The collection of the beauty and elegance of several cards or a series of cards by a great artist is a highlight of many deltiologists. The artist-signed card is more expensive to the publisher to produce so the publisher must maintain a high quality of artwork so that sales at the consumer end are profitable. An artist-signed card may bear an artist's signature or initials; however, publishers often did not allow artists to sign their work in order to avoid their demanding more money as their following increased. No matter, it was the artist that made the postcard great. Artists were paid very little by publishers who saw great benefit of producing cards in sets of series (usually numbering in groups of 6 or 12). The artists discussed below not only produced desirable St. Patrick's Day postcards, but also many other holiday cards.

Samuel L. Schmucker

The most collected artist-signed St. Patrick's Day postcards are by the American art Nouveau artist Samuel L. Schmucker (1879-1921). Even though crippled from polio as a child, he displayed a great passion for art. He received his professional training at the Pennsylvania Academy of the Fine Arts and then at the Howard Pyle Institute. By 1905, Schmucker had established himself as a commercial artist, creating postcard images and making pen and ink sketches for the fashion plates printed in the *Philadelphia Daily Press*. For ten years Schmucker's work was printed by two of the largest postcard publishers in the United States: Detroit Publishing Company and the John Winsch Company.

Schmucker used his wife Katharine as the model for his distinctive wide-eyed woman. Katharine's image was the inspiration for the "Winsch Girl," the Irish Colleen, a design Schmucker is best-known for by the John Winsch Company. His fanciful images, with their intense colors, have long captivated postcard collectors.

One special version of the St. Patrick's Day cards is the series of cards that open and behind Schmucker's beautiful woman is a booklet of poems. These special cards are some of the finest from the "Golden Age of the Postcard" and very collectible.

Beautiful Colleen. An outstanding group of unsigned Samuel Schmucker cards with beautiful Colleen dressed in her finery and adorned with green bows and ribbons. The Irish lass is riding on or holding onto a pipe, or surrounded by a wreath of shamrocks. Published by Winsch. Very collectible cards.

IRISH SYMBOLS. Three lovely cards alive with all the symbols so dear to the Irish: shamrocks, harp, and wearing of the green. Unsigned by Samuel Schmucker. Published by Winsch, c. 1912.

Above and Opposite Page: This very special group of cards, unsigned by Schmucker and published by Winsch, each feature a silk insert of a design that appears on earlier cards. This method allowed a publisher to get more use from a talented artist without requiring new designs.

Ellen Clapsaddle

The most prolific of all the American postcard artists was Ellen Clapsaddle (1865-1934). The Clapsaddle children on her cards are described by many as "charming," "delightful," and "the picture of innocence." The faces of these children are repeated among numerous backgrounds for which Clapsaddle drew upon folklore, traditions, children's games, and nursery rhymes.

Educated in New York, Clapsaddle gave painting lessons as a young lady and then contracted to work for the International Art Company of New York, for which she produced over 3,000 designs. International Art Company manufactured postcards in Germany and a location in Philadelphia. Chester Garre, a partner in International Art Company, noted, "I can remember watching long lines of girls seated at tables either hand-painting or air-brushing each card, passing the cards from one to another to place certain colors upon them."

Wolf Publishing later purchased the International Art Publishing Company. Clapsaddle's cards for International Art were usually embossed; from Wolf, they're not embossed and are usually more difficult to find. Of her designs half are children; the other range from floral to still life in nature. Her children were a reflection of the times and are quite popular with collectors. During the height of her career with International Art Company, she invested her earnings in the postcard industry only to lose everything with the outbreak of World War I, as Wolf closed for business. Once back in New York, Clapsaddle never recovered from the effects of war. She died alone and penniless and, despite the great affection shown for children in her artwork, she never married and had no children, brothers, or sisters. She was buried in a potter's grave, but later reunited with her parents with her tombstone only saying "Ellen."

Celebrating St. Patrick's Day. Artist signed Ellen Clapsaddle cards show families celebrating the holiday by taking a ride on a dirigible aptly named the Shamrock and on a high-speed chase with the wind capturing the top hat. Published by International Art. Very collectible cards.

Irish Colleen. These three artist signed Ellen Clapsaddle cards feature a smiling sweet little Irish Colleen dressed in green with white aprons or petticoats. Shamrocks decorate each card. Published by International Art.

Though unsigned, this card — and the Irish lass featured on it — is strikingly similar to artist Ellen Clapsaddle's "Irish Colleen" images seen above.

These two cards display the same message to the reader: "There's a dear little plant on Emerald's Isle and I've culled a bunch that fortune may smile." Published by Wolf (acquired International Art Publishing Co.), unsigned by Ellen Clapsaddle.

"I've donned the green, so dear to me." This unsigned Clapsaddle card was also published by Wolf, which was later acquired by the International Art Publishing Company.

The Clapsaddle Children. Two of the cards are artist signed Ellen Clapsaddle; the children on the Clapsaddle cards are charming, delightful, and pictures of innocence, as they wish each other a bright and happy St. Patrick's Day. On the third card, a young boy calls out his greeting. Published by International Art.

Gift-giving Irishmen. These artist-signed Ellen Clapsaddle cards show three finely dressed Irishmen presenting shamrocks to their Colleens. The card with the gold border and the one with the green border were published by International Art. The card with no border was published by Wolf. (Cards published by Wolf tended to be simpler in design.)

Artist signed Ellen Clapsaddle. *Top*: The flag adorned with a golden harp was printed by S. Garre. *Right*: Two children, in happier times, display their green. *Far Right*: The sad young soldier offers his thoughts to "Ireland, our home and all her sons where're they roam." The cards were published by International Art.

Unsigned Clapsaddle Cards. Though simpler in nature than the ones designed for International Art, these cards still honor the sweet innocent alluring children. Published by Wolf Publishing.

H. B. Griggs

One postcard artist about which little is known is H. B. Griggs. Today Grigg's gender or what the initials stood for is not known. He (she) designed many signed postcards for the Leubrie and Elkins Company, New York. Only two of the approximately 350 cards designed are signed using the entire name: one is part of Thanksgiving series 2233, the other a very unusual St. Patrick's Day card. Most of her (his) postcards are signed simply "HBG." Griggs had a flair for caricature and humor; these cards are readily recognized by their vivid colors and stylistic writing.

ARTIST SIGNED H.B. GRIGGS. *Above*: A very rare postcard for two reasons: very few cards designed by Griggs contain the entire signature and this particular postcard folds out into a 21" image of a beautiful woman walking her dog (*left*).

ARTIST SIGNED HBG (H.B. GRIGGS). A seamstress embroiders a St. Patrick Cross. "I did with curious work emboss for you a fine St. Patrick's Cross; now, I prithee pin it on your arm, the Saint will keep you safe from harm." Series 2253.

ARTIST SIGNED HBG (H.B. GRIGGS). The cards featuring the women are L & E Series 2253, as recognized by the stylized writing. The woman describes her shamrock as a blend of love, valor, and wit. On the second card, Griggs praises the shamrock as three godlike friends: love, valor and wit.

Gene Carr

A United States cartoonist, Gene Carr (1881-1959) worked from a very early age drawing newspaper cartoons for various newspapers, where he produced the Sunday comics. For two decades, he was a pioneer of the comic strip. Carr also produced forty different designs of postcards for two companies: Rotograph and Bergman. The trademark characters on his postcards were bumptious dogs and nasty little children.

In his St. Patrick's Day series, Carr not only mocked the holiday, but also the Irish. Some of his characterizations were quite unflattering and insulting. This series of six postcards is a parody of the annual New York St. Patrick's Day Parade.

Artist-signed Gene Carr. A comical series poking fun at the St. Patrick's Day Parade; the six cards present various times of the day: getting ready with a bottle of rye; angelic Irishmen instead of the rowdy ones on parade day; an Irishman that has his chance to be "king for a day"; after the parade the swaggering Irishman holds on and gives the dog a peering glance; the "day the Dutch lead the Irish in the parade"; and finally a very stout Irishman with his shillelagh follows the crowd along with the ever present dog and pushy children. Published by Rotograph Co. A very collectible set of postcards.

Margaret Evans Price

A noted children's book illustrator and artist, Margaret Evans Price (1888-1973) was the co-founder of Fisher Price Toy Company in 1930 and eventually became their Art Director. There she designed the push-pull toys based on her characters from her children's books. Her postcards, published by Stecher Lithography, are denoted by small initials M.E.P.

"Wearing the Green." These artist-signed M.E.P. (Margaret Evans Price) cards each feature a young girl in green. "That little Irish Colleen in her auld plaid shawl" and "The lark from her light wing the bright dew is shaking Kathleen Mavourneen" describe two of the cards. The artist outlined the cards both with a wreath of shamrocks and a score of music at the top margin. Published by Stecher Lithography. A very collectible series.

A. Heinmuller

Published by International Art, A. Heinmuller designed not only St. Patrick's Day cards, but also Halloween, Thanksgiving, and Valentines.

Artist signed A. Heinmuller. Both cards display the greeting in a heart made of shamrocks. Published by International Art, Series 4153.

Publishers

Unlike the few number of outstanding postcard artists, the number of publishing companies worldwide, both large and small, that issued postcards during "The Golden Age of the Postcard" runs into the thousands. Just about every subject and view imaginable has appeared on the postcard during this postcard craze. Greeting cards, including St. Patrick's Day cards, were so-ever popular.

E. Nash

The most prolific of all American greeting publishers, E. Nash was responsible for at least twenty-seven sets spanning all holidays.

A young couple enjoy an Irish dance. Published by E. Nash, Series #14. These sweet faces have been reproduced again and again on different holiday cards.

Playing Dress-up. A group of children play dress-up and pretend they are in the St. Patrick's Day parade. Published by E. Nash, Series #15.

Flowers for You. This group of cards, some trimmed in silver and others in gold, have a flower theme: an Irish Rose (*top center*), Irish Forget-me-not (*top right and above center*), Lily (*above left*), and the Irish Daisy (*above right*). Published by E. Nash, Series #5.

Gottschalk, Dreyfuss, and Davis (GDD)

Printed in Germany, Gottschahaulk Dreyfuss and Davis (GDD) cards are usually marked on the reverse with a pillar type mailbox and a person trying to use it in the lower left corner. Underneath the mailbox are the words "Trade Mark."

REMEMBERING HOME. Three of the most typical designs seen on postcards of most publishers: scenes of the homeland, some with shamrock borders (*left column*), others embellished by a gold border (*above*). Published by Gottschalk Dreyfuss and Davis (GDD).

Barton Spooner

Barton Spooner (1906-1915), of Cornwall, New York, published regional view cards and holiday and comical postcards. These cards are recognized by the circled overlapping B S logo.

Wide-eyed innocent looking children join the celebration. Cards have a gelatin finish with gold trim. Published by Barton and Spooner.

Wide-eyed innocent looking children join the celebration. These cards have a gelatin finish with a gold trim. Published by Barton and Spooner.

The young drummer and young girl adorned with shamrocks are ready for the parade. Published by Barton and Spooner, Series 513B.

Left: An Indian maiden; *Center*: A couple, the boy waving an Irish flag and the young girl an American flag, in "a friendly celebration." *Right*: An Irish lass wishing a Happy St. Patrick's Day to the reader. Published by Barton and Spooner, Series #347.

Winsch

Winsch postcards can be identified by the five small windows on the left side of the back of the card. Although Winsch Publishing was located in Stapleton, New York, the firm used superior German lithography, as many publishers did, and had cards printed in Germany and then imported to the United States for distribution. Winsch postcards sold at two for five cents, when the common price was one cent each. While some Winsch postcards were issued in sets of six, most of the better designs were issued in sets of four. The artwork of Samuel Schmucker was published by Winsch. Artist Jason Freixas also worked for Winsch Publishing; his round-faced children appear on many different holiday greeting cards.

Unsigned Jason Freixas Cards. The children designed by this artist are very wide-eyed and innocent looking. Published by Winsch.

P. Sander

Like E. Nash, Barton Spooner, and Winsch, publisher P. Sander produced greeting cards for all holidays.

Two widely different cards illustrating a variety of topics: A simian couple awaits for St. Patrick's Day to arrive while an exquisite woman in a flowing green dress casts her eyes on the "dear isle of my dreams." Published by P. Sander, New York.

Sam Gabriel Co.

Also known as Gabriel & Sons, the Sam Gabriel Company was started by Samuel Gabriel, former manager to Raphael Tuck & Sons, in 1907. The business was family-run for nearly thirty years until it was bought out by the American Colortype Co. Postcards produced by this publisher can be identified by the letter "G" inscribed in a piece of paper with a pen going diagonally through the paper. The Sam Gabriel Co. was not considered a giant in the postcard publishing world. Besides souvenir greeting postcards, Gabriel & Sons was involved with the entire novelty field, including paper dolls.

Bordered by rows of shamrocks, these cards present an assortment of scenes. *Opposite page*: A young boy up in the air on a motored vehicle; *Above left*: A striking looking woman strumming a harp; *Above center*: An Irish lass waves goodbye; *Above right*: A young child with her father. Published by San Gabriel; a most collectible Series #140.

Rafael Tuck and Sons

The firm of Rafael Tuck and Sons had long been established by the time postcard fervor gripped England. Raphael and his sons were quick to grasp the possibilities of pictorial greetings and, in 1880, launched a national contest for talent and original design, but also to attract public attention. In 1900, a competition for the largest collection of their postally-used cards awarded a prize to a collector with over 20,000 Tuck postcards. Tuck, widely known for its high standards and artistic merits, is the "epitome" of postcard publishers and are easily identified by a distinctive signature: Art Publishers to Their Majesties the King and Queen. German bombs destroyed their London factory.

Published by Raphael Tuck & Sons, Series #184 present three young ladies surrounded by shamrocks and "My own little Colleen."

Although the Irish are depicted very unflatteringly, they do look happy.
*(Top row)*The gentleman finally catches the woman of his dreams… "At last!"
(Bottom row) Published by Raphael Tuck & Sons, Series #106.

THE CASTLES OF IRELAND. Six of this 12-card series have a border of shamrocks entwined by gold with most of them featuring one of the many castles in Ireland. One design not often pictured is the minstrel boy gone to war with his father's sword and golden harp on his back. Published by Raphael Tuck & Sons, Series #172.

Stecher Lithography Company

The postcards published by Stecher Lithography Company are easily identified by a mark on the backside consisting of a circle surrounded by the letters "S L C." After moving to Rochester, New York, in 1870, Stecher joined a business that was renamed Mensing, Rahn & Stecher. In 1886, Stecher bought out the company and renamed it the Stecher Lithographic Company; in 1888, it employed one hundred people and had $125,000 in equipment. It published greeting postcards, advertising graphics, and fruit and flower prints.

Published by Stecher Litho Co., Series 39 tells the story of a young boy and girl meeting: she throws a shamrock boutonniere, pins it on, and then enjoys dancing. She is sad to see him go home "with memories of old Ireland."

Published by B.B. London, Series #2602 captures the beauty of the Irish woman. Each is pictured in an insert with a shamrock in the forefront.

B. B. London

A London, England, publisher c. 1905, B. B. London (Birn Brothers) produced embossed cards with greetings of all types. Most sets were in groups of four or six.

Themed Cards

Although many postcards can be identified by the artist or the publisher, there are thousands and thousands of postcards with an unknown artist or publisher. For the postcard collector, it then becomes a large task to somehow organize these cards. As far as St. Patrick's Day cards go, besides classifying by the use of symbols, one way is organizing by various topics of the postcards. Although the most common image is of an Irish woman or child, I have organized the remaining postcards using the following topics: Patriotic, Beautiful Women, Children, Scenes of Ireland, and Special Effects.

Patriotic

The union of Ireland and the United States is conveyed on many cards. Children draped with the American flag or an Irish Colleen kissed by Uncle Sam imparts the feelings of respect and love of both countries. Some of the most desirable postcards feature Uncle Sam, making these the most expensive postcards for the collector. Shamrocks and flags are entwined to give the importance of the relationship of the countries.

Uncle Sam. *Above left*: An Irish lass and Uncle Sam are kissing (Barton and Spooner, Series #7041). *Above*: Uncle Sam poses with both the Irish and American flags (unknown publisher). *Left*: Uncle Sam and his Irishman friend offer a toast to this important day (unknown publisher). Very collectible cards.

Women

Beautifully dressed women were a favorite subject of the turn-of-the-century artist. The influence of the shamrock can be seen, even on cards without a holiday greeting.

Patriotism at its finest. *Above left*: A young woman waving the Irish and American flags "Ireland and America" (Tuck Series #184). *Left*: A young boy is draped in an American flag (artist signed Bernhardt Wall; published by American Post Card, Series 157). *Below*: A young boy dressed as Uncle Sam shakes hands with an Irish lad (published by Winsch).

Three lovely women take center stage on these cards (publishers unknown). Their beauty is second to none. Their reverence of the shamrock is evident. Artist for the postcard featuring the beautiful woman draped in pink is T. Corbella.

Children

Many artists used children as the central figure in St. Patrick's Day cards — mischievous children, sweet demure children, playful children. Many cards show the children surrounded by shamrocks.

Two very similar cards by two different publishers. Ellen Clapsaddle's four children have a sweeter, more innocent look on their faces (published by International Art) whereas the unsigned card with the five children (published by The Robbins Brothers) are seen as more simian, not very child-like.

Two lovely Irish women, one in a flowing green cape (Wolf Publishing Series #1503) and a stylized woman with wings holding on to the harp (F. A. Owen publisher).

Two wide-eyed Kewpies, one adorned with her shamrock pendant, await the celebration. Publisher unknown.

Beautiful children enhanced by a shamrock background. These two series — one with a banner at the bottom (*above left and above center*), the other with a flower border (*above right and bottom left*) — highlight the beauty of young girls. Publishers unknown.

A red-haired child with a cornucopia of shamrocks (publisher unknown) wishes the reader "geluk" — good luck?

A very rare card featuring a black child with a shamrock offering his good luck. Publisher unknown.

Scenes of Ireland

The land of Ireland is one of beauty with the landscape dotted with castles remnants of past days. It is a lush land with soaring cliffs, rolling misty moors, white sandy beaches, and sparkling lakes — a land with a deep history, a home dear to heart of many. Welcome to Ireland!

A welcoming tribute to Ireland. These four postcards pay homage to the country with "IRELAND" written on shamrocks on two Gottschalk Dreyfuss and Davis published cards, which contain the insert "Coming from the bog," while two cards (unknown publisher) identify different castles or rock formations in the country in four-leafed shamrocks.

Published by Raphael Tuck & Sons, Oilette Series 9565 features scenes of the common people of Ireland and Oilette "Irish Life" Series III depicts the real life of many Irish peasants in thatched roof homes surrounded by rock walls.

The Cities

Most of the important cities in Ireland are seaports. (1) Dublin: With a turbulent past, for most of the last 1,000 years, Dublin has been the principle city of Ireland. It was settled by the Vikings and remained under British control until the Easter Uprising in April 1916; (2) Queenstown: A seaport on the south coast of County Cork, it was originally named Cobh, but renamed Queenstown to commemorate the visit by Queen Victoria and then renamed Cobh in 1922 with the founding of Irish Free State. A major transatlantic Irish port, it was the departure point for 2.5 million of the 6 million Irish people who emigrated to America between 1848 and 1950 and was the final port of call for the *Titanic* in 1912; Waterford: Settled by the Vikings, it was considered the second largest city after Dublin. (4) Killarney and its surrounds: Inhabited probably since the Neolithic period, these were certainly important Bronze Age settlements based on the copper ore mined on Ross Island. In the seventh century, Killarney became a focus for Christianity in the region. In the seventeenth century, it developed as a tourist center, an Irish version of England's Lake District.

City of Dublin. Published by Nash, Series #10.

City of Queenstown. Published by Winsch.

"Road to Killarney." The town is located north of the MacGillicuddy Reeks, on the northeastern shore of the Lough Lein/Leane, which are part of Killarney National Park. The town and its surrounding region are home to St. Mary's Cathedral, Ross Castle, Muckross House and Abbey, Lakes of Killarney, Torc Waterfall, and the Gap of Dunloe. Published by Winsch, 1913.

A statue in Cobh, County Cork, of Annie Moore (Jan. 1, 1877-1923): She was the first immigrant to the United States to pass through Ellis Island. She and her two brothers, Phillip and Anthony, traveled a board the steamship *Nevada* leaving Cobh Jan. 1, 1892, her fifteenth birthday. Publisher unknown.

"Eagle's Nest Killarney." The Eagle's Nest is situated on the shores of the Upper Lake on the part known as the Long Range. Here the lake narrows until it reaches the Old Weir Bridge, when it joins with the Middle Lake. The Eagle's Nest is a conical shaped mountain, 1,100 feet high, with a base covered with evergreens, and a rugged precipitous summit, on which eagles once built their nests. Published by Winsch.

City of Waterford. Published by Winsch.

"Gap of Dunloe, Killarney." There is a famous echo at this point. The Gap is a narrow mountain pass between Macgillycuddy's Reeks (west) and Purple Mountain (east) in County Kerry, Ireland. It is about 11 km (7 miles) from north to south. Publisher unknown.

The Castles

The Irish countryside is famous for medieval fortresses, castles, and manor houses rich in Irish history. Some of the most spectacular views of Ireland can be found among them. Most Irish castles are made from stone and date from the 1100s. The Irish began to build fortifications soon after the Norman Invasion, most of which were occupied by invading lords who used them as defensive administrative headquarters. Castles in Ireland were not elaborate dwellings of royalty. While most were owned by the heads of clans, kings, or English gentry, they were fortified dwellings for protection against raids and invaders. The castles were usually dark with very small rooms and small openings.

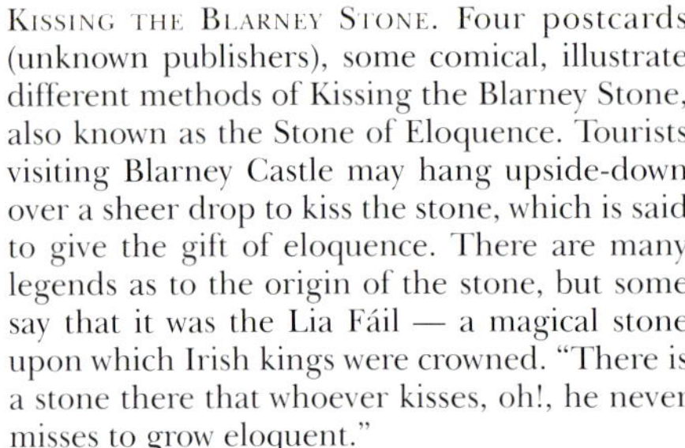

Kissing the Blarney Stone. Four postcards (unknown publishers), some comical, illustrate different methods of Kissing the Blarney Stone, also known as the Stone of Eloquence. Tourists visiting Blarney Castle may hang upside-down over a sheer drop to kiss the stone, which is said to give the gift of eloquence. There are many legends as to the origin of the stone, but some say that it was the Lia Fáil — a magical stone upon which Irish kings were crowned. "There is a stone there that whoever kisses, oh!, he never misses to grow eloquent."

Blarney Castle. Two views of the most famous castle in Ireland; this medieval stronghold near Blarney, County Cork, is probably Ireland's best-known castle. It receives thousands of visitors every year. The one today was the third castle built in 1446 by Dermot McCarthy, King of Munster, and features ruins of a stone keep and towers dating to the 1400s. Legend holds that 4,000 Munster men aided Robert the Bruce during the Battle of Bannockbum; in return he presented half of the Stone of Scone to them in gratitude. Publishers unknown.

Ross Castle, Killarney. Set on the romantic shores of County Kerry's Lake Killamy, Ross Castle was built in the mid-1400s and was the last Irish stronghold taken by Cromwell in the seventeenth century. There was a medieval legend that stated this medieval fortress would never fall into enemy hand unless it was attacked from the lake; therefore, the Cromwellian commander ordered a large boat be transported to the lake. When the defenders at Ross Castle saw this ship, they feared the prophecy had been fulfilled and abandoned the castle. First view: Artist-signed Honeywood O'Reilly card, publisher unknown; Second view: Published by SLC Series 247.

Two Irish Castle Views. *Left*: Dunluce Castle is a now-ruined medieval castle in Northern Ireland. The castle is surrounded by extremely steep drops on either side, which may have been an important factor to the early Christians and Vikings who were drawn to this place where an early Irish fort once stood. *Right*: Since 1345, Shane's Castle was occupied by the royal house of O'Neill. Published by SLC, Series 247.

Kilkenny Castle. Built in 1195 by William Marshal, 1st Earl of Pembrokee, to control a fording-point of the River Noree and the junction of several routeways, the castle was a symbol of Norman occupation and, in its original thirteenth-century condition, would have formed an important element in the defense of the town with four large circular corner towers and a massive ditch. Publisher unknown.

Rock of Cashel. Also known as St. Patrick's Rock, for over one hundred years it was a symbol of power for the kings, and then churchmen, who ruled. It's located in County Tipperary. Publisher unknown.

The Scenic Countryside

Many postcards depict the beautiful views of the country, whether it be lakes, seaports, or castles. Most scenic postcards were sent from one Irish-American to another, tugging at their hearts for their homeland.

Two Winsch postcards with linen inserts capture two Irish scenes.

Special Effects

Postcards with special effects provide the viewer with certain embellishments that add to the joy of the cards. Some postcards are embossed, some with a border of lace-like material, and some have a metallic shamrock attached. Hard to find are the postcards with a small package of shamrock seeds added to remind the buyer of the homeland. Some of most collectible and valuable postcards are the "booklet" type with a cover similar to a book and with 2-4 pages inside offering poems or sayings.

Highly embossed cards. Although the images on these postcards are very common, the use of embossing makes them attractive. Publishers unknown. (Above and opposite top)

These two cards from series 62209 convey the lives of the common folk. Published by Winsch, 1913.

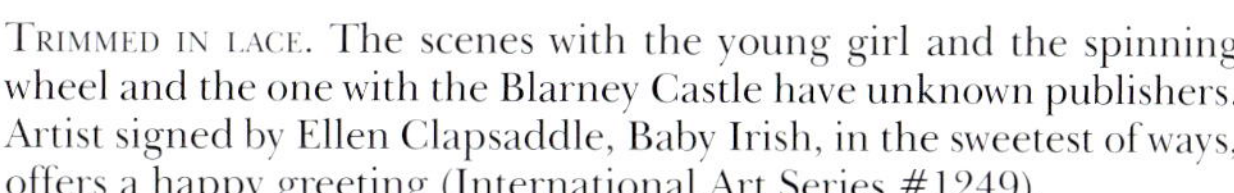
TRIMMED IN LACE. The scenes with the young girl and the spinning wheel and the one with the Blarney Castle have unknown publishers. Artist signed by Ellen Clapsaddle, Baby Irish, in the sweetest of ways, offers a happy greeting (International Art Series #1249).

Bringing Good Thoughts of the Homeland. The shamrock is the center of focus on these cards, whether it be attaching real shamrock leaves (printed by Guy & Co.), being made of dark green felt or a golden metallic decoration (published by Stedman Bros., Brantford, Canada, shown on a card made of leather (copyrighted by S.N. Co.), or with a packet of real shamrock seeds (published by Lawrence Publisher, Dublin).

Booklet cards. Using the same beautiful woman as found on other Samuel Schmucker cards, these postcards are very special because they are "booklet" cards. The ribbon binds a small booklet with an Irish poem inside the cover. Booklet cards are valued between $50 and $100 each. Published by Winsch.

Booklet postcard featuring the golden harp surrounded by delicate white shamrocks. Published by Winsch, 1911.

Series of six booklet postcards. The two postcards that highlight Irish women (artist Schmucker) are designs seen on other Winsch series that are not booklets. The remaining four booklets with various scenes on the front cover have also been used in the more normal postcard design. Published by Winsch, 1912. A very collectible and valuable series.

ROSS CASTLE, KILLARN
ERIN GO BRAGH
DESIGN COPYRIGHTED, JOHN WINSCH, 1912.

SCENE ON THE
MIDDLE LAKE,
KILLARNEY.
ST. PATRICK'S DAY GREETINGS
DESIGN COPYRIGHTED, JOHN WINSCH, 1912.

MC SWINE'S CASTLE,
RATHMULLAN, CO.
DONEGAL.
ST. PATRICK'S DAY SOUVENIR
DESIGN COPYRIGHTED, JOHN WINSCH, 1912.

RIVER SHANNON,
AT FOYNES.
ST. PATRICK'S DAY GREETINGS
DESIGN COPYRIGHTED, JOHN WINSCH, 1912.

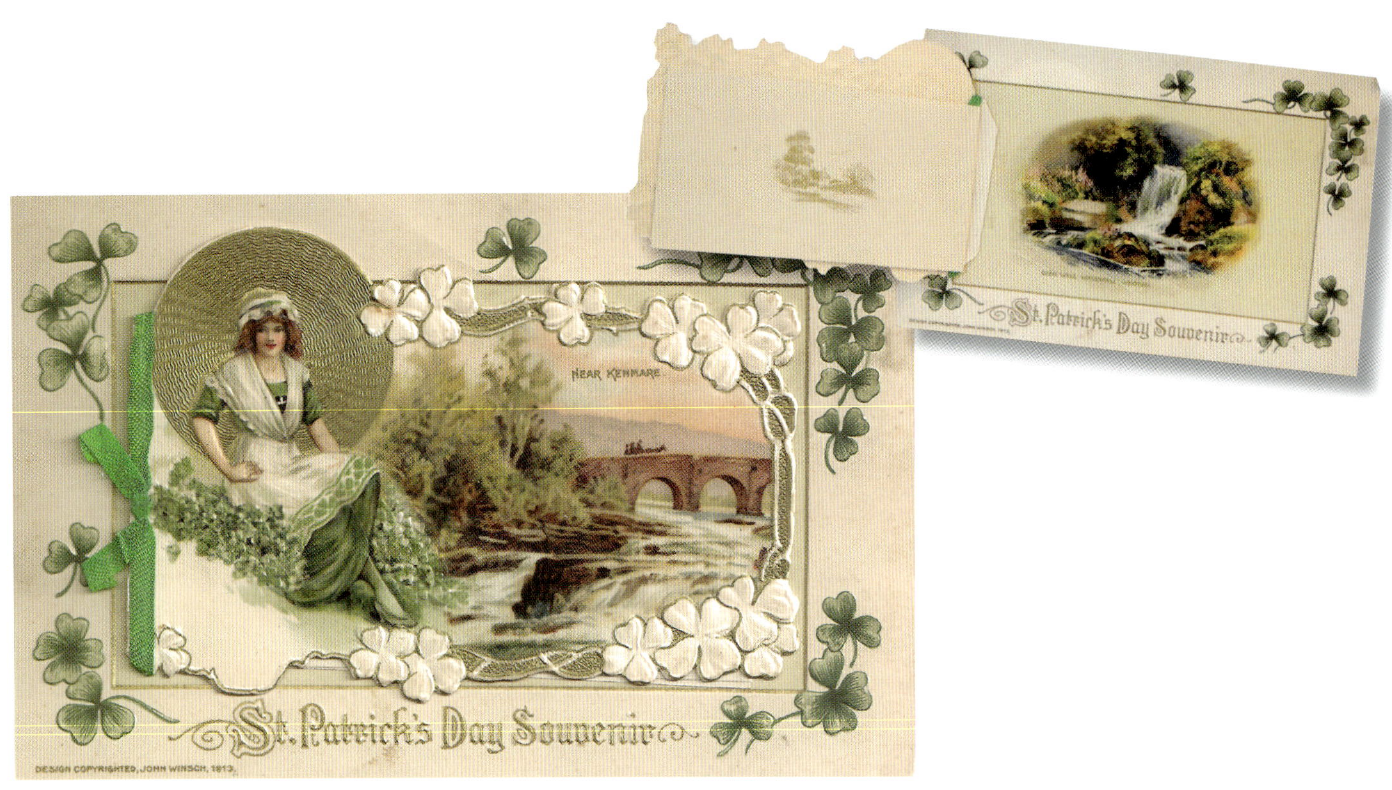

NEAR KENMARE
St. Patrick's Day Souvenir
DESIGN COPYRIGHTED, JOHN WINSCH, 1913.
St. Patrick's Day Souvenir

A booklet postcard displaying a beautiful waterfall with the poem on the inside. Published by Winsch.

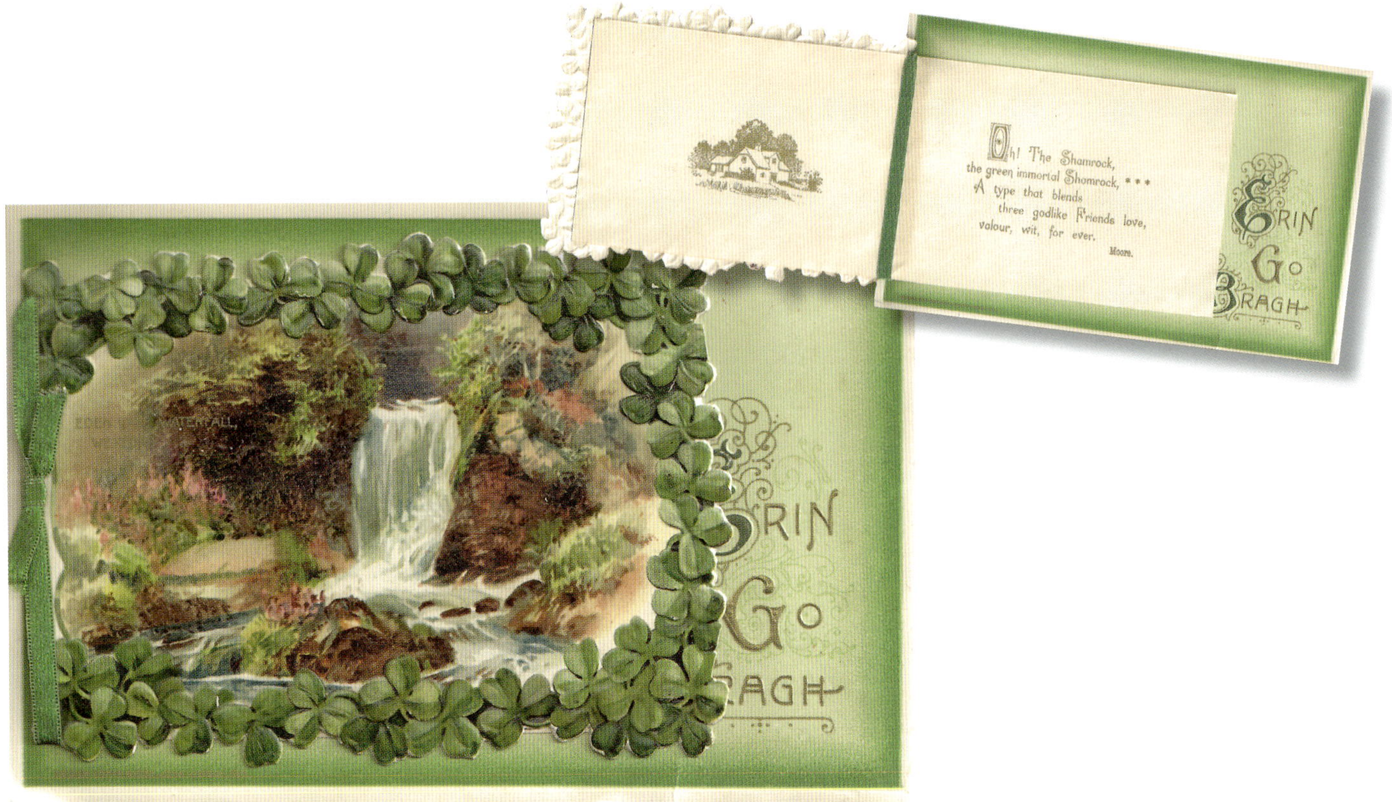
Oh! The Shamrock,
the green immortal Shamrock, * * *
A type that blends
three godlike Friends love,
valour, wit, for ever.
Moore.
Erin Go Bragh
Erin Go Bragh

A booklet postcard with artist Schmucker's Colleen and a bridge near Kenmare. Published by Winsch, 1913.

Greeting Cards

During the 1920s, postcards and greeting cards distributors became producers of greeting cards due to the uneven quality and stilted messages of foreign cards. Both American Greetings (founded 1906) and Hallmark (founded 1910) decided to publish their own greetings cards. While postcards were a very inexpensive means of communication, especially among rural communities, greeting cards were an excellent way to express a myriad of thoughts depending on the message of the card.

After World War II, postcards were reduced to "Wish You Were Here!" travel images or RPPC (Real Photo Postcards), but greetings cards were a great way to express any number of thoughts through humorous images and message. Especially beginning in the late 1950s, when greeting card producers began to acquire licenses to produce images of various cartoon and other popular figures.

Hallmark Cards has been aggressive in not only acquiring licenses, but also forming new divisions within the company to formulate differing messages. Shoebox is one example, as it declares itself to be "a tiny little division of Hallmark." Among the most endearing and enduring cartoon figures were those of Charles M. Schulz' Peanuts line, which still are viable today even after Schultz' death in 2000 after nearly fifty years of his drawing Charlie Brown and the Peanuts gang.

"Irish You A Happy St. Patrick's Day." Peanuts Greeting Card, Hallmark Cards.

Peanuts Greeting Cards, Hallmark Cards.

Peanuts Greeting Cards by Hallmark Cards: "Happy St. Patrick's Day" and "Leprecondos."

"Saint Patrick regrets his decision to drive the snakes out of Ireland." Greeting Card, Shoebox Division, Hallmark Cards.

Magazines

After the Civil War, the tabloid sized illustrated weekly newspapers with their political contents began a slow demise in readership. By the turn-of-the-twentieth century, new advances in printing technology and chromolithography heralded the introduction of a new style of magazine in terms of size, scope, style, bold graphics, and color. The appeal of color was very important to a barely literate and sometimes immigrant audience, as their buying power was important to the inherent longevity of proliferating and competing monthly magazines. As a cultural phenomenon, many magazines sought to shape opinion and foster change while others were published strictly for enjoyment purposes. However, with content becoming important, some of America's greatest literary figures and graphic illustrators formed allegiances with various magazines.

The major holidays celebrated in America, especially during the late nineteenth century to the mid-twentieth century, allowed illustrators, by virtue of their intriguing and skillful graphics, to shape the audience's opinion and understanding of the meaning of these events. This was especially true during the huge emigrant wave that hit American shores from 1850 to 1920. Thomas Nast, for instance, was one of the first illustrators to formulate the way we expect Santa Claus to look as a rotund, jolly-faced, elfin figure dressed in red and white. However, it was also Thomas Nast who drew many St. Patrick's Day images of the Irish as whiskey swilling, simian-looking ruffians.

As the celebration of St. Patrick's Day grew in prominence as being an acceptable event for the greater citizenry, cover illustrators did their best to bring home the idea that the Irish were responsible citizens and not the brawlers depicted in prior years. Foremost among general interest magazines in terms of annual covers devoted to St. Patrick's Day were *The Saturday Evening Post* (1821-1830, 1839-present) *LIFE* (1883-1936), *Collier's* (1905-1957), *Liberty* (1924-1950), and *The New Yorker* (1925-present). Since there was much competition among magazines for the small but expanding literate market, a magazine could not forego colorful attention-grabbing covers, satirical comment, and a weekly publishing schedule that promised that any one entity would not be forgotten in the plethora of magazines offerings.

Today, only *The New Yorker* still publishes on a weekly schedule, and its covers are both humorous and attractive. In fact, except for *The New Yorker*, no other magazine today publishes holiday covers of any consequence (refer to *Chapter 4* for *The New Yorker* covers). The following covers represent a small sample of the diversity of St. Patrick's Day images ranging from the bland to the comedic.

"A Little Sprig of Shamrock for St. Pat." Artist: F. T. Attwood. *LIFE*, March 18, 1897.

"St. Patrick." Artist: Unknown. *LIFE*, March 12, 1903.

"The First Green of the Season." Artist: C. Broughton. *LIFE*, March 1, 1906.

"Saint Patrick's Day." Artist: James Montgomery Flagg. *LIFE*, March 7, 1907; March 19, 1908; March 18, 1909.

"Begorray! If thot iditor ain't Orish, He is but he don't know it!" Artist: Unknown. *LIFE*, March 18, 1918.

"Saint Patrick's Day." Artist: James Montgomery Flagg. *LIFE*, March 7, 1907; March 19, 1908; March 18, 1909.

"The Pipe of Peace." Artist: Unkown. *LIFE*, March 16, 1922.

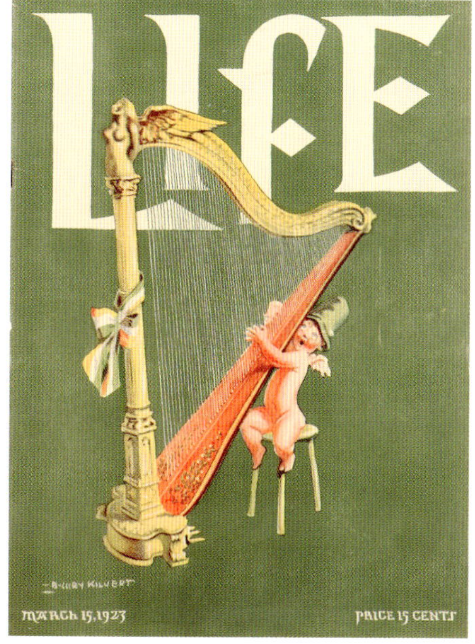

"An Irish putto playing the harp." Artist: B. Cory Kilvert. *LIFE*, March 15, 1923.

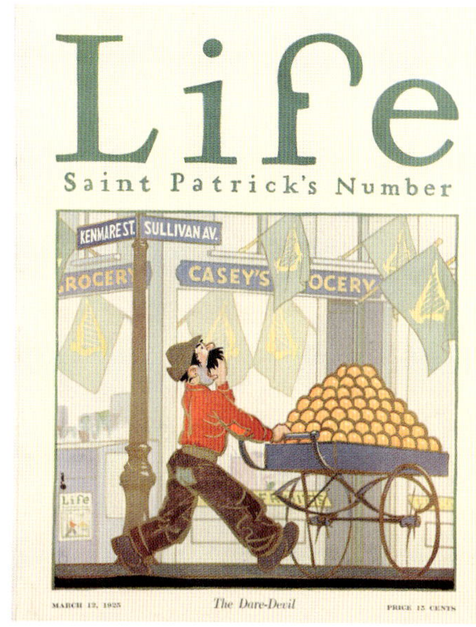

"The Dare-Devil." Artist: Unknown. *LIFE*, March 12, 1925.

"It seems there were two Irishmen..." Artist: Unknown. *LIFE*, March 11, 1926.

"The Wearing of the Grin." Artist: Unknown. *LIFE*, March 17, 1927.

"The Ancient Ardor of Hibernians." Artist: Unknown. *LIFE*, March 15, 1928.

"The Top O' th' Mornin'." Artist: Oreon Lowell. *JUDGE*, March 11, 1922.

Collier's National Weekly, March 24, 1934 and March 18, 1939. Artist: Arthur Crouch.

LIBERTY, March 30, 1937. Artist: Tom Hall.

Liberty, March 25, 1939. Artist: P. Wilson McCoy.

Liberty, March 22, 1941. Artist: David Bugen.

The Saturday Evening Post, March 16, 1940. Artist: Albert W. Hampson.

The Saturday Evening Post, March 20, 1943. Artist: Charles Kaiser.

Motor, March 1936 and March 1937. Artist: Robert Robinson.

Advertisements & Trade Cards

The printed advertisement in a magazine or newspaper contributes over 70% of the revenues of most publications. Special-interest magazines rely even more on advertising cash flow. Many publications over the years, certainly during times of economic adversity, have seen their advertising revenue stream virtually disappear and their circulation base was not substantial enough to cover the overhead necessary to keep in business. As popular as the general interest magazines once were (i.e. *Life*, *Look*, *Leslie's*, *Liberty*, *Collier's*, and *The Saturday Evening Post*), changing consumer tastes, the advent of television, and certain editorial problems all contributed to those magazines' demise as print advertising declined. While today's magazine racks are still full of publications reaching out to virtually every taste, many consumers are getting most of their information from television and the Internet. Still there are over twenty-five new non-trade magazines starting up every year with an equal amount being cancelled.

During the "Golden Age" of magazine publishing, from the start of the 1920s to the end of the 1960s, magazines were full of colorful advertisements that shaped and formed the way we perceived the acceptability of various products. Advertising premiums, especially for children's products such as breakfast cereals, were a great way to foster loyalty as well as the collecting of said items. As all advertising was contained within the pages of a magazine, when the publication was tossed, so were the ad pages. Another advertisement genre was the use of Trade Cards (usually issued in sets) to get one to continually buy the product in order to complete the set. These cards are expensive today to collect. A fair amount of St. Patrick's Day advertisements dealt with the various liquid refreshments to be enjoyed with the St. Patrick's Day meal.

XXXX

THE BEST COFFEE ON EARTH!

The Immense Sales Show the People Know it is the Best.

Chicago Head of the West.
XXXX Head of the West.
XXXX Biggest Seller in the World.

XXXX has the Chicago push, and gets to the right spot.

CHICAGO GETS THE FAIR. YOU GET XXXX COFFEE.

The glazing on McLaughlin's XXXX Coffee DOES THE SETTLING, and is made of corn starch and re-clarified sugar—therefore, perfectly healthful. The glazing SEALS THE PORES of the coffee and prevents the COFFEE OIL FROM EVAPORATING. This costs us ¼ of a cent a pound, but saves the consumer ten times that amount. We buy all our Coffees from the coffee planters direct, and have houses in Rio de Janeiro and Santos, thereby saving the importers, jobbers and commission men's profits. We give all this saving to the consumer, and say, without any fear of contradiction, that we are putting up coffee from 5 to 10 cents a pound finer quality than any other package coffee on the market. The immense success of XXXX Coffee proves that our policy of giving the consumer the cheapest coffee for the money and selling an immense quantity, is the best.

W. F. McLAUGHLIN & CO.,

Chicago, Rio de Janeiro, Santos.

(A Picture Card in Every Package.) (OVER)

"St. Patrick's Day-Drink McLaughlins XXXX Coffee." Advertising/Trade Card. *Front of card*: A sweet young girl holding an umbrella against the rain; this card was one of a series of 12 issued for different holidays. *Back of card*: "XXXX" — The Best Coffee on Earth!

HOLIDAYS

ST. PATRICK'S DAY, IRELAND.

The greatest and best observed holiday of Ireland is St. Patrick's Day; but although St. Patrick is the national patron Saint, the celebration is observed socially rather than religiously. A favorite banner usually seen on that day represents Erin, an allegorical female with green robe, golden trimmings and a gilded harp receiving the Saint's blessing, or kneeling before a picture of the Saint driving the snakes out of the borders of good old Ireland.

"St. Patrick's Day-Ireland." Advertising/Trade Card. *Front*: Beautiful Young Lady with a Harp. *Back*: "The greatest and best observed holiday is St. Patrick's Day." Packed in Duke's Cigarettes, Philadelphia, PA.

"For Those Who Would Be Gay." Automobile Advertisement. "For St. Patrick's Day is dedicated to the gay in spirit...and to you also is dedicated the Studebaker Coupe." The car is superimposed on a shamrock. Early 1930s.

"Top O' The Mornin'...Every Morning!" Advertisement copy: "A bit o' green to brighten St. Patrick's Day! And for a bright start every morning-delicious, sunny-gold, flavor-filled Rice Krispies in a bowl...Lastingly Crisp!" *Collier's Weekly*, March 1941.

"A red-haired Colleen in Irish garb." Calendar: March 1947. Artist George Petty produced many air-brushed calendar pin-ups girls for *Esquire* and *True Magazine*.

"Lucky Charms." Product Box Advertisement, Whole Grain breakfast cereal, General Mills Cereals, Minneapolis, Minnesota. Lucky Charms cereal was first introduced in 1964 with "Lucky the Leprechaun" as its mascot. The sugar-coated oats, with different flavors, are combined with colorful marshmallow bits that periodically change with new marketing strategies. The back of each box always has some sort of game with clues predicated to find some sort of treasure.

"Lucky Charms." Product Advertisement. Back-of-the-Box text: "Legend of the Shooting Star" crossword puzzle for kids. Many back-of-the-boxes have similar brain teasers.

"Keep Smiling 'Fresh up' with Seven-Up!" Advertisement copy: "Shure now and I've seen many a man with a winning smile but niver a wan with a winning frown." Added a 7-Up cutout to the ad. *LIFE*, March 1946.

Colorful rendition of four panels of various "Lucky Charms" cereals, painting, c. 1990s.

Fruit & Produce Crate Labels

Citrus and vegetable box labels occurred as an outgrowth of the need of growers to differentiate their product to far-flung customers. With the completion of the transcontinental railroad system in the 1880s, growers needed a way to identify and advertise a generic product to East Coast buyers dealing in commodity items. The answer was to develop a brightly colored, attractively designed paper label that was attached to the end of a wooden shipping box. Since the many small citrus growers could not effectively market their products beyond their own region, many contiguous growers banded together and affiliated themselves with one of the large co-operative marketing organizations. The growers' co-operatives were responsible for the design and artwork by hiring color lithographers to produce identifying labels for each of their members. From the late 1880s to the mid-1950s, crate labels evolved as an eyewitness to the various trends that transformed America throughout that seventy-year reign of paper labels. In the 1950s, cardboard boxes were introduced as a cost-saving measure. The cardboard shipping box was pre-printed, negating the need for attached labels.

These colorful time capsules of fruit and produce marketing are highly collectible due to their colorful graphic designs. There are many categories in which to collect fruit and produce box and can labels and a favorite way for many is to acquire by holiday(s).

"Lucky Brand Celery." Fruit/Vegetable Crate Label: Bruce Church, Inc., Salinas, California.

"Lucky Find." Fruit/Vegetable Crate Label: Monteleone-Michel Co., Los Angeles, California.

"Irish Castle." Fruit/Vegetable Crate label: Lake County Citrus Fruit, Knowles and Company, Leesburg, Florida.

"Murphy California Vegetables." Fruit/Vegetable Crate Label, 7"l x 9"h: H. B. Murphy Company, Brawley, California.

"Irish Beauty" – Best That Grows. Fruit/Vegetable Crate Label: Packed for J. Bert Moritz Company, Inc., New York.

"Shamrock – The pick of the crop." Fruit/Vegetable Crate Label: Sunkist Valencias, Northern Orange County, California.

"O'Keeffe's Shamrock Brand Tomatoes." Fruit/Vegetable Crate Label, packed Expressly for M. O'Keeffe, Boston, Massachusetts.

"Shamrock." Fruit/Vegetable Crate Labels: Valencias, Marsh Seedless Grapefruit, and Lemons. Packed by Placentia Mutual Orange Ass'n., Placentia, Orange County, California.

"Shillelagh." Fruit/Vegetable Crate Label: Washington State Apples, Yakima Fruit & Cold Storage Co., Yakima, Washington.

Postal History, Special Cachets, and Stamps

A philatelic collection of St. Patrick's Day material would include a range of United States postal history covers covering both military and civilian cachets and cancellations, Irish Post Office special cachet First Day Covers, Franklin Mint offerings of special annual covers with silver medals, and stamps from the Irish Post Office.

For many years there have been firms that specialized in artistically designed hand-painted limited edition cachets on covers or envelopes. The cacheted covers with the new stamp attached are cancelled at the issuing Post Office with the date of issue usually accompanied by a First Day Ceremony. These artistically rendered covers are called First Day Covers (FDC) and are collected by a wide range of postal history and thematic specialists.

In the 1930s, America's naval forces utilized pre-printed St. Patrick's Day cachets on greeting envelopes for the use of military personnel who were generally stationed at sea and far from home. This gave our sailors a chance to bond with the home folk by giving them a reason to send a special cacheted envelope home. In the United States several post offices have represented cities, towns, and villages with cancellations bearing names associated with familiar Irish locations and symbols. Since most of these cachets, both military and civilian, were made with green artwork the senders tried to follow through by using green postal stamps whenever possible to complete the theme.

Military Postal Covers. "St. Patrick's Day" cachets: *USS Northampton* and *USS Pennsylvania*, both 1934. The *USS Pennsylvania* (BB-38) was commissioned in 1916. After spending time with both the Atlantic and Pacific Fleets, she was stationed at Pearl Harbor, Territory of Hawaii. On December 7, 1941, the *Pennsylvania* was in dry dock when the Japanese attacked. She suffered some peripheral damage, but survived the war. After the Pacific War was over, she steamed to the Marshall Islands, where she took part in Operation Crossroads as a target ship for the atomic bomb tests at Bikini Atoll in July 1946. The *Pennsylvania* was sunk in February 1948 off Kwajalein Lagoon.

Military Postal Covers. Special Different Cachets: *USS Ranger* and two *USS Pennsylvania*, all 1935. The *USS Ranger* (CV-4), commissioned in 1934, was one of three pre-WW II aircraft carriers to survive the war.

Military Postal Covers. *Top*: *USS San Francisco*, 1936. *Middle*: *USS Arctic*, 1936 – hand-painted cachet by Lottie Eshliman, #7 out of 15 issued. *Bottom*: *USS Aylwin*, 1936 – W. S. Crosby cachet, real photo.

Special Different Cachets. *L-R*: *USS Manley*, *USS Quincy*, *USS Reina Mercedes*, and *USS Thrush*, all 1937. Hand-painted *Thrush* cachet by Jimmie Allen, Navy Mail Clerk; the *USS Thrush* was a mine-sweeper converted into a seaplane tender.

USS Oklahoma Military Postal Cover, 1939. This ship was commissioned in 1916. After spending years with both the Atlantic and Pacific Fleets, she was based at Pearl Harbor, Territory of Hawaii, starting in December 1940. The *Oklahoma* was moored in Battleship Row on December 7, 1941, when the Japanese attacked. She took a hit of five torpedoes and, within twelve minutes, capsized. She was lost for the duration of the war.

Cachets for *USS Brooklyn*, *USS Dorsey*, and *USS Whippoorwill*, 1938.

Civilian Cacheted Covers. *Top to Bottom*: Hand-painted Hartford, Connecticut, 1931; Jamaica, New York, 1933; Shamrock, Oklahoma, 1934. Tipperary, Wyoming, 1935; Shamrock, Missouri, 1935; hand-painted Saint Patrick, Missouri, 1936.

A Mail-Gram of the Seabees, c. World War II, the Pacific Theater. The Seabees are the Construction Battalions of the U.S. Navy. This censor passed Mail-Gram sent from a Seabee to his wife says: "Standing Pat – It's the same ol' fightin' story of a bunch of fighting Pats, still winnin' fame and glory in chasin' snakes and rats."

Civilian Cacheted Covers. Hand-painted St. Patrick, Missouri, 1937; "First Anniversary, St. Patrick's Day Flood, March 17, 1936," Johnstown, Pennsylvania, 1937; hand-painted Saint Patrick, Missouri; Artist: Gladys Alder (famous cachet designer), 1938.

Civilian Cachet Cover, Saint Patrick, Missouri, 1948.

Special Civilian Cachet Covers, Erin, New York, 1957 and 1958.

Special Civilian Cachet Covers. "Happy St. Patrick's Day" and "St. Patrick's Day," St. Patrick, Missouri, 2004 and 2006.

Special Civilian Cachet Covers. *Top*: 10th Annual St. Patrick's Day Parade, Syracuse, New York, 1992. *Bottom*: Collins' hand-painted cachet "Flag over Field," First Day of Issue of flag stamp, New York, New York, 1995.

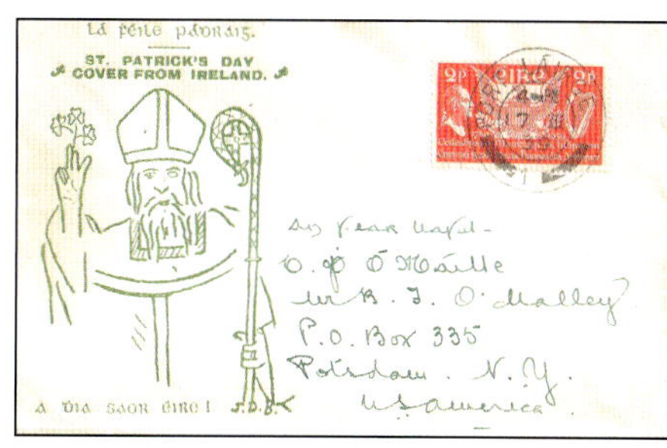

Irish Cover. Special Cachet. "La Feile Padrais – St. Patrick's Day Cover from Ireland," Port Lairge, Ireland, 1939.

In Ireland, as a way of honoring St. Patrick on March 17th, there were specially produced cachets issued over varying periods of time either individually or in a series. For about fifteen years, L. W. Staehle, an internationally respected American cachet artist and designer, was commissioned to produce an annual FDC (First Day Cover) with Irish castles as the main design element. These were issued over a time period of from the mid-1950s to the early 1970s.

Special Cachets produced by L. W. Staehle, New York City. *First, L-R*: "Rathmacknee Castle," "Chair Castle," "Ferricarrig Castle," and "Donegal Castle," Ireland, 1956-1958. *Second, L-R*: "Derryhivenny Castle," "Trim Castle," "Clara Castle," and "Dunsoghley Castle," Ireland, 1961-1964. *Third, L-R*: "Dromoland Castle," "Kilkea Castle," "Ballinlough Castle," and "Birr Castle," Ireland, 1965-1971. (Above, left, and opposite page top)

Irish Cover: "St. Patrick's Day – Newry, 17 March 2006." Text: "God our Father, you sent Saint Patrick to preach your glory to the people of Ireland..."

Special Civilian Cachet Covers. *Left*: Saint Patrick, Missouri, 1960; Erin, New York, 1960; and Erin, New York, 1961. *Right*: Erin, New York, 1964.

In 1974 the Postal Commemorative Society of Ireland produced attractive booklets of annual St. Patrick's Day Covers for five years. The beautiful artwork of the cachets was rendered in green while three Irish stamps completed the cover design. Each of the covers came in a green heavy stock paper folder and was accompanied by a historical vignette of some aspect of the legends and myths surrounding St. Patrick.

SAINT PATRICK'S DAY COVER, MARCH 17, 1975. Issued at Cork-by-the-Sea to commemorate the Legend of Paudrig.

SAINT PATRICK'S DAY COVER, MARCH 17, 1977. Issued at Dun Laoghaire, near Tara Hill, to commemorate the Legend involving Patrick and the High King Laoghaire.

FIRST ANNUAL SAINT PATRICK'S DAY COVER, MARCH 17, 1974. First series of Booklets and First Day Covers issued by the (Irish) Postal Commemorative Society, Dublin, to honor the Patron Saint of Ireland.

SAINT PATRICK'S DAY COVER, MARCH 17, 1976. Issued at Clew Bay, near Croagh Patrick, to commemorate the Legend of Reek.

Saint Patrick's Day Cover and Booklet, March 17, 1978. Issued at Granard, County Langford, to commemorate the destruction of the Druid Idol Crom-Cruach.

From 1972 through 1978, the Franklin Mint issued a St. Patrick's Day Commemorative Medal and cacheted cover. Each year of issue the medal and cacheted cover came in a Kelly green vinyl snap folder. The one troy ounce medal was minted entirely from pure (.999 fine) Irish Silver and is a Limited Edition Proof. After the 1978 striking of the proof medal, the dies were cancelled and presented to The National Trust for Ireland so that these medals can never be minted again. In addition to the cachet and medal, a small history of various aspects of St. Patrick's life was written to serve as background material for each year of issue.

ST. PATRICK'S DAY COMMEMORATIVE MEDAL AND CACHET

The Landing of St. Patrick at Cill Mhantáin — 432 A.D.

This is the first in a series of annual St. Patrick's Day medallic cachets commemorating important milestones in the life of Ireland's patron saint. This year's cachet commemorates St. Patrick's landing in Ireland at Cill Mhantáin — 432 A.D.

The proof-quality medal in the cachet was designed and sculptured in Ireland by Gabriel Hayes O'Riordan and was minted of pure Irish silver by The Franklin Mint. This is the first medal that has ever been made of pure (.999 fine) Irish silver. The cachet was postmarked at Cill Mhantáin (Wicklow) on St. Patrick's Day.

The dies for the medal have now been cancelled and placed in the Maynooth Museum, St. Patrick's College, County Kildare, which was selected by the National Trust of Ireland as the final repository.

The venerated St. Patrick became known as the national apostle who converted Ireland to Christianity. He was born about 385 in Britain, and was 16 years old when he was captured by Irish pirate raiders, sent to Ireland, and sold as a slave.

One night he received a sign in his sleep that he must escape, which he did by walking almost 200 miles to the coast. There he was able to board a ship for Gaul.

Although he commenced studying for the priesthood, the "voice of the Irish" continued to haunt his thoughts and dreams. Finally, in 432, Patrick set off for Ireland as missionary bishop to evangelize the Irish pagans and to preach the gospel. His faith and toil were richly rewarded, enabling him to carry the gospel into regions no missionary had previously visited.

St. Patrick's Day Commemorative Medal and Cachet, 1972. "The Landing of St. Patrick at Cill Mhaniain (Wicklow), 432 A.D." Artist: Gabriel Hayes O'Riordan. Pure (.999 fine) Irish silver proof medal struck by The Franklin Mint, USA.

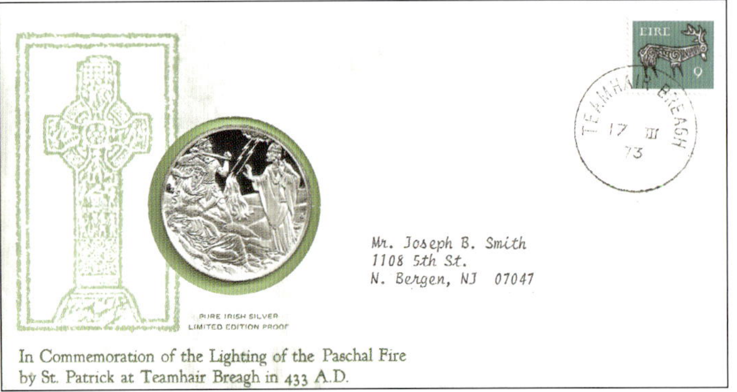

St. Patrick's Day Commemorative Metal and Cachet, 1973. "St. Patrick Lights the Paschal Fire at Teamhair Breagh (Tara), 433 A.D." Artist: Gabriel Hayes O'Riordan. Pure (.999 fine) Irish silver proof medal struck by The Franklin Mint, USA.

ST. PATRICK'S DAY COMMEMORATIVE MEDAL AND CACHET

St. Patrick Lights the Paschal Fire at Teamhair Breagh — 433 A.D.

The pure (.999 fine) Irish silver Proof-quality medal in the 1973 St. Patrick's Day Cachet depicts one of the most dramatic incidents in the Saint's conversion of Ireland to Christianity. This spectacular event took place on Easter Eve, 433 A.D.

That night Logaire, High King of Ireland, and his Druid consorts were holding a special pagan festival at the royal palace at Teamhair Breagh (often referred to today as Tara). The festival was traditionally culminated by the lighting of an enormous fire. And no other fire could be lit within the king's domain prior to this event.

In accordance with the Christian tradition for Easter Eve, St. Patrick lit a Paschal fire. It happened that St. Patrick's fire preceded Logaire's.

In a rage, Logaire and his Druids mounted their chariots and set out to destroy the lawbreaker and quench the fire which so openly violated their rules.

The Druids attacked St. Patrick, only to be stopped in their tracks as a great darkness fell and a terrible earthquake shook the ground. Almost all of the Druids perished. The king and queen retired in chagrin.

The 1973 St. Patrick's Day medal was designed and sculptured in Ireland by the famous Irish artist Gabriel Hayes O'Riordan and struck at The Franklin Mint.

Each medal was then combined with a special commemorative cachet, bearing the St. Patrick's Day postmark of Teamhair Breagh.

This cachet was issued in a strictly limited edition. The dies for the medal have now been cancelled and presented to the Maynooth Museum, which was selected as their repository by the National Trust of Ireland.

Mr. Joseph B. Smith
1108 5th Street
N. Bergen, New Jersey 07047

PURE IRISH SILVER
LIMITED EDITION PROOF

In Commemoration of the Destruction of the Pagan Idol Crom Cruaich by St. Patrick at Cabhán c. 437 A.D.

St. Patrick's Day Commemorative Medal and Cachet

The Destruction of the Pagan Idol Crom Cruaich by St. Patrick at Cabhán c. 437 A.D.

During the early years of his Christian mission in Ireland, St. Patrick achieved one of his greatest triumphs — the destruction of the idol Crom Cruaich. The pure (.999 fine) Irish silver proof medal in the 1974 St. Patrick's Day Commemorative Cachet dramatically depicts the Patron Saint of Erie striking down this pagan idol.

Covered with silver and gold, this massive stone idol stood in the center of a circle formed by twelve stone pillars at Cabhán, on the plain of Slecht, in the ancient kingdom of Connaught. In this open heathen temple the druids of Ireland made human sacrifices to Crom Cruaich in the hope of securing bountiful crops and other favors. The idol's power was believed to be so great that even the high kings of Ireland traveled to Cabhán to pay homage.

About 437 A.D. St. Patrick set out to destroy this center of heathen worship. Miraculously, St. Patrick toppled the idol with a stroke of his staff. The destruction of the idol was an important step in establishing Christianity throughout Ireland.

The 1974 St. Patrick's Day medal was designed and sculptured by the famous Irish artist Gabriel Hayes O'Riordan of County Kildare. The limited edition medal, minted by The Franklin Mint, was then combined with a special commemorative cachet bearing the St. Patrick's Day postmark of Cabhán.

The dies for the medal have now been canceled and have been presented to the Maynooth Museum, which was selected as their permanent repository by the National Trust of Ireland.

St. Patrick's Day Commemorative Medal and Cachet, 1974. "The Destruction of the Pagan Idol Crom Cruaich by St. Patrick at Cabhan, c. 437 A.D." Artist: Gabriel Hayes O'Riordan. Pure (.999 fine) Irish silver proof medal struck by The Franklin Mint, USA.

St. Patrick's Day Commemorative Medal and Cachet, 1975. "The Triumph Over the Devil's Demon Birds on the Mountain Croagh Patrick, c. 439 A.D." Artist: Gabriel Hayes O'Riordan. Pure (.999 fine) Irish silver proof medal struck by The Franklin Mint, USA.

St. Patrick's Day Commemorative Medal and Cachet

The Triumph Over the Devil's Demon Birds on the Mountain Croagh Patrick, c. 439 A.D.

St. Patrick struck down the devil's loathsome birds that had been sent to plague his Christian mission in Ireland. This scene is portrayed on the pure (.999 fine) Irish silver proof medal in the 1975 St. Patrick's Day Commemorative Cachet.

About 439 A.D. St. Patrick returned to the region in Ireland where he had spent his youth as a slave to pagans. With true Christian spirit, the Patron Saint of Eire planned to climb to the summit of Crochan Aigli (later named Croagh Patrick in his honor) and pray for the salvation of the people of Ireland. As he began his ascent of the tall mountain, St. Patrick was attacked by hideous dark birds. But, the man of God fought the airborne demons with his staff and the simple cowbell he carried, soon destroying them.

The St. Patrick's cowbell, as sculpted for the medal by famous Irish artist Gabriel Hayes O'Riordan, is historically accurate. It is based on a relic in the National Museum of Dublin, which still bears the crack believed to have been caused when it was thrown by St. Patrick in his triumph over the demons.

The limited edition medal, minted by The Franklin Mint, is combined with a special commemorative cachet bearing the St. Patrick's Day postmark of Cathair Na Mart, the village where pilgrims from all over Ireland gather each year to make the journey up Croagh Patrick, in the footsteps of their Patron Saint. The dies for this medal have been canceled and given to the National Trust for Ireland so this commemorative can never be issued again.

ST. PATRICK'S DAY COMMEMORATIVE MEDAL AND CACHET

St. Patrick Converts the Pagan Princesses — 441 A.D.

The 1976 St. Patrick's Day Medal depicts one of the most dramatic moments in the Saint's conversion of Ireland to Christianity. The important event took place at Rath Crochan in 441 A.D.

When St. Patrick encountered Ethne the White and Fedlem the Red, daughters of Loigaire, pagan king of Ireland, the curious young girls began asking him many questions. St. Patrick answered extolling Christianity and then said, "I wish to unite you with a heavenly King, as ye are the daughters of an earthly king. Believe." After they were baptized the sisters asked if they could see the face of Christ. St. Patrick explained "Until ye shall taste death, ye cannot see the face of Christ and unless ye shall receive the sacrifice." Then, according to legend, the girls received the Eucharist and fell dead. After a period of mourning, the maidens were buried near the fountain and a church was constructed at the site.

The 1976 St. Patrick's Day medal was designed and sculptured in Ireland by the famous artist Gabriel Hayes O'Riordan and was minted with a full proof finish of pure (.999 fine) Irish silver struck by The Franklin Mint. It is combined with a special commemorative cachet, bearing the St. Patrick's Day postmark of Ailfionn, County Roscommon, the nearest Irish postal office to the sacred ground where St. Patrick baptized the two princesses. This cachet was issued in a strictly limited edition. The dies for the medal have now been cancelled and presented to the National Trust of Ireland.

ST. PATRICK'S DAY COMMEMORATIVE MEDAL AND CACHET, 1976. "St. Patrick Converts the Pagan Princesses-441 A.D." Artist: Gabriel Hayes O'Riordan. Pure (.999 fine) Irish silver proof medal struck by The Franklin Mint, USA.

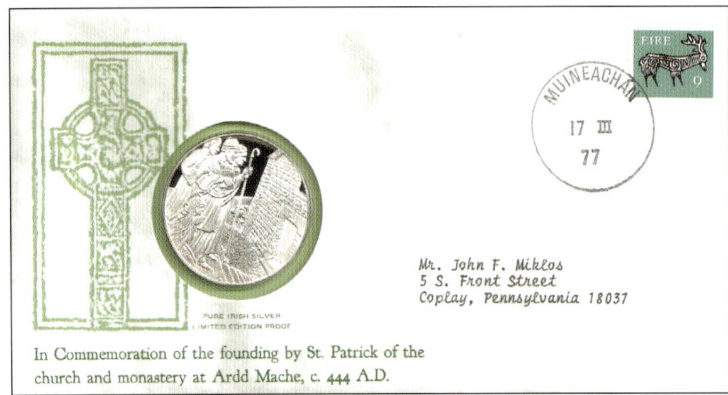

ST. PATRICK'S DAY COMMEMORATIVE MEDAL AND CACHET

St. Patrick Founds his Church and Monastery–c. 444 A.D.

The 1977 St. Patrick's Day Medal commemorates an event that had a momentous effect on the course of Irish history—the founding of St. Patrick's church and monastery at Ardd Mache around 444 A.D., at a site known today as Armagh. The medal portrays the dramatic moment when St. Patrick dedicated and blessed the new church—a house of worship that was to lead the way in the conversion of all Ireland to Christianity.

St. Patrick had spent about four years evangelizing throughout the province of Ulster when he chose Armagh, seat of the ancient Ulster kings, as the site for his principal church in Ireland. The ruler of the district, King Daire, granted him a small tract of land at the foot of a beautiful hill called Ardd Mache. Within a circular space 140 feet in diameter enclosed by an earthen rampart, the saint and his companions erected the crude wooden church and monastery which became the spiritual center of Erin.

Designed and sculptured in Ireland by the famous artist Gabriel Hayes O'Riordan, the 1977 St. Patrick's Day Medal was minted with a full proof finish of pure (.999 fine) Irish silver struck by The Franklin Mint. It is combined with a special commemorative cachet, bearing the St. Patrick's Day postmark of Monaghan—very near to the sacred ground where St. Patrick established his church. This cachet was issued in a strictly limited edition. The dies for the medal have now been canceled and presented to The National Trust for Ireland.

ST. PATRICK'S DAY COMMEMORATIVE MEDAL AND CACHET, 1977. "St. Patrick Founds his Church and Monastery–c. 444 A.D." Artist: Gabriel Hayes O'Riordan. Pure (.999 fine) Irish silver proof medal struck by The Franklin Mint, USA.

ST. PATRICK'S DAY COMMEMORATIVE MEDAL AND CACHET

St. Patrick's Final Years

The 1978 St. Patrick's Day Medal commemorates the final years of Ireland's beloved patron saint—years which he spent in quiet reflection and meditation at Saul, a village in County Down. The medal depicts the patriarch on his deathbed attended by his loyal disciples and his successor St. Benignus.

St. Patrick died on March 17, 493. As the moment of his death approached, he experienced a vision in which he saw Ireland brightly illuminated by rays of divine light. But then clouds gathered over the island and obliterated the glorious light from all but a few of the remotest valleys. Fearing this signified that his life's work would come to naught, St. Patrick was filled with sadness. But an angel appeared to him and assured him his apostolate would never cease.

According to legend, after the saint's death his bier was lit by a heavenly light for days. For a whole year thereafter nights were lighter than usual.

The 1978 St. Patrick's Day medal was designed and sculptured in Ireland by the famous artist Gabriel Hayes O'Riordan and was minted with a full proof finish of pure (.999 fine) Irish silver struck by The Franklin Mint. It is combined with a special commemorative cachet, bearing the St. Patrick's Day postmark of Dundealgan (Dundalk), County Louth. This cachet was issued in a strictly limited edition. The dies for the medal have been canceled and presented to The National Trust for Ireland, so this medal can never be minted again.

ST. PATRICK'S DAY COMMEMORATIVE MEDAL AND CACHET, 1978. "St. Patrick's Final Years." Artist: Gabriel Hayes O'Riordan. Pure (.999 fine) Irish silver proof medal struck by The Franklin Mint, USA.

In 2003, based on the Centenary of the designation of March 17th as a public holiday in 1903 in Ireland, the Irish Post Office issued several sets of stamps to honor the feast day of St. Patrick. The stamps recognized St. Patrick as the Patron saint of Ireland as well as giving homage to the fact that in major cities throughout the world such as Dublin, Ireland, and New York City, major parades are held for the celebration of being Irish.

"St. Patrick's Day–2003" Stamp Booklet. Text: "In 2003, Ireland acknowledges the Centenary of Saint Patrick's Day as a public holiday and recognizes how this day is now a multicultural event celebrated the world over." Three sets of four Irish stamps plus one set of three are included in the booklet.

ST. PATRICK'S DAY 100 YEARS A HOLIDAY

Three stamps, issued by An Post on 28th February 2003, recognise the centenary of the designation of 17th March as a public holiday in 1903. The feast day of St. Patrick has for centuries been an occasion to celebrate being Irish. This celebration of the patron Saint predated even the advent of Canonisation within the Roman Church. The Book of Armagh directed monasteries and churches in Ireland, to commemorate St. Patrick in spring, from the ninth Century.

A parade of Irish Colonial Volunteers on St. Patrick's Day, 17th March 1766 through New York began a tradition that now spans Continents. Parades, festivals and religious ceremonies have become central to this annual celebration of being Irish.

There are a variety of colourful parades and festivals in towns and cities throughout Ireland. The Dublin Parade is now the climax to the first major festival of the year which attracts visitors from all corners of the Globe.

The stamps and First Day Cover were designed by Finbarr O'Connor. The gummed stamps and Prestige Booklet were printed by Irish Security Stamp Printing Ltd., and the three self-adhesive booklets produced by Sprintpak. Design and layout for the stamp booklets was handled by D5 Design.

A souvenir Prestige Booklet for this issue was designed by TroyenKozaki, and produced by Irish Security Stamp Printing Ltd.

Irish Post Office Stamp Sets. Three sets of four Irish stamps: St. Patrick; Dublin Parade; and New York City Parade.

First Day Cover (FDC), 2003. Franked with one stamp from each series.

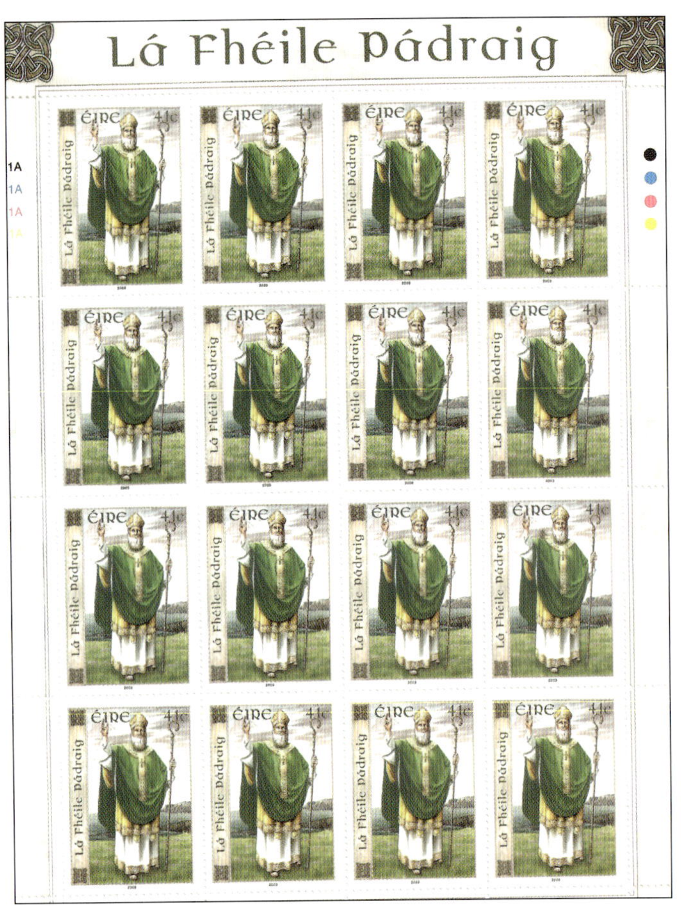

La Fheile Padraig Stamps. Sheets of sixteen Mint stamps feature "St. Patrick," "Dublin Parade," "New York City Parade," and "St. Patrick Stain Glass."

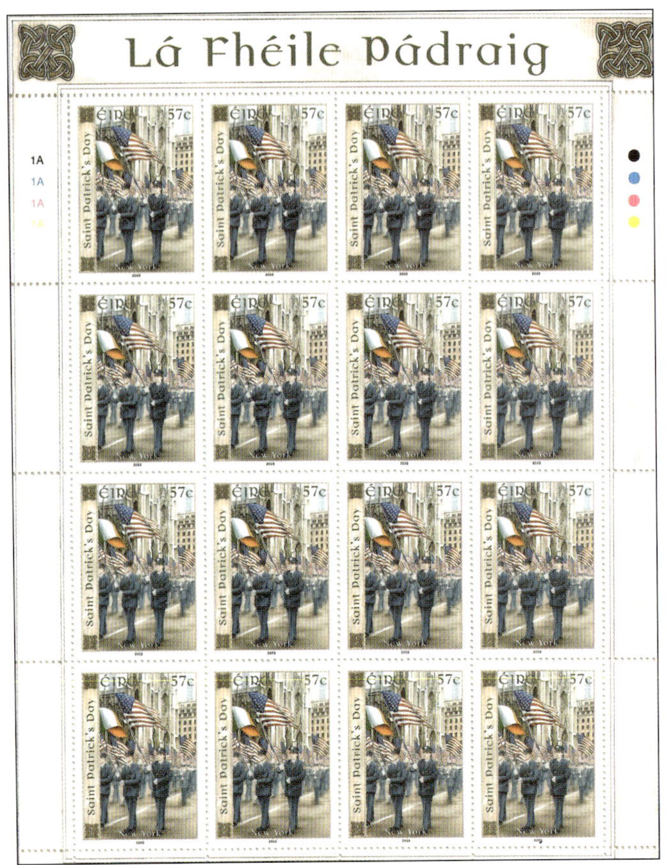

Bibliography

Saint Patrick

Freeman, Philip. *St. Patrick of Ireland*. New York, New York: Simon & Schuster, 2004.

Grace, Edmond. *Saint Patrick*. Dublin, Ireland: Messenger Publications 1992.

Hughes, Harry. *Croagh Patrick, An Ancient Mountain Pilgrimage*. New Road, Westport, Co. Mayo: Harry Hughes, 1991.

James, William F. *Saint Patrick of England*. San Francisco, California: The Grabhorn Press, 1955.

Mullan, Don. *A Little Book of Patrick*. Dublin, Ireland: The Columbia Press, 2004.

O'Farrell, Padraic. *Irish Saints*. Dublin, Ireland: Gill & MacMillan Ltd, 2002.

O'Loughlin, Thomas. *Patrick: Missionary to the Irish*. London, England: The Incorporated Catholic Truth Society, 2002.

Saint Patrick's Achievement. "Dublin Congress of the Patrician Year, 1961." Dublin, Ireland: Frederick Press Ltd., 1961.

Simms George Otto. *Saint Patrick: Ireland's Patron Saint*. Dublin, Ireland: The O'Brien Press, 2004.

The Life of Saint Patrick, Redemptorist Father. Dublin, Ireland: M. H. Gill & Son, Ltd., circa 1910.

Tobin, Greg. *The Wisdom of St. Patrick*. New York, New York: Barnes & Noble Books, 1999.

Saint Patrick's Day

Barth, Edna. *Shamrocks, Harps, and Shillelaghs*. New York, New York: Clarion Books, 1977.

Brogain, Seamus O. *The Irish Harp Emblem*. Dublin, Ireland: Wolfhound Press Ltd., 1998.

Constable, Nick. *St. Patrick's Day, A Celebration*. Edison, New Jersey: Chartwell Books, Inc., 1998.

Crimmins, John D. *St. Patrick's Day*. New York, New York: John D. Crimmins, 1902.

Cronin, Mike and Daryl Adair. *The Wearing of the Green, A History of St. Patrick's Day*. London, England: Routledge, 2002.

Curran, Bob. *The Shamrock*. Dublin, Ireland: The Wolfhound Press Ltd., 1999.

Freeman, Dorothy Rhodes. *St. Patrick's Day*. Berkeley Heights, New Jersey: Enslow Publishers, Inc., 1992.

Kessel, Joyce K. *St. Patrick's Day*. Minneapolis, Minnesota: Carolrhoda Books, 1982.

Kroll, Steve. *Mary McLean and the St. Patrick's Day Parade*. New York, New York: Scholastic Inc., 1991.

Ridge, John T. *The St. Patrick's Day Parade in New York*. New York, New York: St. Patrick's Day Parade Committee, 1988.

The Celts

Davies, John. *The Celts, Prehistory to Present Day*. London, England: Cassell Illustrated, 2002.

Ellis, Peter Berresford. *A Brief History of the Druids*. New York, New York: Carroll & Graf Publishers, 1994.

Hamilton, Claire and Steve Eddy. *Decoding the Celts*. New York, New York: Metro Books, 2008.

Haywood, John. *Atlas of the Celtic World*. London, England: Thames & Hudson, 2001.

Massey, Eithne. *Myths and Legends of Ireland*. Dublin, Ireland: Fall River Press, 2003.

Titley, Alan. *A Pocket History of Gaelic Culture*. Dublin, Ireland: The O'Brien Press, 2000.

Wood, Juliette. *The Celts: Life, Myth, and Art*. New York, New York: Barnes & Noble Books, 2004.

Irish History

Blackwell, Amy Hackney and Ryan Hackney. *The Everything Irish History and Heritage Book*. Avon, Massachusetts: Adams Media, 2004.

Brindley, Anna. *Irish Prehistory, An Introduction*. Dublin, Ireland: Country House, 1994.

Bunt, Cyril. *Journeys through Our Early History – Ancient Ireland*. Hunters Lane, Leavesden, Watford, Herts: The Bruce Publishing Co. Ltd, The Gawthorn Press Ltd., circa 1950.

Cahill, Thomas. *How the Irish Saved Civilization*. New York, New York: Anchor Books, Random House, Inc., 1995.

Clarke, Howard and Sarah Dent and Ruth Johnson. *Dublinia, The Story of Medieval Dublin*. Dublin, Ireland: The O'Brien Press, 2002.

Cronin, Mike. *Irish History for Dummies*. Chichester, West Sussex, England: John Wiley & Sons, Ltd, 2006.

Cross, Tom Peete and Clark Harris Slover. *Ancient Irish Tales*. New York, New York: Henry Holt and Company. 1936.

Delaney, Frank. *James Joyce's Odyssey, A Guide to the Dublin of Ulysses*. New York, New York: Holt, Rinehart and Winston, 1981.

Ellis, Peter Berresford. *Eyewitness to Irish History*. Hoboken, New Jersey: John Wiley & Sons, 2004.

Foster, Roy. *The Oxford Illustrated History of Ireland*. Oxford, England: Oxford University Press, 1989.

Fry, Peter and Fiona Somerset. *A History of Ireland*. New York, New York: Barnes & Noble Books, 1988.

Golway, Terry. *For the Cause of Liberty, A Thousand Years of Ireland's Heroes*. New York, New York: Simon & Schuster, 2000.

Grenham, John. *An Illustrated History of Ireland*. Dublin, Ireland: Gill & MacMillan, 1997.

Kenny, Michael. *The Road to Freedom*. Dublin, Ireland: Country House, 1993.

Killeen, Richard. *A Short History of Modern Ireland*. Dublin, Ireland: Gill 7 MacMillan, 2003.

Lalor, Brian, editor. *The Encyclopedia of Ireland*. New Haven and London: Yale University Press, 2003.

Litton, Helen. *The Irish Famine*. Dublin, Ireland: Wolfhound Press, 1994.

Mac Annaidh, Seamas. *Irish History*. Bath BA1 lHE, UK: Parragon Publishing, 2004.

New Illustrated Irish History. Old Saybrook, Connecticut: Konecky & Konecky, 2006.

MacManus, Seumas. *The Story of the Irish Race, 4th Edition*. Old Saybrook, Connecticut: Konecky & Konecky, 1921.

Massie, Sonja. *The Complete Idiot's Guide to Irish History and Culture*. Indianapolis, Indiana: Alpha Books, 1999.
Moody, J. W. and F. X. Martin. *The Course of Irish History*. Lanham, Maryland: Robert Rinehart Publishers, 2001.
Morrogh, Michael MacCarthy. *The Irish Century*. United Kingdom: Endeavour Group UK, 1999.
Nolan, A. M. *A History of Ireland for Schools, Academies and Colleges*. Chicago, Illinois: J. S. Hyland & Co., 1905.
O'Brien, Maire and Conor Cruise. *Ireland, A Concise History*. New York, New York: Thames & Hudson, 1999.
Pagett, Andrew. *The Way Things Were – Ireland, the Emerald Isle*. London, England: Brockhampton Press, 1999.
Power, Patrick C. and Sean Duffy. *Timetables of Irish History*. London, England: Black Dog & Leventhal Publishers, 2001.
Ruckenstein, Lelia and James A. O'Malley, editors. *Everything Irish*. New York, New York: Ballantine Books, 2003.
Sullivan, Maureen, editor. *A Book of Ireland*. Kansas City, Missouri: Ariel Books, 1996.

Irish Americans

Dolan, Jay P. *The Irish Americans, A History*. New York, New York: Bloomsbury Press, 2008.
Greenham, John. *Tracing Your Irish Ancestors*. Dublin, Ireland: Gill & Macmillan Ltd., 1992.
Griffin, William D. *The Irish Americans*. New York, New York: Metro Books, 1998.
Moloney, Mick. *Far from the Shamrock Shore*. New York, New York: Crown Publishers, 2002.
Wibberley, Leonard and Patrick O'Connor. *The Coming of the Green*. New York, New York: Henry Holt and Company, 1958.

Irish Architecture

Hamlin, Ann and Kathleen Hughes. *The Modern Traveler to the Early Irish Church*. Portland, Oregon: Four Courts Press, 2004.
Harbison, Peter. *Irish High Crosses*. Drogheda, Ireland: Boyne Valley Honey Company, 1994.
Heuer, Ann Rooney. *Irish Country*. New York, New York: Metro Books, 1998.
Lalor, Brian. *The Irish Round Tower*. West Link Park, Doughcloyne, Wilton, Cork: The Collins Press, 1999.
McAfee, Patrick. *Irish Stone Walls*. Dublin, Ireland: The O'Brien Press, 1997.
Meehan, Bernard. *The Book of Kells*. London, England: Thames & Hudson, 1994.
O'Neill, Brendan, editor. *Irish Cathedrals, Churches and Abbeys*. London, England: Caxton Editions, 2002.

Irish Food and Drink

Allen, Darina. *Irish Traditional Cooking*. London, England: Kyle Books, 2005.
Connery, Clare. *Irish Food & Folklore*. London, England: Bounty Books, 2001.
Fitzgibbon, Theodora. *A Taste of Ireland*. New York, New York: Barnes & Noble Books, 1996.
Griffiths, Mark. *Guinness Is Guinness*. London, England: Cyan Books, 2004.
Mulryan, Peter. *The Whiskeys of Ireland*. Dublin, Ireland: The O'Brien Press, 2002.

Irish Folklore and Humor

Anderson, Doug, illustrator. *500 Best Irish Jokes and Limericks*. New York, New York: Bell Publishing Company, 1970.
Bunting, Eve. *St. Patrick's Day in the Morning*. New York, New York: Scholastic Inc., 1980.
Calhoun, Mary. *The Hungry Leprechaun*. New York, New York: William Morrow and Company, 1962.
Curran, Bob. *A Field Guide to Irish Fairies*. Belfast, England: Appletree Press, 1997.
Edwards, Pamela Ouncan. *The Leprechaun's Gold*. New York, New York: Scholastic Inc., 2004.
Haining, Peter. *Great Irish Humor*. New York, New York: Barnes & Noble Books, 1996.
Jacobs, Joseph. *Celtic Folk and Fairy Tales*. New York, New York: G. P. Putnam's Sons, circa 1950s.
Macnamara, Niall. *Leprechaun Companion*. London, England: Pavilion Books Limited, 2002.
O'Gill, Darby. *Walt Disney: A Little Golden Book*. New York, New York: Golden Press, 1959.
Shute, Linda. *Clever Tom and the Leprechaun*. New York, New York: Scholastic Inc. 1988.
Spalding, Henry D. *The Lilt of the Irish*. Middle Village, New York: Jonathan David Publishers, Inc., 1978.
Star Series of Irish Yarns. Racine, Wisconsin: Western Printing and Lith. Co., circa 1925.
The Irish Leprechaun's Kingdom. London, England: Granada Publishing, 1979.
Yeats, William Butler. *Fairy Tales of Ireland*. London, England: William Collins Sons & Co. Ltd, 1990.

All Things Irish

Kelleher, Margaret. *So You Think You're Irish*. New York, New York: Barnes & Noble Books, 1988.
Massie, Sonja. *Irish Pride*. New York, New York: M J F Books, 1999.
McCarthy, Pete. *The Road to McCarthy-Around the World in Search of Ireland*. New York, New York: Harper Collins Publishers, 2004.
Shaw, Antony. *Portable Ireland, A Visual Reference to All Things Irish*. Philadelphia, Pennsylvania: Running Press, 2002.

Newspapers and Magazines

Mellish, Susan Emerson. "Hoping for luck in collecting Irish." *Antique Week*, March 14, 2011. MidCountry Media, Inc. Knightstown, Indiana.